The Diary

The Diary

Life of an
Orthodox Christian Nun
in Her Own Words

Translated from Finnish by EIJA PEHU

SISTER KRISTODULI
Foreword by ABBESS IGUMENIA KSENIA

RESOURCE *Publications* · Eugene, Oregon

THE DIARY
Life of an Orthodox Christian Nun in Her Own Words

Copyright © 2025 Eija Pehu and Lintula Monastery of the Holy Trinity. All rights reserved. Except for brief quotations in critical publications or reviews, no part of this book may be reproduced in any manner without prior written permission from the publisher. Write: Permissions, Wipf and Stock Publishers, 199 W. 8th Ave., Suite 3, Eugene, OR 97401.

Resource Publications
An Imprint of Wipf and Stock Publishers
199 W. 8th Ave., Suite 3
Eugene, OR 97401

www.wipfandstock.com

PAPERBACK ISBN: 979-8-3852-4030-2
HARDCOVER ISBN: 979-8-3852-4031-9
EBOOK ISBN: 979-8-3852-4032-6

Scripture quotations are from New Revised Standard Version Bible, copyright © 1989 National Council of the Churches of Christ in the United States of America. Used by permission. All rights reserved worldwide.

Photographs by Lintula Monastery of the Holy Trinity, Marja and Riitta Lampi, and Nicolas Karellos. Used by permission.

Contents

Important events in the life of Sister Kristoduli | ix

Foreword | xi

Part I: Childhood and youth | 1
    Notes of a little secondary school girl | 1
    Joys and sorrows of teenage years | 9
    The way to the Orthodox Church | 49
    Visit to Bytouma Monastery and studies in Helsinki | 67
    Second visit to Bytouma Monastery | 77
    Student life | 80
    Summer 1969 | 82
    In Helsinki | 86
    Holy Week and Pascha in Kuopio, 1971 AD | 93
    Summer 1971 | 96
    At the seminary | 97
    Winter as a teacher of religion | 100
    Two visits to Bytouma | 105
    Trip to Greece with Sister Riitta | 106
    After the trip to Greece | 110
    Scholarship travel to Greece | 115
    Again in Finland | 122
    The Archbishop falls ill | 128

Part II: In Bytouma Monastery | 137
　First years in the monastery | 137
　Work-filled ascesis | 180
　Archbishop Paul's visit to Bytouma | 214
　The death of Abbess Eufimia | 220
　Thoughts before changes—Homeland on my mind | 225
　The last meeting and the death of the Archbishop | 244
　Longing and pondering in the everyday life of the monastery | 249
　The Philokalia is nearing completion—what then? | 279
　Return to Finland | 306

Photo log

On the kitchen stairs of Mäntyniemi 1957. From upper left down, Anna-Leena, Marja, Antti, and Riitta; in the middle, her mother and Aunt Elsa; on the right, Matti, Irma-Helena, and Kerttu. | 5

Christmas, 1957. | 12

At Rauste summerhouse, 1960. | 16

At Rauste summerhouse, summer 1960. Family Pakarinen visiting. Back on the right, Pekka Vapaavuori. | 19

Children of the Lampi family: Antti, Marja (holding Elina in her arms), Riitta, and Anna-Leena, 1961. | 26

Riitta and Anna-Leena, summer 1961. | 29

Anna-Leena and Marja in Simonniemi, 1962. | 44

High school graduate, 1964. | 67

Anna-Leena spent the winter of 1964 to 1965 in Greece, in Bytouma Monastery. Picture from the spring of 1965. | 69

The guides of the Orthodox Church Museum, Irene Karjomaa, Leo Makkonen (later Archbishop Leo), and Anna-Leena, summer 1972. | 96

Bytouma Monastery. Photo by Nicolas Karellos. | 136

Abbess Euphemia. | 142

Bytouma Monastery. | 145

Sisters weaving. | 150

In the mountains surrounding Bytouma. | 154

Bytouma Monastery, upstairs walkway. | 163

Sister Kristoduli in Bytouma courtyard. | 195

Sister Kristoduli in Bytouma. | 200

Sister Kristoduli taking care of the chickens in Bytouma. | 206

Archbishop Paul in Bytouma, November 1984. | 215

Archbishop Paul celebrating liturgy in Bytouma, May 1985. | 218

Archbishop Paul and Sister Kristoduli at breakfast in Bytouma, May 1985. | 231

Feast of the Holy Great Martyr George. | 239

Last meeting between Sister Kristoduli and Archbishop Paul, April 1988. The Chapel of the Annunciation, Kuopio. | 245

Gardening. | 251

Sister Kristoduli at the Chapel of the Mother of God and Saint Seraphim, January 1992. | 268

Tonsure to a nun, December 14, 1992. | 278

Sisters of Bytouma Monastery: Theodora, Thekla, Parthenia, Kristoduli, Theodoule, and Agne on Patmos, October 1995. | 294

On the balcony of Bytouma Monastery. Photo Nicolas Karellos. | 296

Bishop Seraphim of Stagoi and Meteora (d. 2017). | 305

Sister Kristoduli on her 70th birthday in Lintula, June 18, 2015. | 309

Important events in the life of Sister Kristoduli

June 18, 1945	Born in Helsinki
1952	Schooling begins in Puistokoulu, Kuopio
1956	Starts secondary school, Kuopion Yhteislyseo
February 9, 1963	First visit to an Orthodox Church
May 6, 1964	Joins Orthodox Church
1964	Receives high school diploma
	First trip to Greece, to Bytouma Monastery
	Falls ill
1965	Studies Classics at the University of Helsinki
September 1967	Second trip to Bytouma Monastery
	During university studies, teaches religion in secondary schools in Helsinki, Hyvinkää, Riihimäki, and Lahti; during summers, serves as a guide in the Orthodox Church Museum, Kuopio
1968	Family moves from Kuopio to Helsinki
Summer 1972	Third trip to Bytouma Monastery with her sister, Riitta
Fall 1972	Scholarship trip to Greece, visit to Bytouma Monastery
1973	Earns Bachelor of Arts degree
Summer 1973	Caretaker of the Archbishop in Kuopio

IMPORTANT EVENTS IN THE LIFE OF SISTER KRISTODULI

July 10, 1973	Goes to Bytouma Monastery in Greece as a novice
1974–1997	Translates the Philokalia into Finnish
March 13, 1977	Tonsure to a rasophore (robe bearer) nun
June 1980	Travels to Finland; works on Part I of the Philokalia
Fall 1984	Archbishop Paul visits Bytouma Monastery
Spring 1985	Archbishop Paul visits Bytouma Monastery
October 7, 1985	Passing of Abbess Euphemia
Summer 1986	Serves as interpreter for Metropolitan Alexios in Finland
April 1988	Private trip to Kuopio, Finland
December 2, 1988	Passing of Archbishop Paul; travels to the funeral
October–November 1990	Travels to Finland, finalizes part III of the Philokalia
December 14, 1992	Is ordained as a nun
September 1993	Travels to the Holy Land
Spring 1996	Travels to Finland, lectures on the Philokalia at the University of Helsinki
June 1, 1998	Father's death and funeral
January 2001	Moves to Lintula Monastery, in Finland
December 23, 2020	Kristoduli sleeps in the Lord in the Health Center of Rääkkylä

Foreword

THE INITIATIVE TO PUBLISH Sister Kristoduli's diaries originated from her sisters Marja and Riitta Lampi, who visited Sister Kristoduli frequently in Lintula Monastery during the last year of her life. They also took it upon themselves to select and edit the diary entries included in this book from a vast amount of material.

Sister Kristoduli started keeping a diary in 1957 at the age of eleven, and continued with it regularly until her return to Finland (in 2001), excluding a little more than a year between 1964 and 1966. After her return to Finland, the diaries trailed off to a few sporadic notes. Thus, the regular entries cover a forty-five-year period of her life. There are approximately forty diaries and notebooks in total.

The diaries offer a window into Sister Kristoduli's life and her inner world. They also bring out the bright and difficult moments of her life as she herself described them.

Of the extensive materials, which were excluded from publication? The first culling was done by Sister Kristoduli herself. As she browsed through her old notebooks, she crossed out some words and text segments, and sometimes cut off entire pages. As she wrote in Bytouma on January 4, 1989, "In the past two days I have truly labored to go through my old diaries and censored them briskly. The internal pains and struggles of my youth do not belong to anyone else." On another occasion she censored her diaries in Lintula: "Today I have briskly cleaned up this diary notebook. It is not necessary to leave all the inner twists and turns to be examined by later generations, in case somebody might take interest in them. It can be seen afterwards, what of all the text written is meaningful," she noted in an entry on September 1, 2002. Otherwise, she kept a diary as if thinking it might be of use to someone someday.

Even during her time in Greece, Sister Kristoduli kept in touch with Finland by letters. She closely followed the life and events of the church and commented accordingly in her diaries. The Orthodox seminary and theological education, as well as the work and health of Archbishop Paul, were of continuous interest to her. Greek Church life and politics, news from nearby monasteries in Meteora, and world events—wars and catastrophes—all are there across the pages of the diaries. On the events of the Persian Gulf War alone she wrote dozens of pages.

This volume, however, focuses primarily on Sister Kristoduli herself—her ascetic path and inner life. Over the years and decades, the diary was her channel of release and a place where she could ponder everything around her. During her time in Bytouma Monastery, the diary worked as almost a discussion partner for her, as she was living with sisters who had had limited exposure to worldly affairs.

This book is first and foremost a narrative that depicts an intelligent, contemplative, and shy schoolgirl's development into a nun, spiritual leader, and writer with an enormous life's work. The diary is divided into two parts: her time before entering the monastic life and the years in the Bytouma Monastery.

While compiling this volume, the editors have respected the privacy of Sister Kristoduli's childhood family and of all those who interacted with her at different times. The same applies to the sisters of Bytouma and internal matters of the monastery, which are excluded from the diaries. Additional clarifications and explanations have been added as footnotes. Archimandrite Andreas of Lintula Monastery and His Grace, Bishop Damaskinos of Haapsalu have commented on the manuscript and provided useful advice and additional information.

In Lintula Monastery, on the Feast Day of Saint Anthony the Great, January 17, 2025.

Abbess Ksenia

Part I: Childhood and youth

Sister Kristoduli, Anna-Leena Lampi by her secular name, spent her childhood and school years in Kuopio. Her father, Heimo, was a fighter jet pilot. When Anna-Leena was a toddler, he studied to become a lawyer. Her mother, Anna, worked outside the home, and her father's sister, Elsa, took care of Anna-Leena, the oldest child, while Heimo was completing his law degree in Helsinki. When Anna-Leena was three years old, Heimo returned to work in Kuopio and three more children were born, at two-year intervals: Marja, Antti, and Riitta. When Anna-Leena was fifteen, yet another child, the youngest one, Elina, was born.

In 1958 Anna-Leena transferred to a secondary school in Kuopio, Kuopion yhteislyseo. Her mother was on the teaching staff, but she did not teach Anna-Leena. Religion was not emphasized in Anna-Leena's family, but since she was a schoolgirl, she was certain of the fact that God had created the world. As a teenager she escaped the frost of the winter and went to warm up at Kuopio Orthodox Church. Her path to becoming Orthodox and a nun started from here.

NOTES OF A LITTLE SECONDARY SCHOOL GIRL

I would like to write down all the thoughts and events of my life in this book. I hope that nobody would read my book without my permission.

Anna-Leena, 11 yrs. February 15, 1957

Saturday February 16, 1957
It is so hard for me to be myself; I am pretending almost always. Sometimes I get an odd notion that I should kiss the entire world. For example, when I was skiing alone, the world was so beautiful and fairytale-like. It

is also difficult, when I would like to bring joy to my father and mother and the children, but somehow it does not work, and then it is said that I am no good, even if I tried to be as good as possible.

Sunday February 17, 1957
Oh dear me, now I told a lie, namely to my mother. She asked: "Have you started to use father's aftershave?" I said, "No, of course not," although I had used it.

Monday February 18, 1957
Usually I have two moods, evening-mood and morning-mood. In the evening I am usually kind, quiet, and lyrical, and my mind is much more receptive. In the morning I am boisterous, frisky, and happy. One time in the evening I thought that I would become a martyr and a good and gentle being. Well, when I woke up in the morning, I was happy and frisky and totally forgot my thoughts on being a martyr.

Friday February 22, 1957
I would so like to bake something, but Mother does not allow it. She can tell everybody how bad I am at household chores, but who is a blacksmith at birth? When nobody ever advises you and you cannot even try for yourself, who would learn or could do anything?

Monday February 25, 1957
In the morning we decided to go skiing. Mother and I shared a pair of skiing boots, so she needed to buy a new pair for herself. Because it was the end of the month, she needed to buy them on credit. At the start of the ski trip, I asked Mother, "In your view do I look like someone who could grow to be beautiful as an adult?" Mother replied, "I think you will surely become an ordinary looking girl." Then I decided to become very beautiful.

Tuesday February 26, 1957
While eating I played a small educational prank on Antti. We had grapefruit for dessert, and Antti had naturally gone beforehand and reserved the largest one for himself. He had put two spoons into it as a sign. I ate quickly and went to the kitchen, where I changed Antti's grapefruit to the smallest one. I of course put the spoons in it.

PART I: CHILDHOOD AND YOUTH

Friday March 15, 1957
I just listened to special news on a train accident that occurred in the morning. At least twenty-four dead, thirty seriously injured, twenty lightly. My own things seemed so small after this event. People are continuously exiting from the world's infinity, and I am worried about getting 8.5 and not 9+ in my latest Swedish language exam.

Tuesday March 19, 1957
We argued, Ulla[1] and I—or actually we did not argue but rather discussed—the world's creation and whether God existed. Ulla had discussed this with her cousin's husband. He had staunchly argued that God does not exist, and that supposedly human beings have evolved from a monkey, and a monkey from a cell. But where did the cell come from? Somebody has had to create this world, and I am sure that this somebody is God.

Wednesday March 20, 1957
I have just heard that I am the best student in our class. In all other subjects 9, but in religion 10. It is a pretty good report card, come to think of it, but I am horrified, how could I keep it that way. May God help me in that. I think that when you trust God, you will manage all the difficulties, at least I have managed so far.

Friday March 22, 1957
Yesterday evening I was at a party at the lyceum, Ulla was there too. A catastrophe happened. Nobody came to ask Ulla or me to join the circle dance. The fact that nobody asked me was no wonder, but not even Ulla! Ulla, who is the queen of circle dance in Kuopio.

Wednesday April 17, 1957
Ulla has visited almost all the inland cities in Finland. I have only been to Kuopio, because I live there, to Helsinki some three years ago, and to Lahti about three years ago. In the past three years I have only gone to Litmalahti.[2] Awful, now I will cry! I don't believe in spring fatigue; I could cry like this in the fall as well. The obstacle always is: "We have no money." And if you say something to Dad or Mother, you will immediately get a

---

1. Ulla Ryynänen, classmate and lifelong friend.
2. The Lampi family rental summer house, Mäntyniemi, and the farm of a close family friend, Pakarinen, were in Litmalahti.

flow of arguments from their childhood, how they were always content with everything. Let it be that they were, but I, most certainly, am not.

Friday May 10, 1957
Awful, tomorrow Dad and Mother and Antti leave for Litmalahti, and Grandmother comes to our place. And the worst of all is that I need to keep her company! I would like it best to be by myself. Social interaction is a disaster for me.

Sunday May 12, 1957
We have Grandmother here now, and her presence isn't too bad.

Monday May 13, 1957
I visited the cemetery today. Ulla was with me. We were thinking of finding a small, deserted grave and taking care of it. After looking for quite a while we finally found a small grave. Laina had died at the age of one in 1890. We got money from our paper collection and bought grass seeds and flowers. For the flowers we bought a small vase. Laina[3] is a fitting name for Laina. She has in fact been on loan from God.

Tuesday May 14, 1957
Ah, it is so sweetly peaceful here in the cemetery. People who rest here know what happens after life.

Monday May 27, 1957
I read the Bible a little bit and was taken over by deep repentance when I read Jesus' words: "If you say, 'You fool,' you will be liable to the hell of fire."[4] I have often done that. Said to Marja, "You fool!" Dear me!

Thursday June 6, 1957, in a hotel in Stockholm
It has been lovely here! I spoke a little Swedish. Yesterday we (Mother, Marja, Aili Järvinen,[5] and her daughter Seija) had an adventure in the city hall and the Chinese embassy. Today we rode a motorboat around the city. Yesterday we were at Skansen.[6] We visited its Tivoli.[7] There we rode

---

3. Which means "loan" in English.
4. Matt. 5:22 (New Revised Standard Version).
5. Family friend and science teacher.
6. An open-air museum.
7. A historic amusement park.

the ghost train. To tell all of this would require many pages, therefore I just mention the details.

Thursday June 13, 1957
I don't know what is the matter with me. I am surprisingly down. I feel like perfect happiness does not exist. Here in Litmalahti, which felt like a paradise of happiness in the winter, insects bite human beings, and there are nasty weather conditions.

Monday August 26, 1957
There are plenty of berries here, and we indeed pick them every day. Aunt Elsa and Irma (Elsa's daughter) are here. Granny has visited, as well as many other guests.

Tuesday August 27, 1957
So, tomorrow we leave. Fun! I surprised myself when realizing that I had hoped to go back to the city. In the morning we went mushroom-picking with Dad. It was so much fun to tramp around the autumnal woods in rubber boots.

On the kitchen stairs of Mäntyniemi 1957. From upper left down, Anna-Leena, Marja, Antti, and Riitta; in the middle, her mother and Aunt Elsa; on the right, Matti, Irma-Helena, and Kerttu.

Thursday December 19, 1957
I have not written in a long while. It is lovely that school is out and Christmas is very soon here. I have completed making all the Christmas gifts. For Mother I made a linen cloth, for Dad and Antti I made a clothes hanger cover. For Riitta I made mittens. To Marja I will not give anything, because she told others what I will make for Mother.

Thursday January 2, 1958
Marja has chicken pox. There she is, knitting so peacefully. Sometimes I admire her. Even yesterday, when Antti dropped her leopard Täplä (Spot), she said, "We may not be angry at Antti, it was an accident." She resembles a lily flower.

Saturday May 3, 1958
To me it is totally crazy when girls brag about crying in a movie. Bah, staged events, where nothing has happened to the people!

Wednesday October 1, 1958
Today I have been frustrated many times, but especially by one thing. The history teacher did everything to make Salli a target of the entire class's ridicule. She truly succeeded, the class was rolling in laughter. Salli endured it with remarkable calm. But I did not feel like laughing. I smiled, but with contempt. My expression, which was flaming with anger, probably got our teacher back to her senses, and she said, "Ok, I have already bothered Salli enough."

Immediately after class I went to Salli, making sure that the teacher saw what I thought about her. The reason why I did not laugh is that I have tried to learn from Jesus's rule, "Do to others as you want them to do to you," and empathize with the other person's position. I imagined that I was Salli, how would I feel, if I was tortured like that. Some others would do well to try this trick too.

Tuesday November 11, 1958
"When with clean wings I come to You in heaven, I will receive a new pure spirit as a gift granted to me by my Creator..." Remembering these words from Eino Leino, I always feel myself happy. Especially before exams. I think that what mark I get on my English test, for example, does not have any bearing on whether I can come to my Father and Jesus in heaven. Then I am not tense before the exams anymore.

Sunday November 16, 1958
I absolutely have to share, how wonderful a time I had yesterday. I was namely again with Eeva-Liisa[8] in a youth evening gathering in the new parish hall. Before the actual program started, Toiviainen[9] came to us and asked how school was going, etc.

This evening was an evening of discussion. We talked about prayer. I tried to hide behind a woman, but alas, Toiviainen marched directly toward me and handed me a note and the Bible. I examined the two questions written in it and thought that I would sink below the earth, if I had to answer. I did know the answers, but that I would need to speak and explain the questions, horrible! Well, in any case I had to answer. With a wavering voice I explained my thoughts.

Then Toiviainen said, "Exactly the same answer was at the tip of my tongue. Yes, exactly the same, what Anna-Leena just said." Indeed, God hears the prayers. My Father, I am so happy for this! Thanks be to You!

Saturday November 22, 1958
Today something happened that I want to share. I came to the classroom during recess to open the window. It was a bright morning. The red, recently risen sun was shining into the classroom. I knelt down beside the teacher's podium. I prayed that our Creator would give me strength to lead our pupils to good, to encourage good in my class. The moment was joyful. I sensed the closeness of the Lord.

Monday January 5, 1959
It is so difficult to be good and to know when one has done something right or wrong. I notice also that goodness irritates people. And still, calmness causes people to lose their temper.

Just now Marja came here and asked, "What are you doing?" I answered something and glanced at her. Then she immediately attacked me, scratching and screaming, that I may not keep such a terrible face and speak so formally. I detached her from myself and pulled her hair a little. I am not exaggerating; I really pulled her hair just a bit.

---

8. Schoolmate Eeva-Liisa Flykt.

9. Kalevi Toiviainen, Anna-Leena's well-liked religious education teacher, Bishop of Mikkeli, 1978 to 1993.

Sunday March 1, 1959
Exciting and fun! Tomorrow morning at six I will depart to Helsinki all by myself. I will first travel to Lahti and stay there for a few days and then from there on to Helsinki. It is exciting to travel alone—I have not yet ever traveled alone. I think it is so charming. Truth be told, the trip scares me a little, not so much because of loneliness, but rather because of needing to go there and be criticized in front of the entire family, all of the aunts, uncles, granny, and grandmother and endless cousins. Eek! Although it is still wonderful!

Wednesday March 18, 1959
Probably every young person thinks that he or she will become something special. However, that happens only to a few. All think that they are one of the few.

Good Friday, March 27, 1959
It is raining. Even nature cries remembering the Lord's passing. My Lord was crucified today about 2,000 years ago. I cannot really comprehend it yet. This happened also for my sins. Oh no! I should be happy and joyous, but still it is so tragic. Oh they, who do not know Christ! I pity those millions and millions of Muslims and Buddhists, who fervently pray to their idols. It is claimed that God is the same as Allah. But Allah does not have a son, there is just Mohammed. In fact only a small portion of all the world's people know Christianity. Most likely Allah and Mohammed have the most followers.

May God bless us, especially missionaries, and let them win souls to Him!

Saturday April 25, 1959
I have noticed that all of the beautiful, grand compositions, lovely paintings and buildings have all been done for the glory of God, for example during the Middle Ages. It is so lovely to write this.

Wednesday May 13, 1959
Spring is almost too lovely to be true. Sometimes this beauty even hurts the heart. Every day new flowers open; birds return, and birch leaves grow before your eyes. Why doesn't this continue forever? Soon springtime is over, summer comes, which is equally as wonderful as spring.

Spring and summer disappear, but Jesus's gospel stays. It is always fresh and never withers away. I love Jesus, but my love is deceitful, because no one who does not love the least of his brothers loves Him. And I am afraid that I do not love my neighbor as I love myself. I think that people could do major acts of martyrdom, so that even others would notice. But we succumb to the small adversities of life. They annoy us and make us cranky and snappish.

Thursday May 14, 1959
This is Kuopio's waterless day. Water was turned on at 8 am for just a little while. I just heard through the grape vine that soon it will be on again. Enormous piles of dirty dishes are growing in the kitchen sink. We have not been able to wash them. In the school, pupils are panting in their seats because there is no water. And what about the hospitals! Surgeries could not be done without water. Only now I realize how precious water is. Therefore: all glory to water!

JOYS AND SORROWS OF TEENAGE YEARS

Monday June 1, 1959
I had decided to make last summer a charming one. That it indeed was. This summer's motto is: Vigor and research. I am not going to stay hopelessly crouching over and admiring Litmalahti. I am going to swim often and be happy and active. Deep down I have a tendency for such crouching and dreaming. Therefore I added research. It will focus on nature and especially on the Bible. Even in Särkilahti[10] I will find a place that I like, and in the evenings when it is not raining, I will march there with the Bible under my arm.

Wednesday June 17, 1959
I will be fourteen tomorrow. To me it feels like a lot.

We are now in Särkilahti and this place does not feel too bad. Our milkhouse is a little odd. All the deficiencies are compensated for by a little foal, which the farm has. I like Leija tremendously, and think that Leija is not afraid of me anymore, either. The entire family is embraced with equine enthusiasm.

---

10. The family spent the summer of 1959 at a rental cottage in Särkilahti.

Saturday August 29, 1959
God is miraculous. Always when I ask Him for help, He helps. I have had a chance to experience it many times in my life and especially this summer. I remember once, when I was just a little girl (five years old), I thought: "God exists, if He shuts the door after me." I stepped out and the door slammed shut. It made a huge impression on me. This summer I have experienced my prayers being heard, to my extreme astonishment. I do not at all deserve this kind of mercy. Yesterday a miraculous event occurred. It happened that Mother did not get any teaching hours from our school.[11] It meant that I could not go to England, and that my family's financial situation would be quite tight. I was very sad about this. I prayed to Jesus for help to the point that my heart hurt. I believed that God would help. And it happened! In the afternoon, Mother called from school. From the conversation I detected Dad's words: "—but won't you then get a huge number of hours?" Mother had gotten a position as the acting senior language lecturer in the classical lyceum. Classical lyceum operates in our school building. Now my trips are secured, and our financial situation has even improved. It is only two days before school starts, and the classical lyceum did not have a Swedish teacher. I see God's guidance in this. Thanks be to the Lord!

Monday November 2, 1959
I was once browsing through the pages of the New Testament. Suddenly Jesus's parable of the fruitless fig tree caught my eye. I am like that. I read the Bible and go to church, but then I am as mean or maybe even meaner than before. I don't do anything to advance Jesus's cause. The moment somebody mentions religion, I quiet down and try to divert the discussion elsewhere.

Sunday November 15, 1959
Something horrible has happened. Unbelief is starting to bother me a lot. Whatever I do, it creeps into my mind. I do believe in God, my beloved Jesus, and the Holy Spirit, but sometimes I doubt whether I can ever be a good Christian. Then I feel that Jesus cannot love me, because I am so bad. There is actually real deliberate meanness in me.

---

11. Mother was teaching at the school as a formally non-qualified teacher of languages.

Sunday November 22, 1959
At school I am frustrated during the physical education periods. I am just an extremely clumsy person. I cannot perform even the tiniest move on the gymnastics apparatus. Even now I am completely sore, thanks to Saturday's PE period. My hands are aching and my feet are totally tender. I am sure that I am miserable and awkward. In addition, I feel myself to be awfully ridiculous. I get very annoyed and sometimes tears come to my eyes.

I read a book on Florence Nightingale. I would not like to be like her. Of course, her work in Crimea was remarkable. All that she did for nurses and public health shows that she was a great human being. But she had some characteristics, which I feel to be my vices. For example, her mix of selfishness and ambition. I have quite a bit of that. I would like to be the leader and cannot stand competitors. I saw this also in Florence Nightingale, if it is at all proper to compare a little me with a genius like her.

Sunday December 20, 1959
I got a fantastic report card. I had seven 10s and five 9s in theoretical subjects. There were no 8s or below. I am happy. God has helped me. The 10s included the following subjects: English, history, chemistry, natural sciences (botany), geography, Finnish, and essay writing. Chemistry is a wonderful subject. I am on fire during chemistry lessons. My brain enjoys a little bit of gymnastics.

Yesterday I made a really large himmeli[12] in the living room. It is really beautiful. Even Mother gave me recognition for it. She does not call me impractical anymore, especially not now when my grade in home economics was raised to 8 and handicraft to 9.

---

12. A hanging mobile Christmas decoration made of straw.

Christmas, 1957.

Christmas Eve, Thursday December 24, 1959, 3 pm
We are presently decorating the Christmas tree. The children are radiant. I have prepared a Christmas play. Marja is Mary, Riitta-Liisa[13] is Joseph, Antti is a wise man, and little Riitta is dressed as an angel. She is darling in my nightgown with a candle in her hand. Christmas, now is Christmas! Oh Christmas, dear Finnish Christmas!

New Year's Eve, Thursday December 31, 1959
Actually one should now make good resolutions. I decided that after school starts I will go to bed by 9:30 pm at the latest. The day after tomorrow I will go and see Granny in Lahti. From there I will go to Helsinki. I will go to Svenska Teatern[14] to see "My Fair Lady." It will be performed in Swedish, but never mind that!

So tomorrow starts the 1960s, the decade of my youth. Next year is likely to be educational for me. For the summer I will go to England.

13. Riitta-Liisa Kinnunen, our downstairs neighbor.
14. Theater in Helsinki, with performances in Swedish.

Tuesday January 5, 1960, in Lahti
Children here in Lahti as well as in Helsinki speak strangely. The words, which in Kuopio are "twisted" (vowel shifts and rhythm changes), are here pronounced purely without "twisting" in standard Finnish. But here other words are modified, and people use strange verbs, apparently of foreign origin. Whatever does duunata (adopted from the English verb "to do") mean! I still don't know what the foundation of that word is. Sometimes the boys of Viirala, my cousins, ask me, "Don't you know what this means?" And often I, the "country bumpkin" (or whatever it is), had to answer, no. In Savo we say tiiä ("to know," in standard Finnish, tiedä). My aunt insists that I speak Savo dialect. That I don't actually do, because I have not mastered Savo dialect even if I do understand it. I simply speak in a different way than those in the humming Helsinki.

Sunday January 24, 1960
My life has felt quite monotonous lately. Mother says that it is abnormal, that I do not have friends whom I would meet outside the school. Yes, I do not have even one. But the girls in our class are just so emptyheaded. At least, the topics they discuss are totally stupid—sometimes dance courses or boys or clothes, other times fabric for a skirt or some simple homework. I cannot bear to listen to it sometimes.

Monday February 1, 1960
This morning I met Tapani, the new pupil in our class, on the way to school. I continued on my way, and he came after me. I did not quite know what to do, so I increased the speed. I was really embarrassed and felt quite shy. During this time the boy probably gathered courage to talk to this strange sphinx, who only talked when answering questions in the class. His steps started to get closer, and I, feeling ever more shy, increased my speed. But it did not help, because fairly soon he was walking beside me and started a conversation. I chatted back. In this way I walked all the way to the school. In fact, it was not anything extraordinary. It was like chatting with girls. Ulla and Marjukka[15] walked behind me, and Ulla looked awfully astonished. Even Anna-Leena dared to speak with a boy. Imagine!

---

15. Marjukka Huttunen, schoolmate and friend.

Saturday February 6, 1960
Boys never tease me, but rather talk matter-of-factly. Even in the street they greet me almost like they greet a teacher. This is not always so pleasing.

Monday February 8, 1960
It is nice to go to bed. Every day after evening prayer I have a sweet moment. I call it "on Jesus's lap." I namely imagine that the Lord and I sit in Gethsemane and below us is Jerusalem. I rest my head on his knee and He strokes my hair. Then I tell him the worries of the day and all the things that are bothering me. All this is so vivid that I nearly feel Jesus's hand on my hair, but I do not see His face clearly.

Thursday February 18, 1960
My life is turning into one great adventure. Apparently I will be sent all by myself to England for next summer. That is going to be very exciting. I will make it, I will have to.

Friday February 19, 1960
I was appreciated beautifully today. An examiner came into the class when we had Swedish lesson, and Pekka, one boy in our class, had not done his homework. During the previous class I offered him my notebook so that he could copy the assignment from it. He gratefully accepted the offer. After the Swedish lesson he looked at me seriously and said, "I wonder what would have happened to me, if it were not for you!" Usually I don't share my notebook, except in a real emergency. You don't learn anything by just copying from another. But now I was happy to have done that.

We were having a meal in the home economics class, and I felt myself awfully uneasy and clumsy. Suddenly the teacher with whom we were discussing the topic of being thin said, "Oh how Anna-Leena has so delicate limbs and slender body." Ha ha! Delicate limbs! I take it as a joke.

Sunday February 21, 1960
I went skiing with Marja and Antti. Wind was blowing and it was snowing. I enjoyed the weather, as so many times before I have derived joy from the unleashed powers of nature. Then I feel like a fighter, who is bravely pushing ahead in spite of all the difficulties.

Thursday March 17, 1960
I was at the seamstress fitting my new dress and heard how she and Mother talked about other people, and not a good word was uttered about any of them. I, who am fighting against gossiping at school with all my strength, hear it every day at home. I hate it. Always when I hear slander, I become awfully ashamed.

Good Friday, April 15, 1960
Tomorrow, Dad, Antti, and I will go to Litmalahti and the Rauste summer house.[16] My sister Marja is a sweet creature. First the thought was that only Dad and Antti would go. Marja and I presented our firm objection. Marja might have even wept a little. We just could not go. Suddenly Marja said that I can go, and she will remain home with Riitta. I would have never suggested something like that. I am impossibly selfish.

I attended a mass where communion was offered. The priest said gently, "Come to me, all you who are weary and are carrying heavy burdens, and I will give you rest."[17] Then they all took their coats off and went to meet Jesus. I could not go. I am just fourteen years old. In other words, I have not had my confirmation yet. I felt extremely lonely and abandoned. Nobody understood me. Why can't I go to Jesus's mercy seat? I was crying because my heart was hurting. Jesus never said that you need to be fifteen and confirmed before you can have Holy Communion. It is wrong. I so miss it.

Easter Sunday, April 17, 1960
Our new summer house is charming. The building is white. There is a porch, a balcony, and an upstairs. There are quite a few small rooms in the house. Mixed forest dominated by birch is growing in the large plot of land. In the yard there is a little vegetable plot, and there are also flowers. I am not especially interested in going to England. I almost feel that this summer house is nicer than Mäntyniemi itself.

Now I will go and see the "The Nun's Story." I have waited for it all fall. Now in the spring it finally came.

---

16. Rental summer house in the summer of 1960.
17. Matt. 11:28 (New Revised Standard Version).

Friday April 22, 1960
The film "The Nun's Story" was miraculous. The nuns, who always tried to forget themselves, were magnificent. After seeing the film, even I behaved in a dignified and composed way for a while. Instinctively I wanted to pull the sleeve over my hand. Nuns could only have their hands exposed when they were working. If I lived in a Catholic country, I might think about becoming a nun. I don't, however, think that I would join a monastery. Then I would need to forsake family and friends, the entire world.

I am going to be a doctor. Maybe that would be the best way to be useful for the world. I would like to, before I make my final decision, hear the call of Jesus. A vicar came to our school to give a talk. He told us about his youth. He had suddenly heard the word "Come!" over and over again. Nobody was talking. Oh, how I wish I would also be called to work, where I could be of most use. I would not, however, like to leave my beloved homeland for too long. Help is needed here too. Mission work would be difficult precisely for this reason. I would always be homesick.

At Rauste summerhouse, 1960.

Friday May 6, 1960
My eyes are becoming a problem for me. It is sad to have poor vision. And besides I hate eyeglasses. They probably make me look uglier. At least Mother has said so.

Saturday, May 7, 1960
I heard a song, "Jo Karjalan kunnailla lehtii puu."[18] Then I understood how it feels when fathers had to leave their home region. It would be upsetting if I had to leave the woods of Litmalahti, especially if they were left to the enemy. I feel pity when I hear Dad talk about his long hikes in the forests. His most earnest wish would be to one day be the judge of the jurisdictional district of Sortavala. Poor Dad, that will probably never happen.

Thursday May 26, 1960
Oh, what news has come to my attention. Mother said that we will get a baby. It is as if a bomb would have dropped. A baby! Mother is over forty, and our youngest child Riitta will be seven in the fall. I could not have expected this. I will soon be fifteen years old and will still get a little brother or sister. To me it is all the same, if it is a boy or a girl. Happy child! Just like this I would have liked to be born—with many older siblings. This one will really be a favorite child. She or he will be spoiled rotten. Mother told us the news out of the blue when we were at the dinner table. Riitta is totally beside herself with joy.

Monday June 6, 1960
The great adventure has started. I am happily in the ship. There are four of us girls in the cabin, including one who speaks Swedish. And we three from Kuopio speak it also. It is good practice. The cabin is cozy. I am just annoyed when I lift my eyes and see a red flag flying on the bow and mast. It is a mishmash of languages. We girls speak Finnish, Swedish, and occasionally English. In the ship people speak Finnish, Swedish, English, and Russian. The sea is completely calm and the sun is shining. The food is good here. Homesickness is not bothering me.

I will soon go for dinner. It will be at 9 pm. One of the Russian waitresses is beautiful. It is odd to be served. I am the youngest in this cabin. I would, however, like to be a little livelier.

Dad's last words were, "Remember that you are representing Finland there. Based on you, they will form their opinion of Finland." I have decided not to dishonor my beloved country.

---

18. "In the rolling hills of Karjala, tree leaves are budding."

Monday June 27, 1960
I have been in England for a long time. I can speak the language quite well. I have seen London and many other places.

Right now, I am in the countryside in Norfolk. I like this 300-year-old house. I like the Green family a lot. Mr. Green is very sweet to me and takes care of me like a baby. Mrs. Green is funny and the center of the family. I spent a week at the farm of the eldest son William. His young wife Christine is sweet.

Thursday July 28, 1960, in London
The day after tomorrow I am going to Finland and home. I am so happy. Soon I will be able to see Finland, our own forests and lakes. I love my country even more. We are so happy, because we are so few. England is a country packed full. Oh, my Finland, my dear Finland. I can't wait. It is wonderful to feel like being one of us. My country is a lovely, heavenly place. I pity foreigners. Homefolk, how I love you.

I spent two more weeks at a boarding school. It was like in books. I got many new friends. I am sure that the trip has been useful for me in many other respects beyond the language. I have learned to take care of myself. I have seen a lot. My worldview has expanded greatly. But returning home is the greatest joy of the entire trip.

Wednesday August 3, 1960, in a boat along the coast of Sweden
I am on the way home. In this ship there is a famous Finnish beauty queen, Marita Lindahl.[19] I have talked with her. My sister Marja will be delighted to hear about this.

Friday August 12, 1960, in Litmalahti
I am rowing to a small island near Lehmäsaari. The waves are splashing, and suddenly I remember the gray, hopeless, working class living quarters in London. Gifts of lady luck are not shared evenly.

This summer weather and feel is new to me. You don't know anything about summer in England. Water is wondrous. It feels velvety and looks like crystal. Summer will be over soon. In the city I am likely to get my own room, because we will get a day helper. I do not yet want to think about the end of summer. Mother is starting to look quite round. We are

---

19. Miss World 1957.

guessing whether the baby is a boy or a girl. The latest assumption is that we will have twins, a boy and a girl.

Monday August 29, 1960
This is like a dream. I am sitting in the most charming small room. There is an old-fashioned desk and a bed with a new and becoming cover. The windows have light curtains. A mirror and a few paintings enliven the walls. The ceiling has a light fixture, and in addition the desk has a table light. The room has a new green chair, and there is a yellow pillow on the bed. I can see the sunset in between two buildings. The room has been recently cleaned up, and it smells fresh. And this room is my very own. At last, I have gotten my own room. I am so thankful.

I spent a wonderful August in the countryside. In Litmalahti I met a boy, and we became friends. He is a few months older than I and already in the sixth year of secondary school. He worked in the house. Pekka's father died recently. Poor Pekka had to earn some money in the summer. We had great fun guiding little children around the fields and threshing barns. Pekka got along exceptionally well with children. Little Tapani was actually the one who introduced us, because he was quite attracted to both of us. "Anneena and Pekka, here!" insisted Tapani.

At Rauste summerhouse, summer 1960. Family Pakarinen visiting.
Back on the right, Pekka Vapaavuori.

Tuesday September 6, 1960
Our new baby can be born any day now. When I heard the news of the baby's birth, something jolted in my heart. I had in there a little structure, with an assumption that there would be four of us. I had to reorganize myself, so to speak. I am reading Dostoyevsky's *The Brothers Karamazov*. The book gives a lot to think about. All the time when reading, I struggle to overrule Ivan Fyodorovich's odd thoughts about religion.

I wonder what would happen if someone would get me to believe that God does not exist. Then everything would collapse. Therefore in my view it is dangerous to read books by Voltaire. Voltaire does recognize that God exists, but his God is quite different from the one presented in Christian teaching. I don't yet have enough counter-evidence. That's why it is dangerous for me to read philosophical books by deniers of God.

There are so many different kinds of people. Why is it so difficult for me to be free or at least natural with people, when Irja can shout to a new gymnastics teacher, that she cannot put on the new pants, because when trying them on in the dressing room she noticed that they were tight from behind? It bothers me to be unnatural and clumsy when I am in the company of strangers.

Wednesday September 7, 1960
I will go for my evening stroll, my "thank you" walk. That is when I recall all the fun and happiness that happened during the day.

Monday September 12, 1960
I got a tennis racket. We played for two hours yesterday. Tennis is an ideal sport. Blood starts to circulate faster, one gets livelier.

My own room. My favorite dream has come true. I can be in complete peace. It is so wonderful, beyond words. Siblings are good to have, but oh, how they sometimes get on my nerves. Then I go to my room, close the door, and throw myself on the bed and read with an apple as my snack. That is real relaxation.

Monday September 19, 1960
I have started confirmation school. I know that it will lead me to many spiritual pains, but will end up in a lovely meeting with the Lord at the Communion table. In the first hour of the school, a thought was stinging my mind: "Now I will leave behind my childhood." My childhood has been so bright and happy, I hope it is not over yet.

I hate domestic work. I will never be a good matron of the house. I could not satisfy my need to create with cooking or baking. Poor man whom I will marry, if I marry at all. I think I would like to dedicate my life to my work, especially scientific work, to which I am drawn.

Monday September 26, 1960
I try to clear my own path. In this world there are so many public highways and smaller paths, but there are also still many unexplored areas. I want to clear such an area, provide milestones for a short path that others could continue. Thus the world would move ahead even with my help.

Sunday October 2, 1960
Hurrah! I am a writer's daughter. Werner Söderström announced a big writer's contest. Dad wrote in the attic of the summer house the entire summer. Today at the 100-year celebration of the publishing house, the results were made public. Dad did not win the first prize, but his book was among those selected to be published. In all, 161 books were included. It was a great national contest. Finnish News Agency called. The title of Dad's book is: "—and your neighbor as yourself." What will the teachers and our class say! Maybe I have inherited some of my talents from my dad. Our father is a writer! What a news item! That also means money. The award is 500,000 marks. We will buy a new, bigger car. Many things are happening to me. Thank you, dear God! I have received everything from You.
    P.S. How does it feel to see a book in the bookstore written by your own father? I have no experience.

Saturday October 8, 1960
It is hard to be fifteen years old. Mood swings from dark despair to elated joy. All the little details bother me. One needs to desperately try to contain oneself. I have complexes. Eyeglasses are the worst of them. The way I look annoys me. I have not yet found my own style. The hair is what it is and pimples appear on the face. One does not ever again experience a sincere joy emerging from nothing as one did as a child. At least I don't.

Friday October 21, 1960
School is fun. We are like one big family. We have our shared sorrows, but also numerous joys. Girls and boys are not shy in each other's company anymore, but rather talk constructively and freely.

Monday January 9, 1961
Sometimes it feels incredible to think that I am walking around here in Kuopio as one insignificant being. An enormous globe gushes around me and an infinite space surrounds me from everywhere. All of the stars circulate there in a noble way as they have done for millions of years. Maybe there too are millions of living creatures. It is selfish to think that only we would be living beings, given all those hundreds of thousands of other places. And over here am I! After thousands of random events, exactly me. One would think that God would not find me even with His microscope. But He does.

Friday January 13, 1961
Mother said today that it is awful to see a young girl who does not care about her appearance. She meant me. In reality I do care somewhat how I look. I definitely want to be clean, but I do not accept anything artificial. I don't want to spend two years of my life at the hairdresser, and therefore I am growing long hair. I get to hear about it so much that I am becoming immune.

My mother, as I have mentioned earlier, is a great materialist, or at least she looks like she is. It is hard to know what emotions are truly meaningful to her. All ideals are banned. All "whims" like patriotism, faith, and other such will apparently shake off as time goes on. I said, "I want to always do my best." "Oh, I see, you are still in that world-saving phase," my mother remarked sarcastically. I am no world healer. I will try to do my best even at the smallest thing, as I have done until now. I am just a fifteen-year-old schoolgirl who above all else does not have any special talent. I got the best grade in many disciplines.

Saturday January 21, 1961
I am again in such a "fermenting" state. Nothing has happened to me for a long time. I would like to talk with Pekka of course, but of course not. Pekka's class had a Swedish exam today. Nice to see Mother grading them. I have my thumbs up for Pekka.

Sunday January 22, 1961
I was quite depressed this morning, but then I went skiing. The weather was wild. I glided with my knees shaking down the hills of Antikkala. Once I had to fall intentionally. Otherwise, it might have been disastrous. I was intensely trying to slow down, so I would not dive down the worst

hill of Antikkala, when I saw Pekka. In a brown woolen pullover he was energetically skiing up the hill with a classmate. I finally got myself to stop. Pekka greeted me and smiled with a mysterious, happy twinkle in his eyes. Our secrets are the small, fun moments of the summer. For my part, I was also smiling happily, and uttered an embarrassed little, "Hi!" Nothing else happened, but oh, how brightly the sun was shining. Even the people seemed so happy. All tiredness was gone. I skied as fast as I could and kept on smiling. In my view it is really odd that such a small encounter affects me like this. From the viewpoint of others, very little actually happened.

Tuesday January 24, 1961
"You are sweet!" said a Brownie hanging from my arm. It is nice to be recognized, even if it comes from a little Girl Scout. "From the mouths of babes we hear the truth," as we say. I would also like to be sweet in the opinion of others. But I think that the girls find me a little odd and serious and above all, even a little proud, "because her father is Court of Appeal Counsel and her mother a teacher." I have hardly ever heard a more false accusation than that. Yes, I probably am not sweet, because I am not boisterous or funny. I hope, however, that at least some would notice my tendencies for honesty, righteousness, and friendliness.

I have a strange mania for writing. I could well continue for another couple of pages. Writing is my favorite hobby. I would love to have a gift for writing, even a major one. Then I could write life-promoting positive books, which would give renewed belief to readers in the beauty of life, and they would continue their daily work happy and refreshed.

Thursday January 26, 1961
Today Ulla praised one girl. I also joined in that praise from the bottom of my heart. Ulla said that that girl is never proud, even though she is the daughter of the senior physician of Nivala Hospital. "Unlike some others," added Enni, an assistant. They talked about other things too in the same way. The fact that I walk in the playground during lunch break is absolutely not from pride, but rather I sometimes want to be alone and get some healthy exercise. And because they don't understand the joy of being alone, they accredit it to pride. What a net of gossip intertwines my oblivious being!

Saturday February 4, 1961
At the start of every week I decide this and that, but regularly at the end of the week I realize that I have fallen in everything. Jesus, I cannot endure this forever. Even my prayers are mechanical procedures. My room and my things are in disarray, I have snacks as much as before, I talk in a mean tone, I forget the golden rule: "Do to another what you would like the other to do to you."

Saturday February 11, 1961
The Kukkonen family is visiting us. Mother asked me to appear as little as possible; apparently my hair is awful. Mother wants to hide me from guests. She is criticizing me day after day, and she gets angry when I don't even blink an eye. She cannot imagine how I would like to be a pretty, mediocre, well-behaved, and nifty "ordinary girl" who does not think too much. Nobody understands me. People see me as a ridiculous idealistic fool.

Monday February 13, 1961
I have probably been awful. I have been condescending, lazy (i.e., I did not wash the dinner dishes), disrespectful (i.e., I declared a few unpleasant truths), blunt, weird, and stubborn. Mother is probably bemoaning "teenage youth" right now. She sees me as a model piece.

Saturday February 18, 1961
I am impossible. I believe now myself, what Mother has been trying to tell me for years. I am lazy and disobedient, a stupid dreamer who can never get anything. I am always so hurt and sad at home, that I don't care how I behave. Besides, I cannot tolerate my brother Antti. He is not stupid, but his actions and deeds demonstrate a complete lack of self-control. Sister Marja is the only one whom I like wholeheartedly. Everybody likes Mammu.[20] She is so happy and open-minded. There is still one more in our family, whom I despise and loathe. And that is me myself. Not religion, nothing helps me. If I blame myself, I also blame God. He was the one who created me.

---

20. Marja's nickname.

Tuesday February 21, 1961
I like physics. Most girls don't understand any of it. In the corridor they were enthusiastically wondering how I can get it so fast. "I don't understand physics, but it would be even harder to understand Anna-Leena," said Enni. I really enjoy physics lessons.

Friday April 7, 1961
I cannot tolerate that I am treated as a girl. Girls don't understand these things, this is a boy's thing. This does not interest girls. Why wouldn't guns, politics, technology, and other such things interest girls just like they interest boys? I for sure am interested. I guess girls should in a feminine way think about fashion, their appearance, boys, and housekeeping. I am furious. This is a country of equality. Why is there a demand that girls should be soft, feminine twits? Not me for sure, although many fit this role perfectly. In my view, in school there should be no attention paid to whether one is a boy or a girl.

Wednesday April 19, 1961
I was home alone with our half-a-year-old Elina. Little Ekku is a gift from God. I am so happy when I can press my cheek against hers, when I can touch her chubby arm, when she grabs my finger with her little hand, when we talk in Ekku's own language. She is lovely.

Friday April 21, 1961
Mother told me that the history teacher referred to me as her right hand. I know history so well. She also said that despite my knowledge I am modest and pleasant. Besides, I am supposedly much more advanced than my age group. Because of this I am undergoing a bout of self-confidence and superiority. It is dangerous to hear such admiring talk.

Friday May 12, 1961
These days I have suffered from a deeper than usual feeling of inferiority. I am so ugly. I only have my intellect, and even that may not be anything so special. The price of that intellect is that I don't have beauty, singing talent, charm, or sweetness. I am so serious. My ugliness has started to bother me. My hair, to use my mother's favorite word, is coarse and messy. I have noticed that I have beautiful hands. Fingers are long and slender. I am thankful for them. I am trying not to pay attention to my looks. Mother just keeps on reminding me of their awfulness.

Saturday May 13, 1961
I confess that my confidence in God has been a little bit shaken. I am fighting against it tooth and nail, but this has happened. My emotions are like those of Job. I am in rebellion. Lord, help me! I am drowning. Don't forsake me, the one possessed by the devil, to use my mother's only religious term.

Children of the Lampi family: Antti, Marja (holding Elina in her arms), Riitta, and Anna-Leena, 1961.

Monday May 29, 1961
Our class field trip is over. Everything was like a wonderful dream—shared accommodation, meals in a bar, and conversation! I got to know the class better and to love it even more. It feels awful to think that tomorrow we will be together for the last time. Us, the whole class. Then dispersed in the wind.

Tuesday May 30, 1961
I am becoming an adult. Already for years I have thought of many things as an adult, but now my thoughts have changed to be more mundane, and I can no longer shift to the worlds of imagination as easily as before. Just now I got a burning desire to imagine from the bottom of my heart. My

hungry soul wants to experience something merry, if not in reality, then by imagination.

Thursday June 15, 1961
Grandmother and I debated about Noah's ark. Grandmother believes in it absolutely firmly, as she believes everything said in the Bible. It is certainly quite clear that it only describes how God saved His created beings. Deluge has existed and remained in the tradition of the people of Israel as an account of Noah and his ark; it is a beautiful, poetic story. I expressed this view to Grandmother. She became quite agitated and started to talk about how every word in the Holy Bible is the real truth. I disagreed. That is merely a medieval perception. "Yes indeed, we will see. You are sinful and carefree people," said Grandmother. She would one day sit in her bright white gown in the golden city, while we poor relatives would be scorched in the fiery lake. I am sorry that I surrendered to [the desire to] argue. Someone, I think it was Kalevi Toiviainen, said that people believe in different ways. Others like that, superficially. They are offended if the Bible is doubted. Toiviainen said that you may not offend such people. Their faith is good in its own way. Once when I was younger, I asked Grandmother if there is a forest in the heaven. My goodness, a forest! That does not grow in gold. But I know for a fact that in my heaven there is a large, tall forest. There in a small cottage I would live with all those who had been my most beloved in the world. And it would not be too crowded . . .

Saturday June 17, 1961
Tomorrow is Jukka's[21] and my birthday. I am already sixteen years old. I sense myself to be so childish and immature. It feels like I have not changed at all since I was eleven years old. Sixteen is already a lot, a whole lot. I will soon be an adult. How awful. I am not ready for it.

Wednesday August 23, 1961
I went to a hairdresser. I certainly did not want my long hair cut short; no, since even the hairdresser said, "My goodness, I hope Miss Lampi is not going to have her hair cut short. So long and thick!" She definitely knew how to charm me. Therefore, only bangs were cut, which apparently fit my high forehead perfectly. The ponytail was lifted a little higher and

---

21. A cousin in Helsinki.

split hairs were trimmed, and look, even Mother was content. This really builds one's self-confidence. I am satisfied when realizing that I am not as ugly as I thought.

Thursday August 24, 1961
Mother and I were on an evening stroll. These days we get along splendidly. Mother is after all funny and special. I hope that the times when I argued with Mother have already passed.

Monday September 11, 1961
I got a gift from God. That gift is a little bit of humility. I did not get angry when little boys were laughing when I did the high jump, nor even when the gymnastics teacher said that I run heavily.

Thursday September 28, 1961
A very exciting and horrifying event happened to me. I had just left for school and was going across Puistokatu when, right in front of me, a motorcyclist crashed into a car. He had been looking over his shoulder and did not see it. Neither the car nor the motorcyclist had time to brake. I turned totally pale and stood motionless. A horrible crash sound was heard. The motorcyclist flew backwards and remained lying in the middle of the street. I rushed to him. Blood was flowing profusely from his head, and he was wheezing terribly. Of course the poor man was unconscious. Against my thinking, the driver and another man dragged the victim into the car and drove off to the hospital. My opinion was that he should not have been dragged like that, but rather they should have called for an ambulance. The police arrived, and my name and address were recorded for later investigations. I remember the blood, the wheezing, and the flight in the air vividly, but did not lose my composure. I think I might be fit to be a doctor. I prayed all day for the man. In tomorrow's paper I can read if he died or not. I don't think so, the speeds of both the car and the motorbike were quite low.

Saturday September 30, 1961
The man is alive. I went to the police station to be interrogated. I told them what I remembered seeing. I am likely to be a witness in the municipal court.

Thursday October 5, 1961
I am enchanted with life. I observe everything with active interest. Every day brings something new. I love this deficient world. All the hustle and bustle is endearing. I could almost say that I am happy. Isn't it happiness that you are waiting for every new day with joy?

Riitta and Anna-Leena, summer 1961.

Wednesday October 11, 1961
For a few days now I have seen everything radiating brightly. It is so peaceful in the class. I like my classmates. Sometimes, quite suddenly I have felt myself to be happy, and in some ways have glided on the surface of the ground. I look at the [new high school] class in the afternoon light, I walk along wet Kauppakatu at sunset. Everything feels so good. I have gained some inner peace. I thank Jesus for it. Saima Harmaja[22] is mys-

---

22. A Finnish poet famous for her religious poetry.

terious. I get an inferiority complex reading her poems. I have not been created to be a poet. Maybe there is some hope for me in fiction.

Monday October 16, 1961
It seems impossible that I would live to be old. How could I ever find equilibrium? I often wonder, now as before, what is the real meaning of my life. Recently I feel my life has become more organized and that my path is leading somewhere. I cannot say what such a feeling results from; it simply is the way it is. Why do I need to suffer so? I walked along the streets. The neon lights were shining unpleasantly on the wet asphalt. My foot was hurting. I hope God would not make me a writer! A human being, who would only start living after death. I want to become deeply happy. Deeply.

Monday October 23, 1961
We were doing the high jump. I was so afraid, my hands got moist. I got cold feet. I ran, closed my eyes, but my jump was weak and the bar dropped. Teacher asked me to try again. I could not. With my lips quivering I explained that I could not try again. The moment was unbearable. I felt like crying, my throat choked. The teacher looked at me and said that I don't have to jump anymore. She was so friendly. Merely from the relief I was about to burst into tears again. Imagine that the teacher understood me!

Tuesday October 24, 1961
The geometry exam did not go well. This matter felt so small when watching a tiny evening star. Enormous planets circulate along their orbits according to God's ordered sequence. What am I, what is my exam? A delicate glow illuminated the day. I want to surpass envy and anger. Because nothing is important besides salvation of the soul. I want God to be satisfied with me. I will need to fight a lot more.

Friday November 10, 1961
A poor girl was standing in the corner of the gymnasium watching how others were hanging from various pieces of equipment. Cold sweat made my hands moist. When my turn came, my performance was really bad. But my nice teacher comforted me, saying she had heard how "awfully good" I was in many subjects, and of course one cannot be good in everything.

Tuesday November 14, 1961
This evening we had a meeting of the Christian teenage guild at our school. I went there casually, not anticipating anything. Pekka was also in our school's teenage guild. I was a little surprised about that, but then I heard that the classical lyceum does not have one of their own. Finally we got into a very intense debate. Even though the topic was the good old story of creation, something deeper was involved. As it happened, Pekka and I agreed on this matter, namely that the story in the Bible is true, even if it needs to be understood as having happened within a long time period. When I said that we were debating, I mean that Pekka and I were on the same side, and Terho[23] and Olavi, students in our school, were on the other. The debate continued long after the meeting. Pekka and Terho, and Terho and I, confronted each other furiously. Terho nearly condemned Pekka and me to hell. That kind of debating is useless, that we all agreed, but we still wanted to talk about things.

Friday November 17, 1961
Russia plays around with us like a cat with a mouse. God, You need to help us. You are stronger than nuclear weapons.

Wednesday December 20, 1961
Maybe it has started now. Namely, purification by suffering. I was in an evening service in the church. Pekka was sitting there between his sister and another girl. They were chatting and singing from the same hymnbook. I wonder if Pekka anticipated then, that behind him, a modest girl with a gray coat was observing him with desolation in her heart? The girl found herself to be alone amongst people, her tender small dreams bitten by a frost. Pekka did not notice while laughing with the other girl that a tear rose in the eye of the backbench girl. She was weeping because of her orphanhood and went to Jesus. The world was so rude and hard. The girl herself was also rude and hard, she wept about that too. About her non-understanding mother she wept.

Thursday December 21, 1961
I need to fight to keep my thoughts at bay. I would so love to escape to dreams and daydreaming. I read from the psychology book that those are the drugs of the soul. I could spend hours dreaming, my imagination

---

23. Terho Pursiainen, theologian, politician, social scientist, and journalist.

does not set any limitations. It would be so easy and wonderful to escape reality, simply to refuse to see the facts and go around them. Just like a drug, so refreshing is a dream.

In our famous Friday evening debate, Terho mentioned that a human being should not use his intellect when thinking of God and His creation. "Faith alone!" God has given us our intellect, and I for one will use it as much as possible.

Saturday December 23, 1961
Children asked me what I want for Christmas. "A Christmas card," I replied. The children laughed, but it is really true. If I got a small, cheap card from Pekka, I would be very happy. Or if my biology teacher Muhonen remembered me with a Christmas card from the far-away India, my joy would be endless. Both alternatives are totally unlikely. I don't even think about them seriously, although my imagination can usually make the impossible possible. Will I become a lonely, quiet sufferer or a balanced, peace-radiating Samaritan? Let it be whatever, as long as I will not be mediocre. If I forget my brain and my goal to do good, I have become one in the masses.

Boxing Day, Tuesday December 26, 1961
I remember my primary school times well, even if I recall them ever more seldom. I even remember my seat, where I sat, when I got a little paper slip that said, "Why are you with Ritva?" Ritva was bullied, despised, and seen as a weird girl in the minds of the others. I was with her because already then I defied the society. I am and will always be on the side of the loser. My schoolmate Aune was suspected to have stolen a coloring pen. Later on, it became clear that she had indeed taken it. As the investigation proceeded, all of the girls had their nose out of joint and avoided Aune. A Thief! I was with her. We played hide and seek, horsed around. She insisted that she was innocent; I believed it, I could not doubt her yet. I did talk about the ugliness of stealing, though. We were together all the time. I rebel against the prevailing opinion and therefore defend those oppressed by it. Maybe during that time, when I felt the great joy of faith, fulfilling the will of Jesus influenced my deeds. That was a wonderful time. Nothing had collapsed yet.

A psychologist would say, "Being disappointed in an attraction, the patient seeks a replacement by transferring her affection towards an older person; in some ways one's emotional life develops backwards, because normally the period of idealizing and worshipping teachers occurs in an earlier phase of puberty. In addition, the patient seeks replacement from religion." I am angered by this, and I know it is not so. First, I liked Muhonen and was seeking Jesus already when I liked Pekka a lot. Therefore, they cannot be any kind of replacements. I love Jesus for His kindness; similarly I like Muhonen for who he is.

Saturday December 30, 1961
I am in the beginning of my life's journey. I am setting out on the path on which most fall. They will arrive as materialists; they cannot reach the "brightness of the peaks," as [the mountain climber] Carrel says. I have to get there; my spirit has to elevate. I will do it; the carpenter from Nazareth will lead.

Sunday December 31, 1961
During this year I want to get some glow of God's love in my face. My aim is to become an open, refined person who understands her neighbors. I can reach this only by strenuous daily efforts.

Tuesday January 2, 1962
I have gotten to know two sweet little American girls. They are visiting their grandparents, Dr. and Mrs. Hublin. The eldest one is ten and her name is Carita, and the younger is five and her name is Pami.[24] Neither of them can speak any Finnish. Marja got to know them in the yard and needed an interpreter. I by and large understand Carita, and she understands my English. "Tell the girls," Carita starts the talk. She and her little sister were playing with us today. I guided their work. My experience as a Girl Scout leader was very useful. I remember a whole bunch of different games. It was fun to speak English and fun to listen to Carita speak. All of a sudden it was very important to me that those girls liked to be with us and in Finland in general.

I fell asleep yesterday, overcome by a miraculous feeling. I felt that I was very high and Jesus was closer to me than ever before, after my childhood years. I got strength from Him. It flowed into my heart. An unknown peace filled my mind. I love Jesus and I know that He exists. But it cannot be explained by one's intellect.

24. Carita and Pamela Sztybel.

Thursday January 11, 1962
When my pen pal Susan told me about her dances and cocktail parties, Mother said to me, "Doesn't your life feel colorless? In a few years you will also get a similar experience, if you ever will get one." "No, I will not get one," I answered with a smile. My life is now so full of content, it is so pure and organized. I have my everyday struggles, I have Jesus, whom I believe. Even my mind also believes. The Lord has been and will always be.

Friday January 12, 1962
I am free. At last! My suffering, which has taken over two years, is over. I do not like Pekka the same way as I did before. Now he is just an ordinary boy to me. I realized it finally today in the Christian guild event.

Sunday January 14, 1962
I have again suffered losses. For the life of me, I cannot control myself when Father and Mother are present. I talk sarcastically and am probably appalling. The follower of Jesus disappears every Sunday.

Yesterday I forced myself to invite a classmate over. She is a country girl, and her roommate had gone to visit her home. I was quite annoyed. When she finally came, I spent a few hours with her. And it really was not much fun for me to talk so much. I have a strange tendency to keep people far from myself. I hate small talk between two people. I love discussion and opening up between two people.

Sometimes I feel that I have a boy's soul in my girl's body. I would want to do all kinds of things, but Mother says that hardly anything is proper for a woman. Ha ha, and why not! Are we in some ways weaker weapons in God's hands? When God uses His weapon, be it a man or a woman, the impact is equally strong.

This world feels so heavy, so impossible to win. If I were Catholic, I would consider going to a convent. Then I could leave everything, witness my faith wearing a nun's habit, and serve God with hard work at a mission center. Jesus did not mean that people should go to a monastery, but these days He would not be sorry about it either.

Tuesday January 16, 1962
It is difficult, or should I say impossible, to become a saint with my kind of character. I am not referring to a hypocrite, but rather to a genuine

person following the will of God and living in communion with Him. I am so intense and selfish. My sense of right and wrong is strong, when it is a question of myself. St. Paul, I guess, was even more intense.

Tuesday January 23—Thursday January 25, 1962
Father will become the judge [of the municipal court] of Juva. We will move, but I will stay here. Where will I stay, how do I feel? I am not going to burden myself with that this spring.

I want to stay here to continue my schooling, even though we will move to Juva. Mikkeli is closer; however, I will stay here.

Sunday February 4, 1962
I fought so hard today that I am still feeling weak. I was asked to empty the waste bucket, but I said I will do it as soon as I have done my homework. I shut myself in my room, but Father got one of his disciplinary attacks and insisted that I need to go IMMEDIATELY. He turned the lights off from the main switch—quite a good illustration by the way—so I could not read. It is rare that a child is punished by being prevented from doing her work. That should only encourage me. I was ready to stay in the dark the entire evening and decided that I would not empty the waste bucket at all, not even if I would lose my head. Father probably imagined that he was very witty by turning the lights off, and the most horrifying thought is that he probably thinks so even right now. I took the bucket outside pretty soon after the lights were turned off. I struggled and clenched my teeth, and I almost broke the window by pushing it. It was so disgusting, so humiliating to my nature to obey a command only because of the punishment. I am still totally furious. But I had to! "If any wish to come after me, let them deny themselves and take up their cross and follow me," said Jesus.[25] I was very sweaty, just about to burst into tears, and my feet had no strength. But I had to do it, because I want to follow the Lord.

Wednesday February 7, 1962
I am beaten. I am sorry, so sorry, that I feel like I could not stand up ever again. In the morning I got so furious that tears welled up in my eyes. You see, Mother insisted that I need to move to Mikkeli for school. It has become an obsession for her. And I am not going there! I will escape from home if they do that. Tears were again in my eyes.[26]

25. Matt. 16:24 (New Revised Standard Version).
26. The family did not end up moving to Juva.

Friday February 9, 1962
"Please come here, Anna-Leena. I have something to tell you," said lecturer Kallio-Kokko after the lesson. She asked me to take two girls for tutoring. They had lecturer Havansi, dear old Pökö, in English, and these naughty girls did not follow the teaching at all. In other words, I will become a public servant! I will give English lessons, how glorious!

When I stand in admiration of our untouched landscapes, I sometimes feel that I live in the middle of a disappearing idyll. Soon the city will encroach all the way to the edge of the sky. The skiing field is already being destroyed fast. Nature changes, and the people change. "The image of our homeland, its friendly mother's face has been carved into the depths of my heart forever"[27] during the summers in Litmalahti and winters in Puijo.

Sunday February 11, 1962
There is also joy in the world. There are two kinds, and I have familiarized myself with both. When we had the Christmas party for the class, I noticed that I was asked to dance quite a bit, and I felt myself jolly and maybe a little triumphant. Already the same evening I regretted and thought about my behavior. I have chosen a different kind of joy. It brightens the everyday, and you don't need a party for it to be born. It is joy you don't need to regret. It is a great holy understanding that flashes in the glances of two people. It is the friendly smile of a teacher. It is the beauty of the horizon. It is the Bible, and for me it is also my fountain pen. Writing allows me to capture the time. Otherwise a day goes, another one goes, and nothing remains.

Monday February 12, 1962
I have learned to realize there are other values besides intellect. There is courage, self-denial, being considerate, ability for self-sacrifice, etc. However, a certain amount of intellect is needed for these too; for example, a fool cannot be considerate.

Wednesday February 14, 1962
Another happy, brilliant day. I gave my first tutoring lesson. The teaching was wonderful. My students learned so fast that right then and there I felt

---

27. From the poem *Kansanlaulu* ("A folk song"), by Aleksis Kivi (1834 to 1872).

satisfaction. Being a teacher, at least in our school, would not be boring. I thought it was so much fun, I was burning with enthusiasm.

Sunday February 18, 1962
It is lovely sunny weather. A real wintry "jewel" of a weather, as I call it. There is diamond dust in the air, and snowbanks are shining. I take my skis and glide ahead with long strides and slide down the hill and embrace nature and smile at the sun. That is how my skiing is.

Sunday March 4, 1962
It is already 9 pm and I have not eaten even a crumb all day. I decided it last night. I want to feel the pain of hunger, which is so often described, and, I hate to admit, reduce some weight. Simeon the Stylite could fast forty days every year. Why could I not therefore even just one? Quite a miracle, I guess I have been able to. I don't feel particularly hungry. I'm just feeling a little weak. I had been mean and stupid, I could hardly even pray anymore. Then this idea was born. I decided that if I have even a little bit of strength in my character, I will fast this day. Now I go to bed after having had no food. In total the fast will be thirty-two hours. From this I notice one of my characteristics: There is no middle way for me. Either all or nothing!

Saturday March 10, 1962
We had a party at school. Rauha, Pirjo, and I were sitting in the dark teachers' room and were talking. We talked about this and that, among other things earthly and heavenly love, which I think was a great problem for Rauha. There was hardly a happier girl at school than I. Most likely not on the dance floor while crashing music is playing. In the teachers' room it was dark, and we were discussing life's problems. Oh, how good everything was! How pure I felt my mind to be.

Saturday March 17, 1962
I came home from school with a girl. Her strange opinions and talks both astonished and amused me. Oh poor girl, what she can understand! She has not yet been able to get to know life other than very superficially, as has none of us. We lack experience and knowledge. We have barely gotten to know other countries. And then such people criticize everything and abandon, supposedly after long, deep pondering, all old, great, and good ideals, for which many have fought for hundreds of years. They are full

of themselves and do not understand that they are dust in the enormous globe God has created.

Monday March 19, 1962
We have bought a summer house, in fact two. They are both located in the same plot of wooded land of five hectares on an island rather close to Litmalahti. I have not seen the place, but Father and Mother are enchanted.

Friday March 23, 1962
When coming from the teen guild meeting, I chatted with Pirjo[28] for almost half an hour in the street. We always have such a good time. I am happy that Pirjo is in my class. Even I have got a "best friend."

Yesterday, sounds of movement could be heard from the attic of the house. One unhappy neighbor of ours had shot himself. Many times I had curtsied to him and taken the elevator together. The man had a burning look, I saw that he suffered. I remember how this winter, when going up in an elevator with him, I thought: "Here are two people. Why do we discuss the weather, when there is something else, more important?" It did not, however, occur to me to say something—that would have been so inappropriate.

Sunday March 25, 1962
Oh how I look! Poor posture, hair hanging down the neck, stain on my blouse—and I have had so many apples that I can hardly close my skirt. Now is again one of those rare moments when my appearance annoys me. It is only a small detail compared with everything else. If I will ever be better, it will be a miracle from God, because natural prerequisites I do not have. My own will does not suffice even to begin with. If I will become something, it will be a great miracle from God.

Saturday April 14, 1962
Pirkko asked the whole class to her birthday party next Tuesday, of Holy Week. Of course there would be dancing. I was a little taken aback, but then I was told and I believe that it was the right voice: "Anna-Leena, if you stay away, you will hurt Pirkko, spoil the joy of the class by declaring: 'I for one will certainly not dance during Holy Week.' Seldom do we have

---

28. Pirjo Hartikainen, classmate and lifelong friend.

a reason for joy, you are not going to muddy it. Holy Week is celebrated for the glory of Jesus, he does not die then anymore."

Tuesday April 17, 1962
The great tragedy of dancing: I obviously am not very popular. I danced three times. Many girls could dance much more frequently, and boys went to ask some girls for a dance several times. The tragedy of the life of a young girl: she is not popular!

Good Friday, April 20, 1962
Pirjo, thank you Pirjo, I like you so. She called from a phone booth, and we walked, just the two of us. Walking was not tiring at all, when one could talk. Pirjo has the gift of kindness. She can really console. She smiles and is sweet. We talked about God, and I felt much better. Pirjo really likes me, and prays for me. Oh how lovely that is! Thank You, God, for friends! Bless Pirjo, she is the sweetest girl on earth.

Tuesday April 24, 1962
It is so hard for me to be so alone. I often think about nuns. It would be good to be one of them. I remember one French nun, whom I saw in the London Underground. She was very beautiful, and her beauty was just the kind I would hope to get: purity of the soul. She looked happy. Just at the last moment before the train left, she jumped in the wagon, and the black gown got caught between the automatic doors. She wasn't startled, but rather laughed as if totally sure nothing bad could happen. If I converted to Catholicism and went to France to be a nun, I am afraid that I would never manage to gain peace. I could not bear to be separated from my fatherland and from my mother tongue, not even for Jesus. The little Protestant, poor thing, longs for the confession chair. Why don't we have such a thing? Poor little Protestant cannot let this become an obsession, because the poor little Protestant is and will stay Lutheran until the end of her life. Only if our Lord Jesus Christ appears to me, so that I can touch Him, and says: "Join the Poor Clare nuns!" I will obey. I would be happy in a nun's garment. There is something definitive in it, which we here in the "middle of the world" can never reach.

Thursday May 3, 1962
I went into that museum.[29] Undeniably it was magnificent. Gold, silver, jewels everywhere. However, the greatest impression on me was made by the ascetic instruments monks use, heavy iron crosses and chains with which they whip themselves. Then Kallio-Kokko, teacher of religion, asked, "Is Anna-Leena ill?" I came home and took my temperature. It was 38.5 C. I had some aspirin, and the fever was reduced. However, I did not go to school. Later Ulla came to visit. She was happily talking about the events in the class. Then suddenly, maybe even too lightly and in passing, I asked, "Did you change places?" Yes, they had changed places, and apparently, I got the first desk of the row by the wall. My wonderful view to the outside is gone. And above all it was the loss of Pentti's company, of safe, friendly Pentti, who already for three months had delighted my going to school. This is what I was afraid of, but I could hardly imagine how hurtful it would be. We read together and did math together. I think I have tears in my eyes. I am stupid.

Saturday May 12, 1962
This is like a fairytale, so grand, so lovely. I am sitting on a high, steep rock. In front of me is the calm open water of a lake on which clouds are reflected. Light radiates as rays through gaps in the clouds. There are no people, no human voice. There are great forests beyond the reach of the eye and a vast eternal open water of the lake. This is Finnish nature, which I love so that it hurts my heart. This place is an island close to our summer house. There are high rock formations, pure old forest, and plenty of animals here. No foreigner can understand us. This does not exist anywhere else. Our nature is the most beautiful for me, I cannot imagine that anything more beautiful would exist. Thoughts change, worries and nuisances remain somewhere out there, for whatever they are worth. Here by the wide-open lake in God's silence there are eternal peace and rest and balance.

Sunday May 20, 1962
We were in the countryside. Marja and I were running around the island. We climbed on the rock, sank in the swamp, and laughed. Laughter rang happily. We even sang together. It was miraculously wonderful. I jumped around in the field and ran in long strides on the rocks. The water

---

29. Orthodox Church Museum of Finland in Kuopio.

glittered, the sun was shining and made me tanned, healthy, and happy. It was uncomplicatedly beautiful. I am going to enjoy my summer. Although it is still seventeen days before moving to the countryside for the summer.

Monday May 28, 1962
Let me describe a party at the school. The description is rather subjective, but then again, this is my diary. We carried the mead buckets to the lower level hall, where they were testing the record player. When dragging the mead bucket, Olavi from the teen guild rushed beside me and asked to carry it. "May I?" he asked. "Yes, you may, thanks a lot!" I answered. He likes me. I noticed it again when serving the mead. He said in a Kalevala[30] rhyme, "Good hostess, beautiful hostess, give me some brew." It was the first time, by the way, anyone had called me beautiful even in Kalevala style—any boy, I mean. It is nice when someone looks at you in such a friendly way. However, I should not play around. We sang together as a group during the meal; even a few speeches were given. Our chairs Aulis and Eeva taught us a circle dance called "Kuusankoski pastor had a watermill" or something of that sort. The boys retreated as an unorganized herd towards the door, and Aulis commanded that the girls should come and ask them to dance. Unpleasant. Well, others were courageous and went. Aulis came to me and told me: "You will ask Pentti." And I did. I stopped in front of him and said bluntly: "I got a firm order to come and ask you." Pentti did not seem to mind at all. With pleasure he took my hand and walked with me. It was fun.

Wednesday May 30, 1962
I got a 10 in geography as well as four other subjects, and in music. So: essay writing, Finnish, history, biology, geography, music; average 9.25. The statistics have hereby been recorded.

Friday June 1, 1962
In the afternoon I was with Ekku in the War Memorial Park. We ran and played on the sand and grass. We horsed around and understood each other excellently. Ekku is a smart little girl. I periodically notice myself behaving towards her as an equal. Then we found a little baby spruce. Ekku was a little surprised when the baby clearly waved to her; the wind was hard you see, but then she waved back at the baby spruce.

30. Finnish national epic poetry.

Saturday June 2, 1962
I have been rushing around all morning in the kitchen. I baked and cooked food. Our maid Kirsti is in the hospital. I am not fit for domestic chores. I do not like doing them, and they don't go so well. Kirsti was able to achieve twice as much with half the struggle.

Tuesday June 5, 1962
This is totally crazy. All of a sudden I got an idea to go to Lahti. In spite of Mother's objection I went to buy a train ticket. With my eyes strangely glowing and even myself wondering about my courage, I walked to the bank and withdrew some money from my account. I continued walking towards the station and with a wavering voice asked if there were free seats on the fast day train. Now I feel very anxious. First, I angered Mother. Second, I missed a lot of fun; for example, tennis lessons and Poukama-evening gathering on Wednesday. The best part of the whole thing is that I realize my own stupidity and on return will see the beauty of my hometown. To the last moment Mother kept her proud, spiteful attitude, even though I hoped she would soften. For sure, she had full right to act as she did, but if she were a real mother, she would have accompanied me to the station.

In Lahti. I am writing this in the street. Grandma was not at home. What will you poor girl do now? I don't know Aunt Eeva's new address.

Later. I am at last here in Grandmother's house. I was walking along Aleksanteri Street when Grandmother walked towards me.

Thursday June 7, 1962
My Grandma is just amazing. If I could accomplish even half of what she has been able to in her life, I would be very satisfied. Even if she does not talk so much, one just gets the idea. I respect her and am very thankful that I have gotten someone like her as my relative. So fondly I listen to my Grandma's stories of old times; I listen and am ashamed of myself. Don't I wish I had inherited something from my Grandma! I have certainly gotten a lot of seriousness and love of nature in my character, but not her level of energy. I need to try to be better and always remember to love my Grandma. I hope I can come and visit her more often. I would like to hear a lot. Grandma shares many things with me and I am proud of that. She told me how she cried through the nights, and how early in the morning she went to Grandpa's grave, but during the day she had to

pretend to the children. For sure Grandma and Grandpa will meet again, God has arranged it.

Monday June 18, 1962
The seventeen-year-old got a fountain pen as a birthday gift, for which she was very happy. I had lost my beloved green one and was totally miserable, because I cannot stand pencils. We just had birthday coffee on the porch. There were fancy cakes and sweet juice for us children. Marja and I rowed against the waves and swayed in the wind. I enjoyed the thrilling feeling when we reached the crest of a wave.

Midsummer Day, Saturday June 23, 1962
I spent the night in Litmalahti. I stayed there when we got our things from the Rauste summer house. Dear Grandma borrowed her nightgown, and I slept in the bed of the drawing room as I had done many times before. Little boys were hanging around me and were sweet like bear cubs, but in spite of that I had time to do some work with Sirkka. We cleaned and fetched lily of the valley flowers to the tables. We weeded the vegetable garden, and the world went dark in my eyes when I got up. With the master of the house in the lead, we fixed the midsummer birches in the yard. Liisa, the madam of the house, unfolded her best light-colored carpets on the floors, rowanberry trees were brought in the family room, and vases were full of lilacs and lilies of the valley. The scent of the fresh bread grandma made fused with the fragrance of the flowers. Then the people went to sauna and came from there dressed for the celebration with a reddish face after the sauna. Then guests started to arrive, our family and villagers among others.

After the coffee we walked to the bonfire cape, where the midsummer bonfire has been burnt every year as long as people remember. The men of the houses, our father among others, sat on the grass and shared fishing stories. The women were chatting gently and happily, and the children were running around the bonfire. Then suddenly the bonfire flared, and all were busy explaining that they had never seen as nice a bonfire as this one. In the quiet evening we walked to the house while the bonfire embers were fading, and the sky glowed wondrously red. Lilacs and rowanberries give out their fragrance in the Litmalahti home mound. The flag in the mast waves a little. I so love Litmalahti, as it is like my homestead. I am always welcome there, there is always a drawing room bed available for me. When the evening was quieting, as the house was sleeping, I padded along the bumpy floor to the bookshelf and read a little. Then the family room clock strikes, I close the book and view the fields and the lake out there in the background. It is nice to sleep on the soft mattress and in the morning again to wake up for the chores of the house. Thank you, good God, for Litmalahti.

Anna-Leena and Marja in Simonniemi, 1962.

Sunday July 1, 1962
We came to town with Mother, who oversaw the annual exam re-takes for those who had a poor grade in a subject. I went to the movies with Marja to watch "I Saw Him Die," which I did not like at all. I am completely tired of those eternal Roman legions that are busy running around in these films. Then I came home to hear that Grandma will be sleeping in my room. Oh no, no, how disgusting! And I have to sleep between Marja

and Cousin Irma and listen to their stupid chatting, into which they often draw me too. I cannot stand others sleeping close to me, but it is a must. Oh, how I was thinking of staying up in the evening, staying up and praying, because, Jesus, that is what I need.

Monday July 2, 1962
I walked around the city, weird and afraid. Everywhere was rattling and squeaking. Cars put their brakes on, and I stopped, feeling horrified. Unknown people, smart looking young girls, boys in their bright colored shirts were walking towards me, and I thought that if they noticed me at all, they despised my ankle socks, ponytail, and insecure expression. I am so different. I can never become like that. In the middle of all the noise and my insecurity I thought of the peace which is above all understanding and which I want to reach. Help!

Monday July 23, 1962
I went to the grocery store. The wife of the grocer more or less did all the shopping for me, declaring how all kinds of things would be just right for us. I dragged the bag to the boat and rowed the two kilometers back. I again felt tired. It is really nice to feel tired after doing some work. Then you really feel satisfaction. And besides, I have the tendencies of a masochist. My tyrant-like spirit really enjoys when my body needs to fight opposing waves. The stronger the wind, the better, because the more tired one is after the trip.

Thursday July 26, 1962
The trees are humming, and the lake is splashing, and it is beautiful, but the mere beauty and staring at it tires a human being. Beauty should be the frame for life, not the main thing itself.

Sunday August 26, 1962
We have just come to the city. It is so nice, when our maid Kirsti has cleaned up the entire apartment. Even my room is sparkling clean and lovely. This summer was much nicer than the last one. I was really happy laboring with the twigs and walking around in the woods. I hope that the little crumb of peace I achieved would last through the winter and strengthen me. I wish I could smile warmly and chase away all the inferiority complexes.

Monday August 27, 1962
My hair is nice now. I got new clothes, and I almost feel pretty. Of course I am happy about that. When thanking God for all of this, I must pray that it would not become too important for me. I would not like to think about my hair and mirror myself in the showroom windows. The goal would be that my long curly hair would interest me only once in the morning and would then free me for the entire day, whereas the ponytail bothered me all the time. I am from the bottom of my heart thankful to the Father in Heaven. However, I am bothered by the thought that so much money was spent on that. There are people in the world who go hungry. How can I have the right to have expensive perms on my hair? It says in the Bible, "You shall love your neighbor as yourself,"[31] not "more than yourself." From my heart I would have wished a nice hairdo for a girl who for a long time would have been ashamed of her impossible hair. When that girl happens to be me, I guess I can award that for myself too.

Tuesday August 28, 1962
Our kind Kirsti is in the hospital, where she was operated on. Mother and I went to see her today. I was enchanted by the atmosphere in the hospital. It was peaceful and quietly bright. People talked peacefully, white beds stood in rows. It smelled mysteriously medical. I was overcome by a strong enthusiasm to once be able to work in that large friendly house, help people while thanking God, and to surrender to their death and comfort them. I wish God would have chosen that as my part. Kirsti was a little pale, but she will make it.

Wednesday August 29, 1962
I have all my life wanted to be a doctor, but only now I feel it to be my real calling. I think I would love that work. The hospital in my mind is magnificent. It would be great to work there. It would of course be more noble to go to more primitive circumstances.

Tuesday September 11, 1962
I returned home from the teen guild under a starry sky. "The Lord is my Shepherd," I said, and my heart was full. Under His stars, even in the middle of the universe, I knew that I, just a single particle, am striving toward the Lord, and He will notice me and will take me as His sheep. He

---

31. Matt. 22:39 (New Revised Standard Version).

will direct my steps, and I do not need to fear anything, not even death, because then I will finally reach Him. I can imagine the sweetness of seeing Him and am going towards it. He will forgive me during the trip.

Thursday October 4, 1962, morning
I woke up half an hour early. It is raining. That does not affect my mood. I again have a kind of nice feeling, that something may happen. I feel like that often in the morning. And indeed each day something does happen. It is interesting to observe life. Annoyances and worries belong to it. I have a tendency to analyze them objectively, even when I encounter them myself. Mood swings are part of life. Boredom and depression are part of it, as are childish enthusiasm and noble goals to move upward. If joy and enthusiasm are sometimes lacking, one can make observations of the opposite feelings! Oh this day, I wish there were red [happy] moments! Help, good God, so I could arrange a red moment to somebody's day.

Biology is totally magnificent. We talked about human genetics. It was so interesting. Then lecturer Muhonen talked about twin studies. I could even discuss these topics with myself in this diary. What a great combination. Interesting topic and respected, well-liked teacher! What else can a pupil hope for?

For me it is very comfortable to be in rooms full of books. So many areas of life are present then.

Monday October 8, 1962
In the afternoon I went to the hairdresser and had to stare at myself for almost an hour. I looked quite moving. Pale, sad, thin, of poor posture she was, that Anna-Leena.

Thursday November 1, 1962
Before algebra lesson, Pirjo and I were sitting on our desks and swinging our legs. We were happily carefree, we laughed and chatted. I felt like a young girl. Periodically we have so much fun, when we girls go as a group and are joyful. We are young and worry-free, the sun is shining, have a look!

Friday January 4, 1963
I long for something other than well-being, riches, money. I believe that I belong to that young generation, which in all quietness is rising and to whom material things are not enough; they have realized the hollowness

of it. Such serious, quiet young people exist, and I believe there are many searching around here.

Friday January 18, 1963
The school day was rather stormy. During the last three periods, the class was making a lot of noise from the mere relief of pulling through two periods of mathematics, where six-decimal logarithms got our heads heated. To the substitute teacher of church history, we declared with one mind our assessment of the subject: "Dry as purism and in addition useless!" One period should be merged with general history and the other allocated to teach dogmatics.

Monday January 21, 1963
Waking up this morning was gloomy. I realized for a passing moment that everyone's secret power is found in the hope that one day we will not need to get up again. Those moments of waking up in the morning show the world in the light of blatantly hard truth. It is hard to watch and difficult not to throw the alarm clock against the wall, because you know so clearly that all is absolutely in vain. Soon those moments are over, and the human being again gains his/her naïve but necessary optimism.

Tuesday February 5, 1963
Suddenly I heard a strange hollow sound from the living room. After a while Marja rushed into my room and shouted with a high-pitched voice: "Annuski!" I ran to the living room, stopped in the middle of the floor. Tears started to run down my cheeks. A new, shiny piano was standing by the wall. We have a piano! An expensive, great piano! I can hardly grasp it even now. I just cried, and then played it for a few hours. Although I write about it relatively seldom, I go many times a week and play the piano at school, but after this I will not! I have progressed quite rigorously, and now will progress fast. I play, I play, how truly beautifully it plays! What have I done to deserve this? God, You let all my dreams come true, even if I am so bad. Oh, God, I have not deserved a piano, I can never express to my parents the joy it gives me. The best gift back to them is just to rejoice from the bottom of my heart.

THE WAY TO THE ORTHODOX CHURCH

Saturday February 9, 1963
I went to an Orthodox Church for the first time. I said it like that, because it will not be the last time. When walking last night, I saw a door to a small temple open. I walked around it once and then steeled myself to go in. There was a small congregation, they were standing and kneeling, bowing and crossing themselves. I looked at the people, old mamas, who had come from as far away as Karelia, from the lands of songs. They had the "true faith" in their blood. One could see that their ancestors had prayed the same way. But I did not focus so much on the people. A strange mood overcame me. I felt I was serving God as it had been done since the time of the apostles. The Orthodox Church is original and has remained united, the mysticism of ancient Byzantium and the sighs of the Slavic world echoed in their church singing. I listened to them, mesmerized. The hymns, even as performed by the small parish of Kuopio, had wondrous attractiveness; they were old, enhanced by centuries, and beautiful, full of piety and praise. The difference with Protestant hymns, which everyone sings with their own style, was remarkable. I listened to the Akathist hymn to the Virgin Mary, "the Mother of God," and prayers of thanksgiving to Christ and God, where it was said that He "loves mankind." The plea "Lord, have mercy" still echoes in my ears. In that had been crystallized the cry of humankind. So beautiful were the songs; and beautiful was the small church also. There was something eternal, holy, and sanctified. When I watched the people kneeling down, I wanted to throw myself on my face on the floor. God was there in that church.

Divine Liturgy is most certainly an oasis for members of the Orthodox Church. They receive beauty, they can sense the presence of great mystique, they can feel a miracle, which the Lutheran pastors just keep on explaining after explaining. Even in modern times, the Orthodox Church has retained its age-old inheritance of Christianity. Therefore, I will go there again next Saturday. The core of the issue has now become clear to me: In the Orthodox service God is worshipped; in the Lutheran worship the parish is served, which sits there criticizing. That is it.

Tuesday February 19, 1963
In the street I saw the Orthodox Archbishop Paul. He is a very modest-looking, thin man. Deep life wisdom can be seen in his face. In some independence celebration I heard Bishop Paul speak, and I immediately

admired him. I have sometimes seen him in the street, always alone and looking pensive. One would not think that this man is an Archbishop, but he can be recognized as a Christian immediately. Today it seemed that he really noticed the people walking towards him, and suddenly his blue, pure glance met mine. I was close to curtsying, even though Bishop Paul had probably not ever seen me before. I pondered that there are still true Christians and people, who really know Christ and live in Him. New hope, new belief in life made me straighten up and smile. Bishop Paul's blue glance got me thinking of sincerity and innocence, which is not naïve. There is something harmonious about him.

Friday February 22, 1963
We had "kicking-out" celebration[32] at school. Luckily it was just for junior and senior classes. Tomorrow evening our class has a "class party." I do not like parties. I get an uncomfortable feeling, when I should have fun, and at that moment I do not have fun. Stupid. That disturbs my peace of mind. But I have to go to the celebration, and I guess also the class party; I will go, but will not expect anything. Oh, what a pity about tomorrow evening, when I cannot even go to the Orthodox Church!

Later. I slaved away the whole time. I carried tables and chairs, teacups, coffee cakes, water jars. I served the teachers and washed all the dishes in the school kitchen while others were doing circular dances. Nobody asked me [for a dance]. Marjukka and Rauha from both my sides were led to a dance. I escaped with cheeks burning from the hall. That hurts me. I feel ridiculous. During normal days, I think that the boys in our class like me and enjoy talking with me, but when not even one of them asks me, I think that they talk to me from pity and outright laugh at me. I cannot bear that thought. I do not want to be subordinate to their tyranny. Thus I was washing dishes in the kitchen and thought, how good the new humiliation had been for me.

Saturday February 23, 1963
I wanted to cry at school. The seniors were rowdy. It makes me shiver to think that next year we need to be like that. I do not know how to be cheerful. I am always criticizing. I did not go to the class party. It makes no difference whether I am there or not. I despise fancy clothes; rivalry between girls is despicable. I am poor at pretending. It would be fun to

---

32. When the high school juniors bid farewell to the seniors.

know the extent to which the fact that I am not popular influences my thoughts. Maybe it is good fortune. I am vain enough as it is.

I do understand the danger of being isolated. I become strange; I close up so that I cannot open the cover. But I cannot help it. I have a passionate longing for loneliness, as well as to closeness with souls, but I detest the middle ground. I am alone.

Monday February 25, 1963
I have been thinking that I would need a nun's gown. It would help me to be watchful, even if it could not save me from the Devil. I do not know what to do. I try to resort to the Bible. The word of God is there. It will expel the Devil.

Tuesday March 5, 1963
If this country were Catholic, this little girl would have gone to church this evening. At the moment, when the evening sky is brightest, she would have stepped into the old church, into the dim light of stained glass windows, and lit a candle for the Holy Virgin, because the geometry exam had gone really well. She calculated exactly and cleanly like a machine and got almost everything right. A weight had been lifted from my shoulders, because I had been worried that geometry would yet cause an awful catastrophe.

Thursday March 7, 1963
Morning prayer
God, give me humility and patience. Don't allow me to expect great things from this day, let me be content with the small opportunities I encounter and use them. You will teach me. Let me be faithful in small things and to remember my helplessness. Let me humble myself before everyone, because I am the most worthless. Let there be at least one person to whom I can bring joy to without even knowing it. Bless those I will hurt, and You, please heal their wounds. Let me hear and obey Your voice. Let me have Your strength for the battles of this peaceful day.

Friday March 8, 1963
Suddenly during the last lessons, I am overcome by a panic; I have to get home with a book in my hand. Then there would not be my life anymore for several hours. I live in the book.

Friday March 15, 1963
Antti gave me a serious lecture on how mean I am at home. There was a lot of truth in it. I asked Father and Mother, what was the meaning of their life. They were infuriated by the question.

Monday March 18, 1963
I was fetching food from the school kitchen when Mother came there with red eyes: "Father had a heart attack!" Mother had been at home for two hours in the middle of the school day. I almost dropped the macaroni casserole for our class on the floor. "What!" Mother explained that the doctor had come to our house and asked father to lie down quietly until Thursday, when he can go for further diagnostic tests. If something happens before that, we must call the central hospital. Father is tar-colored, very serious and looks around in a strange way. Mother has been able to control her hysteria. I don't want to think of anything. In the evening we had a relaxing time. Father lay on the sofa; we all gathered in the living room and were talking about the most fun things we knew.

Friday March 22, 1963
I was in the Girls' Lyceum listening to a presentation on mountain climbing in Pamir. We saw beautiful bright slides of the trip. An Englishman was narrating. I enjoyed the event, pictures, topics, profuse English, which flowed from the lips of the man. Two climbers lost their lives on the trip. After hearing that, my mood changed. At first mountain climbing sounded like refreshing, exciting play, but when I saw the two men blue from lack of oxygen at the peak of the mountain grieving their two companions, it got to be too much. But I cannot condemn it. Maybe the satisfaction after the effort is so magnificent. The whole of life is similar to mountain climbing. One just needs to try, even if the goal is not worth the effort. This is the nobility of a human being.

Sunday March 24, 1963
We visited Litmalahti. Mother was driving, because Father needed to avoid any exertion. After the initial shock caused by the news of the heart attack, I have continued my life as before and almost forgotten the whole attack. Maybe it is because the thought of Father's death feels so utterly unreal, that I have not been able to really believe it even for a moment.

I horsed around outside with the little boys of Litmalahti. They are loved and well taken care of, but nobody has time to listen to them.

Therefore, I hear a flood of questions and explanations. Enthusiastic talk spills out uninterruptedly. I remember how their brother Seppo followed me often all the way to the lake shore, when I went to fetch milk from Mäntyniemi. He wanted to hear endlessly about foreign countries, animals, machines. He listened with his eyes wide open and periodically asked: "But what about if . . . ?"

Monday March 25, 1963
I listened to my Christmas gift record, *Messiah* by Händel. Harmony and even a sensation of physical pleasure overcame me. I can still hear the music. It has been playing in my mind the entire day. Händel himself must have been surprised hearing the opus being performed the first time. I believe that all great works are attached to mystical external power that penetrates the worker and makes him work in such a way that he himself does not know what will be born from it. I think that this is called inspiration. It can result in divine accomplishments.

Friday March 29, 1963
Pirjo's fourth grade sister said she heard, that I, if possible, wanted to become a nun. It had been told to her by a girl who had heard it from Kaisa, who in turn had heard it from her mother, who apparently had talked about my latest essay, which apparently had been read in the teachers' room. And I am of the opinion that apparently, as long as the story still goes around, it will return to me saying that I am already in a monastery. I wrote a short story where the two main characters were nuns. I did not, even in one word, refer to myself wanting to go to a monastery. On the contrary, I said that my interest in the institution of monasticism is evidence of my naïve character. From that statement a rumor started, that "if possible" I would go to a monastery. The most splendid thing is that even if the story is pulled from thin air, there is an unsuspected amount of truth to it. Often, indeed, nun-temptations have bothered me. The unconditionality attracts me, but on the other hand the restrictions make me too anxious. I could not just close my eyes and obey. Besides, the idea is impossible.

Sunday March 31, 1963
In the morning at nine I went to the Orthodox Church. There were a lot of people. To my surprise I saw another Lutheran, my schoolmate Raija.

The service lasted for two hours. I stood the entire time, not leaning on anything. I felt a little weak. Even Bishop Paul had strength to stand. In his wondrous golden garment, he seemed directly from Constantinople. Communion was celebrated. The Archbishop shared it, and the parishioners kissed his hand. Even small children received Communion. Nowhere in the Bible does it say that you must be fifteen years of age. Orthodox people must have lovely childhood memories of their trips to church. There was also a sermon. Bishop Paul talked about Communion and some upcoming reforms of the Divine Service. He wanted the congregation to also hear the early church prayers, which priests nowadays mumble in a low voice at the altar. The doctrine is as pure as that of the Lutherans, but the beauty has not been ripped away. There is a prayer for those who look for beauty from the church. My heart moved warmly.

Monday April 1, 1963
It is likely that Father needs to be in the hospital a long time. He is being thoroughly examined. They need to be able to achieve a fundamental healing. Neither my mother's nor my nerves could take living in constant fear of an attack.

Saturday April 6, 1963
Father was not released yet to come home. That is good. Feeling calm, knowing that he is in the hospital.

I have set my fasting rules. No eggs in the morning, no sandwiches after dinner. I will not eat a lot during meals. In addition, I hope I can fast completely on Good Friday.

Wednesday April 10, 1963
I made a mistake and left with Mother to go to the countryside to Simonniemi and got completely exhausted during the ice road portion of the trip. Mother was running far ahead of me. I tried to drag myself after her. It was quite fun once we got there. There were already some patches of snow-free ground. I sat on the porch railing. Sun was warming the air, and there were already weak scents of summer. While going, we used the ice road in Puutossalmi, but when returning, the cable ferry was already in operation. In town, Marja found the first coltsfoot.[33] Spring is apparently coming.

---

33. *Tussilago farfara*, which blooms early in the Spring in northern Europe.

Saturday April 13, 1963, or actually Sunday April 14
"Christ is risen from the dead, trampling down death by death, and upon those in the tombs bestowing life." Archbishop Paul sang with such a luminous voice, the choir sang so quietly and slowly and strongly. Bishop Paul said to the congregation, "Christ is risen." "Truly He is risen" was the reply by the parishioners, and I also replied, because He really did resurrect. I was in the Paschal service, which lasted from 11:30 pm to 3:00 am. May Christ be glorified.

Sunday April 21, 1963
My soul rests in the small church. I don't have to guide my thoughts at all. They stay with what is beautiful and good on their own. I lift up my heart to the Lord. Sunday is a day for recharging. Then I go to the little church to refresh myself. I have not in general admired Greek Catholicism.[34] It has always come across to me as stuffy and conservative and something that leads to unhealthy movements. This is surely so in Russia and elsewhere in the Slavic world, but our church is different. It is totally independent, and hence there is brightness and clarity in this small room of God's; not a trace of stuffiness, not to mention resistance to development. Simply put, God's gifts are being offered steadily. "Drink from it, all of you."[35] I have come to drink.

Wednesday April 24, 1963
It is amazing to know that we do not need to worry. Every day comes from God. He is raising me for something. Be that place however small, it is meant for me, and someday I must be there. The most wonderful thing is that the best in a Christian's life is last. Last breath, and then we are free from everything that prevents us from rising to where God is. One can sigh one's last breath in the hands of the Lord and be sure that He will take care, come what may, because He has already taken care of it on earth. Of course, I wish that all knew that. I wonder if missionary work is meant for me?

---

34. During this time period, Orthodoxy was called Greek Catholicism in Finland, even though now the term refers to Eastern Catholic Churches that use the Byzantine-rite.

35. Matt. 26:27 (New Revised Standard Version).

Saturday April 27, 1963
I told Elina about Jesus. We were looking through pictures in the big family Bible, which Elina insists on calling "Jesus-book." The name is actually a really good fit. Finally Ekku got an inspiration for a very powerful song: "Jesus was born at Christmas in heaven." He repeated this theme. We were at home, just the two of us. Ekku becomes serious and attentive when we speak of Jesus and always asks me to tell more. It is not a fairy tale for him. Telling a two-year-old about Jesus is challenging. I try to firmly stick to what I know myself and not to blabber children's tales. Many things seem to be outside Ekku's circle of concepts.

Labor Day, Wednesday May 1, 1963
The month of wonders has come. God lives! Flowers are rising from the ground, birds are returning. Nothing lasts, not spring nor summer nor anything else on earth, but God lasts forever.

Father traveled to Helsinki today to undergo more tests. I wish they would identify a cause which is not too serious, but rather easily helped. The cause in any case needs to be found, because we cannot bear to live in uncertainty.

Saturday May 4, 1963
Father returned from Helsinki. The prescription is: 10 kg thinner. A fatty diaphragm is pressing on the heart. There we see what a high living standard can cause. Otherwise, Father is in good shape.

I went to church in the evening. "Teach me Thy statutes!"[36] was ringing in my mind. Lifting up my heart to God fills me with pure joy and elevates me from the mundane world. During the week I often miss my oasis moments. I guess this is how one should feel, and thus the little church is the right church for me.

Tuesday May 7, 1963
Without You, my Lord, I am nothing. Don't ever leave me, don't let me doubt, and give me belief that what I have done, even if in the eyes of the world is strange and abnormal, is according to Your will. Strengthen me. I have jumped into the unknown, and there is no return. Sometimes I am horrified. What if I am not standing on the rock? Help, Lord, let me try

---

36. Ps. 119:12 (New Revised Standard Version).

to do as You say, even if it would look foolish to others. "In the world you face persecution. But take courage; I have conquered the world."[37]

Wednesday May 8, 1963
I have nobody, and being alone can easily put off the flame, but I cannot get attached to the people I know, because there is the world. I live from oasis to oasis and trust that You, Lord, will take care of me. Monastery, give me a monastery! I just want to watch Him, Lord Jesus, and when I die reach perfection in my watching.

Thursday May 9, 1963
It is hard for me to live like this. At home I am not understood at all. From all sides I am being pulled to worry about vain things, and I cannot watch You, Christ, in peace. I feel like an outsider in the world, but I cannot detach from it fully. All kinds of noise and hurrying, the goals of which are completely counter to what I have now found as my eternal goal, make me sometimes doubt. Maybe the ordinary suffices.

Friday May 10, 1963
I bought a little Bible. I told Mother that I would need a hymn book, but lying did not work at all. I said straight that I want the Bible. Mother thought I was crazy, but gave me the money. During the day I will have moments when I can read it.

Friday May 17, 1963
Oh, my God, don't ever let me collect possessions. I hate money. Lust, selfishness, and beastliness are linked with money.

In a heated moment I hit Marja. That's the way to go! Tomorrow, oh tomorrow, my God, I can go to church, me the languished, miserable soul.

Wednesday May 22, 1963
We talked about medical school at home. I said I am not so sure if I will become a doctor. I want to hear God's voice. "I cannot be pressured," I said. "No, no," answered Mother. "Do what you want, as long as you don't go to a monastery." They seem to be secretly afraid of that. Then they started to badmouth the small Orthodox Church. Strange that civilized

---

37. John 16:33 (New Revised Standard Version).

people can talk like that of the faith of others. "They lie down on the floor in front of images and worship people," said Father and continued by telling what crimes Orthodox priests had done. I interrupted him by saying, that yes, I do believe that all Orthodox are crooks and criminals. Mother intervened by explaining, how low and primitive Orthodoxy is compared to Lutheranism. As if she knew anything about it! It was miserable to listen to. Mother tried to insist that my "weirdness" was because of puberty and laughed in contempt. "After a year you will already think quite differently." Poor thing, puberty cannot be an explanation much longer. The influence of Christ, our Lord, those secretly extremist Lutherans don't even seem to think about. Savior, Lord, be with me. Save me from discussions with my parents, because they do not understand at all. I just become too agitated.

Wednesday May 29, 1963
In the reading room I read about the history of the Orthodox Church through the times. Recently it has gotten closer to the Protestant Church but has not lost its centuries-old mystical feel of holiness. Our independent church is apparently a pearl among the other Greek Catholic Churches, too. Pure, beautiful word of God is unwaveringly available.

I also viewed pictures from Karelia. If I would pray and believe, God would give us Karelia, but I don't believe strongly enough to even try. If I did believe, it would happen, but I am not brave enough to believe the impossibility.

Friday May 31, 1963
We got report cards this morning. My average in theoretical subjects was 9.23, which is undeniably great. Suddenly I felt gifted, able to do anything. I felt hope for the country resting on me. I knew how false, wrong those sentiments were, but I was like a full-blown balloon. I am talented, I am genius, what will I still accomplish! Little gray mouse cast triumphant looks around her. It forgot for a moment to be bad, mean, lousy, ugly, and it forgot its infinite helplessness.

In the evening the whole class was at Erhola. There was no dancing; we chatted and listened to records. I shifted my glance from one person to another. How good it was for us to be! We did not do anything bad, we were expecting a joyful youth and pleasant life. I looked at the boys. They seemed honest and smart. How safe it would be if the strong arms of a boy would protect me through life. No, no, no! I have chosen an impossible way, impossibly difficult! Oh, my God, help me, strengthen me, give me certainty that I am right. I must stay free so I will always be ready to follow Your voice.

When visiting Heli's high school graduation party next door, my ambition was aroused. The most important thing in the world is a smart career. The entire world's recognition and respect will follow—the world's, my Lord, but not Yours.

Saturday June 1, 1963
For my mother I am just a teenager grown crooked, and this view of hers she repeats to me day after day. She gnaws at my faith, whispers wrong advice, squirms and penetrates into my impressionable mind. Alone I would have collapsed a long time ago, but God has helped me. Sometimes I feel like I cannot take it anymore. Mother is my worst enemy. I write this totally without anger; on the contrary, I am on rather good terms with my mother these days. But that is the truth. I need to close my ears when Mother is talking. I really am not crazy when seeking God.

Thursday June 6, 1963
I have started my academic studies in the summer university and am leading a hardworking, peaceful life. I live alone here at home. I read, play the piano, and listen to records. Today with the money I got from father I bought a *St. Matthew Passion* record. I am going to chemistry, Swedish, and English lectures, in total five-and-a-half hours. Chemistry is interesting.

I have done something. I wrote a letter to Valamo Monastery. I asked if they would have work on the monastery farm for a schoolgirl. I attached a return mail stamp to the letter. I am not nervous. What is for good will happen. It is just interesting to see, what is for good.

Saturday June 8, 1963
I guess what will happen in the end is that I will join the Orthodox Church, if I will be accepted.

I remember the first time, when God led me to the small church. Being hesitant, I first walked around the church. It was winter and dark, golden light flashed towards me, and then my glasses steamed. What came after that first visit? Several, innumerable visits, first only Saturdays, later also Sundays, followed by awakening, a final decision, a turn in my life, the greatest joy and peace that I have felt.

Monday June 10, 1963
I believe in the Devil! Temptations are tearing me apart. A young mother with a white scarf came into the bus and with a smile put her child on her knee. Then for the first time I was overcome with an intense desire to be able to hold a child, my own child in my arms. That somebody would say to me "Mother!" and would trust me more than I trust God. I would have a child, whom I could love, for whom I would suffer and sacrifice. But all that is a temptation for me, my part is not in that. I will not have children. God is leading me somewhere else.

Tuesday June 11, 1963
There was a letter on the floor in the hallway. I went to the kitchen and sat firmly in a chair. The letter was from hierodeacon Jonah. It was written in large, old-fashioned handwriting, endearingly sweet and a little clumsy. It ended, "With respect," and I thought that it was far too much. The letter said that right now they do not have suitable work in Valamo, and besides Valamo is a men's monastery, well ok, even though the youngest monk is fifty years old, and they have female labor taking care of livestock. Hierodeacon Jonah advised me to inquire from Lintula and even gave me the address and wrote, "For sure You can get in there." I immediately wrote to Lintula. I greatly miss peace; I would like to get to know nuns and that whole life. I would be modest, quiet, and would work to the best of my ability or actually even more. I certainly don't have a romantic misconception of Lintula. I know that it is a little, dilapidated farm and that the nuns are old, perhaps quite strict and smallminded, but I would like to get to know that life before it fades completely.

Wednesday June 12, 1963
The great mirrors of the vocational training school[38] show a girl wearing a long blue dress. The dress makes me look even more angular and shows my poor posture, so the ensemble is fairly miserable. The girl looks very modest and serious, her expression is quite ardent, hair pulled back. Periodically I get amused by her frightened and solemn appearance. It is only me wandering there, full of basics in chemistry.

---

38. The summer university that operates in the school's facilities.

Thursday June 13, 1963
If the Lintula nuns follow the example of hierodeacon Jonah, I will get a letter tomorrow. I want to get into a monastery. It will be a great disappointment if they do not accept me. Even if I did not like Lintula, it would in any case be an experience for me, a memorable event, and a unique experience, because after ten years Lintula will hardly be there anymore. I would get a taste of an old way of life. And there would be peace for sure! Oh, how I wish . . . I need to stop excess imaginations, so my disappointment will not be too heavy. I will wait patiently. Take me!

Friday June 14, 1963
The family returned to the city this morning. Noise came, nagging came, stupid talks and adoration of mediocrity. I almost cried; it was somehow so hopeless to start living in that old turmoil. I had gotten used to silence. Now I am just one odd phenomenon in this family circle. They include me in the family, although I belong to it fairly loosely, hardly at all. It would be much easier both for them and for me if they succumbed to the fact that I am primarily an independent person and I answer for myself, and thus my deeds are not the deeds of the family.

Sunday June 16, 1963
The family finally left. I behaved inferiorly. I did not control myself at all. So this is the way I follow Christ!

Tuesday June 18, 1963
Eighteen years is already a lot. So now I am expected to live the joy of youth, the happiest period in a person's only life. And what do I see? I see that I have not actually ever really had fun. Those rare parties I have had in my life, I haven't been able to enjoy. Fun, what is fun? Most likely I will never get to know it. I have drifted to a point where, even if I wanted to change my style, become happier, dress differently, dance—I don't mean a dark-eyed streetwalker but rather a sweet family girl—I could not anymore. I would not have fun, and besides, changing my style would be impossible. In relation to boys, I am extremely shy. It is a total impossibility that I would ever walk hand in hand with anybody in the park.

Thursday June 20, 1963
I came home and decided to have a party, my kind of party, which hardly anyone else would have thought of as a party. First I went to the store and

bought white ankle socks. I changed into a cotton dress, took a basket in my arm, and went to the market square. It was hot. People were bustling in the street. I bought a huge apple from a smiling market-grandma and parsley from a middle-aged woman, and from a man, radish with a discount. I like walking around in the marketplace. It is colorful and busy there. I walked to the park to have my apple. Carefree, I watched alternately glittering birch leaves and people, who walked below. Lastly, I went to the reading hall to browse through English magazines. I enjoyed myself!

I am starting to doubt that they will not answer me at all from Lintula. That would be impolite! Hierodeacon Jonah was fair at least.

Sunday June 23, 1963
We have celebrated Midsummer night. On Friday I drove directly from the city to Litmalahti, where the rest of the family came later. It was fun to come to the yard decorated with birches and peek into the festive family room. Children ran towards me, Grandma greeted me warmly. All were happy about my arrival. I kept on answering Seppo's endless flood of questions, watched calves with Sirkka and the small boys.

If I haven't received an answer from Lintula by Tuesday morning, I will write there again.

Monday June 24, 1963
I don't know if this is just my own laziness, but I think that God's purpose is not for me to spend many, long bleak years in Helsinki studying and using the family funds and my own precious young years. Heavy and bloodless is that kind of life. I shiver to think of next winter, when I will be the embodiment of my parents' and teachers' ambition, and I should gather all my strength to beat everyone else and to glow in front of everybody. Vanity.

Wednesday June 26, 1963
I mailed my appealing letter to Lintula and called the Salvation Army. They are organizing a trip to the monastery on Sunday. I fit in. The woman who answered the phone was very friendly. It is fun to leave alone. Nobody knows me or has any preconceived idea of me. Maybe I can also familiarize myself a little with the Salvation Army. I am not suspicious. I want to be free to like everybody who loves the Lord. But above all on Sunday I will see real monks and nuns! I am childishly excited.

Saturday June 29, 1963
I am going to have a fasting day. I understand why Christ tells us to fast. In the beginning, like during the first Lent, it felt humiliating and fixed the thoughts even more on food. But that phase is now over. Fasting elevates the mind and gilds the thoughts. I am always going to fast before going to church.

Tomorrow real nuns and monks! It is a pleasure to get a little diversity.

Sunday June 30, 1963
Joy swirls, bubbles, trembles. I am so happy right now that it is hard for me to stand still. I got it! Next Sunday I will travel, God willing, to Lintula Monastery. It is a beautiful, white manor house by a lake. A long alley lined with birch trees leads to it, and behind it is a well-tended garden. The yard is a wide-open grass field. Towards the end of the trip, I was very excited. After the cars stopped, all rushed to the hallway of the house to buy postcards. A very young nun, under thirty years old and apparently some kind of novice, was selling the cards. At the church door stood another older nun with her hands clasped. I was truly not disappointed. She was very thin, translucent even, and her eyes were very large, deeply dark, wise, and beautiful. The novice had a long gray dress; the nuns had a black gown and a headpiece. The nun watched us tenderly and spoke Russian with one of the men. Strange, her voice was low and sweet like the voice of Archbishop Paul. When the people had dispersed, I got encouraged. "Can you speak Finnish?" I asked. Restrained shake of a head. "Russian, German." "Deutsch?" I uttered almost delighted, but then sighed inside and started hard work. "Ich bin . . . das Mädchen . . . die . . . das zu ihnen geschreiben hat."[39] "Geschrieben" she corrected. From there things started to get clarified. She had apparently heard about the letters. "Es ist schwere Arbeite,"[40] she noted smiling. "Wann kommen Sie? Nun?"[41] "Nein," I said, almost insanely. "Eine Woche."[42] "Nach eine Woche?" "Ja!" I had not thought of German for a month, and the situation came so suddenly. I at least understood what she said. "Willkommen, willkommen," she nodded and smiled. To be sure I still talked with the novice about it. I felt miserable when she told me that the abbess had previously said

39. "I am the girl who has written to you."
40. "The work is hard."
41. "When can you come? Now?"
42. "After a week."

that she cannot arrange accommodation for such a young person. "But," I motioned toward the nun, "she said, that I could come." "How old are you?" The novice inquired. "Eighteen." The nun had come beside us. She and the novice spoke in Russian. Miraculously I understood that she also asked about my age. "Achtzehn," I answered and looked at her appealingly. "Eighteen," the nun said for some reason in an amazingly wistful voice in Finnish. "We still need to ask the abbess," said the novice, and shouted in a surprisingly loud voice in front of a door: "Mother Abbess, Mother Abbess!" and then something in Russian. A long while passed. The nun had disappeared, and I did not see her anymore. I got nervous. I thought that the whole world will crash into a black darkness if I cannot get in. At last, the novice came. She explained that I can come, but warned me that the food is bad, one must take provisions (well, I can take some crispbread), no coffee (does not bother me), accommodation poor, together with another summer guest, some teacher in the outbuilding. She said that I can leave whenever I want. She did seem quite doubtful. Well, at least I have been warned. What is bad food like? What is poor accommodation? I think that despite all I will get along and will experience something I will never forget. Maybe I will learn humility and gentleness. I will work to the best of my ability, as hard as I can. I will try to be humble and helpful. God, bless and help me!

What a lunatic I was, emptyheaded, nutty, I got to hear I was after returning home. What else could I have expected?

Tuesday July 2, 1963
Everything seems to be going very well. I got my driver's license today. I passed the written exam, and my driving test went excellently, as the inspector noted. It is a relief that it is now over. Apparently, it is a useful skill.

I am of course thinking of Lintula. During the lectures I look at the girls, and a sense of joy comes over my mind. Soon I will not need to see high heeled shoes, nor ornate hairdos, nor fashionable clothes, although I will for sure intensely stare at the gowns. I notice myself acting like Martha and thinking more about clothes than I have in a long time. During the past couple of evenings, I have removed ruffles and laces from my white blouses, sewn seams, and fastened buttons. I need to look neat but very modest. After long consideration I have decided to buy a new skirt. I wish I could find a gray one, made of strong fabric.

Wednesday July 3, 1963
After going shopping a few times, I found a straight gray skirt, just the kind I wanted. However, it had to be reduced in width by 10 cm, but that will be done in the store. I apparently look poor and modest, because in stores I am often treated quite contemptuously. In fact I am poor, I do not own anything, thank God. Other saleswomen, especially young ones, look at me from head to toe and ask abominably without a smile, "What would you like to have?" Humbly I present my case. It is totally different to be shopping with Mother. Saleswomen whirl around, presenting their best merchandise, and Mother shoots out her firm opinions. But there are also friendly saleswomen for sure. They smile encouragingly and serve each client eagerly. The woman from whom I bought the skirt treated me maternally, protectively, and even said, "You are really thin!" A friendly attitude melts me, it warms me up.

Thursday July 4, 1963
All obstacles evaporate. Father called me from the countryside in the morning and talked in a friendly way, he urged me to come to the summer house for at least part of the summer. Yes, I will go. I had been a little afraid that Father would rush over here on Saturday, excited by Mother, and would shout, "Come home and get rid of those thoughts!" Although it would not have helped any, the law is on my side: eighteen-year-olds can themselves enter into employment contracts. Father understood that such conduct would not have helped. I think that he actually understands me in quite a few instances, even if he does it in secrecy from Mother. I believe that what is happening in me is quite familiar to Father. He has never said that I am crazy, even if he dutifully has gone along with Mother. He does not want to prevent me walking the path he did not follow, but to which he has certainly been pulled. Let's see how long I will be in Lintula. I think I will like it, but it can of course be that I get fed up and cannot endure it. Then I will have made a mistake, but it is my own mistake. I will have to suffer because of it. I have the right to make mistakes, and it is none of my parents' business. I read a little German.

Friday July 5, 1963
I already feel that a cross is standing between the world and me. It feels good and safe. From behind the cross people are watching—quiet, kind, and peaceful. I wonder if finally I am on the right side of the cross?

Savior, God, my Lord, can I sometimes go and help unhappy people with Your message of joy on my lips? May I walk under Your eyes, led by the Holy Spirit with the gospel in my heart? There would be no fear, complete trust, Your peace. I don't ask for a lot. If I could just be Your little, worthless, poor servant, who even in the smallest way would do your work, there would lie eternal happiness for me. I hear in my heart, "Anyone who comes to me I will never drive away."[43]

Saturday July 6, 1963
Unexpectedly one of my worst temptations rose for an attack. "You," said the Devil, "you think of some old-fashioned Jesus and are going to old, superstition-demonized nuns, while the entire world is waiting for research. There is a myriad of things we need to get to the bottom of. What can the human being still achieve?" Perhaps God someday will let me do research on something and in that way uncover His greatness. But I always want to remember to be small, childlike, because for such people God's secret will be revealed.

No obstacle has emerged. Hence, I am really going to the monastery tomorrow.

Monday October 14, 1963
In Lintula I found the way. I got a teacher, Sister Maria.[44] I got to hear things that I could not have ever anticipated. I saw peace and humility in the midst of all scarcity. God had mercy on me. Maybe my road will lead to a monastery. I think so. In any case, one period in my life is now over. There will still be many temptations and difficulties, but they come from God, because I believe that He will not throw me, a sinner, out.

---

43. John 6:37 (New Revised Standard Version).
44. Sister Maria (Smirnoff), later schema nun Seraphima, d. 1986.

High school graduate, 1964.

VISIT TO BYTOUMA MONASTERY AND STUDIES IN HELSINKI

A lot happened between October 1963 and the next diary entry in the summer of 1964. In May 1964 Anna-Leena joined the Orthodox Church. She fulfilled the expectations of her parents and school and received six laudaturs, or highest grades, in the matriculation examination. As was prevalent in those days, she was interviewed by the local papers. Later, on the wish of her parents, she traveled to Helsinki with the intention of applying to the Faculty of Medicine. In the end, she did not take the exam.

June 1964
I have received great help from the monastery and from Archbishop Paul. I am at home in the city and will not go to the entrance examination of

the Faculty of Medicine. I am lazy and depressed and unbelieving. I eat too much and don't have strength for anything else but to say "no" to my suffering parents. I have tasted the Lord's goodness, and I don't want anything else. In a few days I will be taken to a psychiatrist in Helsinki. I am powerless, sinful. Around me is the suffering of my parents and the mockery from the surroundings. I myself am like a torn, worn-out floor rag. At this moment I have no enthusiasm, no wish, no goal. But hope I do have! The Lord will not forsake me, I trust that, I, the most miserable of all sinners.

After this entry there is again a pause in the diary. Upon the suggestion of Archbishop Paul, Anna-Leena went to Greece, to the Monastery of Bytouma. Even her parents agreed, although with a heavy heart. Anna-Leena's private, deeply felt monastic calling spread to the public by newspapers. Privacy was not respected, and the entire family suffered from unpleasant gossip. For Anna-Leena, the combination of it all—the matriculation exam, with all its associated huge expectations, hurting her parents' feelings, gossip about personal matters—all this weighed heavily on her mind when she left on her journey. The small monastery in the middle of the mountains felt heavenly. In the midst of all the pressure, her mental health faltered, and she had to return to Finland. Years afterwards, she experienced a deep sense of failing, even though the doctor stated that the psychosis she went through was comparable to a bout of fever, which did not leave a negative trace on her character.

But God's providence and guidance is strongly expressed precisely during the difficult turns of life. After all that had happened, in the fall of 1965, on the suggestion of Archbishop Paul, Anna-Leena started her studies in Greek, which later enabled her to translate the Philokalia, a revered collection of Greek Christian monastic texts of the 4th to 15th centuries, into Finnish.

The subsequent diary entry (April 12, 1966) is from the spring of her first year of studies.

Tuesday April 12, 1966
I went to meet Archbishop Paul in the morning. I was very nervous. For a long time I stood in the stairway ready to dive down the stairs after hearing even the slightest cracking sound. Then finally I dared to ring the doorbell. Fortunately Father Archbishop opened the door and kindly encouraged me to come in. I promised to go to the museum and the

summer university. If it is not the will of God that I go to Greece, it is all the same where I go. It is only that sometimes a shivering goes through the whole body and tears come into my eyes, because I miss Mother Euphemia so.[45] But Father Archbishop knows everything, and it is good to live in obedience. I wish I could just wander in humility and simplicity. Lastly, I got a blessing for the trip.

Anna-Leena spent the winter of 1964 to 1965 in Greece, in Bytouma Monastery. Picture from the spring of 1965.

Wednesday April 13, 1966
If somebody wants to go to a monastery, it is good to get used to acting against one's own will. Now I don't expect anything special, but rather I experience every day as it is given to me.

    I am not one to be a Helsinki inhabitant. I miss Kuopio, because it is fun to do practical chores at home. How good it is that I can go to Kuopio for the summer. I need to have a role model in my Christian life, and if I cannot go to Mother Euphemia, let Father Archbishop Paul be my role model. On Holy Friday, quite abruptly I told him, "I detest all of the life in the world and want to go to a monastery, nothing else, and this is the truth."

    45. Abbess of Bytouma monastery.

Thursday April 14, 1966
You must coldly deny your own will. Everything with me is outwardly fine, and I can endure the summer; even school[46] will be over in little more than a month. How much longer do I need to live in the world? One needs to remember that all depends on God. If He wants to let me go to Greece, Father Archbishop will suggest it one day. Although right now I don't understand how I can make it from year to year without hope of going back. But I cannot show my distress to Father Archbishop, and I have to curtail it also in my own mind. Everything will go well. God will also give me refreshment and will not leave me alone to fight and suffer mental and spiritual death. One should not be afraid of a little crying and longing in the summer. It is only natural.

Friday April 15, 1966
In any case, I need to try to rise from this hole. I need to do this battle myself, nobody can fight it for me. I need to start to live like other people, to study and be awake and be happy sometimes and patient with others, even if my heart is bleeding. In the coming years it seems that there will be a constant battle against melancholy and overeating. Lord, You see everything, You see the three years of waiting, You see my earnest wish, have mercy on me, a sinner. Let me at least shed some tears so the anxiety will lighten a little.

When I told Father Archbishop that I am attending lectures on modern Greek, he said that I will probably not be needing it soon. Without your suggestion, Father Archbishop, the idea of Greece would never have crossed my mind. And now when I sold my heart to the Bytouma mountains, I may not go back, and I need to forget the language as well. What on earth will become of me?

Saturday April 16, 1966
I got the biography of Saint Seraphim of Sarov in German. He is very dear to me. I will go and pray in front of his icon in Uspensky Cathedral.

Sunday April 17, 1966
It is not right that behind Father Archbishop's back I pray, "Lord, let me get to the monastery!" No, one has to pray, "Lord, give me obedience and

---

46. In addition to her studies, Anna-Leena served as a teacher of Orthodox religion in the schools in Helsinki.

patience and strength to endure all, what I need to endure, and to do the work you have put me in." Now I feel that I cannot talk even an hour, not with the students or anyone else. Tomorrow morning again those three boys!

The craziest thing about this is that I have been in a monastery, and there developed a mental disorder, although there are several explanations for what really happened. And now it is perfectly clear that I will not be allowed to return, even though my mind, oh how strongly, wants to go back. The situation would be completely different if I had not had that mental episode. Monastic life, you see, is poison to me, they say. Despair tightens my throat when I think about this all.

Wednesday April 20, 1966
I wrote to Mother Euphemia, told her about the summer, and asked that if Father Archbishop—who very well knows how I love the Holy Monastery of Bytouma—someday will let me come to Greece, would she accept me there. As Mother Abbess is far, and it is probably not possible to meet her for a long time, I am writing to her boldly.

I treasure every hour when I do not need to speak. It would be great just to listen. For sure the Lord will give me opportunities to be silent.

In connection with teaching church history, I have tried to acquaint myself as much as possible with the biographies of holy people. They are the source of inspiration and power. Such a high example they set in front of us, and what demanding challenges they have had to endure. They live for us. St. Seraphim is most likely the closest to me.

I go to sleep and try to remember, always, that "For nothing will be impossible with God."[47] It is exciting to observe how God's guidance also influences my life. I should just not become too passive an observer, but to pray in front of the icons more frequently and read the Bible more diligently.

Saturday April 23, 1966
I don't want to teach others, but to be quiet and learn myself. In Greece I would just be an ordinary novice, maybe a little despised, and that is why I would like to go there. But it seems that I will not be able to go anywhere for a long time and it breaks my heart. In the summer, three years of waiting have passed.

---

47. Luke 1:37 (New Revised Standard Version).

Monday April 25, 1966
Getting ill was actually a real sign of God's mercy: all confidence in one's own strength left, or at least it should have. On the other hand, it made me like an invalid for the rest of my life.

If I had to live in the world, I would feel good doing practical chores, for example, amid a large crowd of relatives. But I would not under any circumstance like to be the mother of a large family. I would like to live my own life while being of some use to others. Even at home I enjoy busying myself with making coffee in the morning, and later in cooking and other small tasks. Here I am alone, and I cannot do those things for others.

Tuesday April 26, 1966
I have asked for help from St. Seraphim, and he will give it. I want to believe and trust that by the grace of God he will liberate me from sorrow and fear. I am afraid when praying. I am afraid of any experience of the grace of God and any level of my heart being moved, because I start to think that it is the beginning of a mental disturbance or at least self-deception. It is this fear I am asking God to relieve me from and am turning to St. Seraphim for intercession and his presence. I would like to be sure that all is not just imagination. St. Seraphim, please, help!

My parents just called. It was good and gave me joy, but there is also something bitter. First, they ask how I am, and of course it occurs to me that they think I might have fallen ill again. Secondly, we talk about the studies, and they remind me of people in their social network who, in spite of years spent in the university in vain, have become senior lecturers. But the core of the matter is that I will not become a senior lecturer; I certainly don't think of it as my goal in life. And I know that I will, yet again, crush their growing hope, and the more they hope, the more bitter it will feel. They even suggested paying for my education, but I don't ever again want to be economically dependent on them, because I want to become a nun, and Father Archbishop reminded me of the words of Christ: "Mary has chosen the better part, which WILL NOT BE TAKEN AWAY FROM HER."[48] From me they want to take it away by force.

---

48. Luke 10:42 (New Revised Standard Version).

Wednesday April 27, 1966, remembering Bytouma Monastery
The mornings were dreary in mid-winter. At 4:30 am we heard the sound of the *simandro*. I usually woke up a little before that. It was pitch dark if the moon was not shining, often even almost freezing inside, and I still wanted to sleep. One could hear how sister walked around citing a prayer. It was not pleasant to stand up on the ice-cold floor. We had half an hour to dress and read morning prayers, and then we went to the church. We were not pampered in any way, but that is also not the point in a monastery. We did not wear shackles, we did not fast strenuously, but we woke up every morning at 4:30 and celebrated Matins and Vespers, relatively short (about two hours), but regular. We ate nourishing food twice a day, and in the morning we had coffee or tea with milk, but nobody had even a little piece of bread in their cell. What we ate we ate together and publicly. Everybody went to church, and everybody worked.

Thursday April 28, 1966
It would be better to hang a millstone about the neck of those who offend the youth. God save the youth from liquor and bless them, that they would not need to regret tomorrow. I especially remember the high school seniors: they are celebrating May Day for the first time "in freedom." Everything secularizes, and I cannot prevent it; I cannot prevent the fact that grown boys think of Christianity as an ideology among others and don't understand its life-giving meaning. In the old times many escaped secular life to the wilderness. I would like to do so also. The wilderness is Bytouma by name, and generically a monastery.

Friday April 29, 1966
May Day has such an unpleasant ambience about it. One would think that youth would soon get tired of dirt and mud.

Thursday May 5, 1966
Yesterday ended in a deeply depressing way. I went to the Latin exam, but it was over already. If I had gone to the university fifteen minutes earlier as usual, I would have been accepted to take the exam. My delay was caused just by me dropping in here to get an attendance certificate. I had lived a hope-filled, optimistic life studying Latin. I imagined how I could surprise Father Archbishop and the whole family by passing the pro exercitio exam already now. And I would not have needed to go to the summer university! In the beginning my mistake totally stunned me.

Colors disappeared from my life; everything is bleak and irrelevant. I merely cause everyone disappointment. It seems that my studies will not lead to anything. What is really expected of me? What was the meaning of that incident? Roads are closed to every direction. Life has no meaning. Lights go off.

Why? I must get some explanation to have strength to believe. Leena is namely a teacher of religion. Children are in any case a source of comfort for me now. I can forget my own disappointments, at least for a few hours.

Saturday May 7, 1966
I went to give Pentti an examination.[49] It was quite extraordinary. I did not ask questions, but rather we discussed. We talked about church and churches, war and hunger, the goal of life and culture, true Christians, who are the light of the world, duties of the priests, meaning of divine services, orthodoxy, ecumenism. Especially heartening were Pentti's words, "I would also like to be like that" (namely a Christian preaching with his life). Hooray, he wants that! When we were discussing, I observed that Pentti was sometimes listening to my opinions, looking solemn and respectful. It astonished and even frightened me. Usually I get embarrassed if I notice the students taking me too seriously.

The university finished for me today. I got "good knowledge" of Greek. After three weeks this winter is over. It feels even a little nostalgic. I don't know why. There will not be another one like this, and that is good. Happy days are rare. Melancholy has weighed like lead on my heart.

Sunday May 8, 1966
Mrs. Nikkanen, the translator of *Sisäinen kauneus*,[50] has invited me to her home in Herttoniemi on Thursday at 6 pm.

Monday May 9, 1966
I read about the construction works at Lintula. There was a frightening thought in my mind, that I am somehow predestined to go there. And then I will be busy my whole life hurrying between all kinds of practical

---

49. Student of Orthodox religion.

50. Meaning "inner beauty." Sisäinen kauneus. PSHV 1965, the first small collection of the Philokalia texts in Finnish translated by Irinja Nikkanen from German. Later on, Irinja Nikkanen became the editor of the Finnish edition of the Philokalia and an important background influencer.

tasks and arrangements, and I will never really have an opportunity to be silent and contemplate and learn to pray, and when I die after being almost all my life in a monastery, I realize at the moment of death that I haven't really even started real monastic life and I don't know Christ or anything of anything. If I always need to do practical work, I will lose an internal ability for being silent, and even if I get opportunities for it, I would not be able to do it. Protect me from that, Lord, and make me an ordinary Greek novice.

During my school times I often had to bear responsibility in the class and among the circle of my friends. Everything was routinely pushed on my plate. And now again I need to take responsibility. Lord, Lord, give me a carefree period as a novice without any responsibility. In my childhood I stood up directly from crawling without a period of being on all fours, which is why I have had poor posture since I was small. Now I want to be on all fours, and for a long time, and to take my first cautious steps supported by the hands of mother (or father), and to learn the basics in depth. I have had to do so many things, which I don't really know how to do well.

Don't worry Leena, maybe your road will lead again to a mental hospital! With this I mean: let go of all vain worrying and distress. God will make you fit for what you have been "predestined" to, be it becoming a patient in a mental hospital, Abbess of Lintula, Greek novice and nun, or what might be more likely, a teacher of religion, or Master of Arts (unlikely).

Thursday May 12, 1966
I met Mrs. Nikkanen. I visited her home in Herttoniemi for about three hours. She has translated *Sisäinen kauneus* and is excited about all that involves monastic life and ascesis,[51] and especially literature on these topics. She is a mother of four, and her husband chatted with us. He approaches his wife's hobbies a little amused and arrogantly, however, positively.

I have translated three sheets of canons, and it has taken at least six hours. Over half are remaining. Let's see if I can finish this assignment, so I can have something to meet about with Father Archbishop by Pentecost.

---

51. Practicing self-discipline for spiritual goals.

Saturday May 14, 1966
I went to church. "Holy Master, bless!" I am especially attached to those words because they indicate a bishop is in the church. As all the others, I got a blessing from the Archbishop.[52] With my knees shaking I went to get the blessing, and Father Archbishop looked at me gently and smiled a little. It is probably quite confusing when you are a monk and an Archbishop, and all of a sudden you are given a full-grown daughter, who above all behaves like a little child.

Wednesday May 18, 1966
It has been a year now since I started the diary to lighten the restlessness of my mind. Today is also the day when I met Father Archbishop the first time after returning from Greece. I would so like to meet him now and be able to confess.

I wish I can endure these last days. Hooray, I get to go away from Helsinki! I will go to Kuopio and don't want to come to this big city for a long time. Let's see if the summer will go along the track of university-museum.[53] August is still open. I think it will be spent in Lintula.

Feast of the Ascension, Thursday May 19, 1966
Next week, God willing, I will already be in Kuopio. I become poetic thinking about my hometown. The old cemetery with its stone fence is a wonderful place. And how about the pond of Valkeinen, and Väinölänniemi and the surroundings of the port. Hundreds of times during the school years I wandered, crisscrossing the town, fall and winter and spring. In the summer I did not need to be there ever, but now I am thankful also for the summer. There is my home church and home parish, where I am known and accepted and where the atmosphere is solemn and homey.

Thursday May 26, 1966
I got the canons finished; I can die in peace. It felt festive to finish them, and now I have a reason to meet Father Archbishop. I was close to missing the train but made it after all. Great thankfulness came over me when thinking about the winter that just passed. God has taken care of me; at the station I inhaled the air of Kuopio. I sensed the fresh scent of spring.

52. The Archbishop was visiting Helsinki.
53. Refers to her summer job as a guide in the Orthodox Church Museum.

At home I opened the local newspaper, *Savo,* and immediately my eyes spotted the Orthodox service schedule.

SECOND VISIT TO BYTOUMA MONASTERY

Friday August 25, 1967
The departure from Kuopio is in front of us tomorrow morning. All the luggage has been packed, and everything is ready. Father is here. It hurts my heart to think of all the sorrow I have caused him. I have ignored the wishes and insistence of the parents to have a return ticket.

Sunday August 27, 1967
The ship is already sailing in the sea. An American girl I met in the church museum is sharing my cabin. Similarly among the Germans, there are some acquaintances from the museum. It is unsure whether I will be in Greece for a week or the rest of my life. Let's see if I will meet Grandma ever again.

Wednesday August 30, 1967
Somehow war comes to mind when traveling on these railways. We left a while ago from Nuremberg, arriving soon in Augsburg and then on to Munich.

I have crisscrossed Munich and finally rescued myself on a park bench. Undoubtedly, I am most interested in nuns over here. One can see many Roman Catholic sisters. And when I see them, I become happy: Only two days and I will meet Abbess and the sisters.

I went for an hour-long sightseeing tour. We passed many Roman Catholic churches, and by the end of the tour I set a goal of getting into one of them. I have never been in a Roman Catholic church. I rushed towards the two domes of the Church of the Virgin Mary, and after walking at times under the ground to cross the street, and having a lemonade, I succeeded in getting there. The atmosphere was about the same as in an Anglican church. Even though the chapels and crypts are dim and have a peaceful ambience, I don't feel a particularly special solemnity there. The church art, Virgin Mary with her flying hair, red-cheeked and flourishing, is not appealing to me, nor the sentimental and almost deliberate way of expression appealing to one's emotions. Even in the church the most interesting were the nuns.

I went to eat in a sophisticated and quite reasonably priced bar. I could barely find the bill, which was tucked behind the armrest. New currency, tipping, etc., practices make you feel quite helpless.

Friday September 1, 1967
We are approaching Athens. I feel nonexistent and worthless. I have come from afar. Have pity on me, Lord, and let me find what I am looking for. In Athens I met the secretary of the consul, Mr. Heinonen, and everything went smoothly: From their point of view I can stay as long as I want.

I am in Trikala, almost halfway home. I came by bus. For me, Greece actually only starts in Lamia. These villages in Thessaly, which smell like barns, are magnificent. A little boy brought my luggage to the house of the Metropolitan.[54] There were priests, a sister of Father Metropolitan, and her driver. The reception was heartfelt. "Eleni came,"[55] people were saying, almost laughing. Of course, people asked about my health especially. Then I sat in Father Metropolitan's office waiting for him. He came, and again peace and joy were ignited in my heart. I am very fond of Father Metropolitan. He has a peaceful, thoughtful, and firm way of doing things. Father Metropolitan told me about Father Archbishop's letter, which said that I can stay here for a month. Father Metropolitan was surprised about that. I explained that for the first time I got a blessing from Father Archbishop to stay in the monastery for a long time, but that lately, under pressure from my parents, he has started to backtrack.

At Father Metropolitan's house I was served food—rice, tomatoes, melon, and grapes. "Eat, eat, my child," encouraged Father Metropolitan gently.

Saturday September 2, 1967, in Bytouma
Glory to you, oh Lord, glory to You! Most Holy Mother of God, save us!

I am again at home in Bytouma. One of the happiest moments of my life was when I stepped down from Metropolitan's jeep in the yard of Bytouma, and Abbess hurried towards me with her eyes shining, just like I remembered.

Sister Eusevia took care of me, showed me the monastery and school. We have a new workshop here. I was put in a room which a little

---

54. Metropolitan Seraphim of Trikke and Stagoi.
55. Anna-Leena's baptismal name was Helena, or Eleni in Greek.

bit resembles a guest room, but luckily I am treated as one of their own. First, of course, Abbess and I went to the church. In trapeza my place is somewhere in the middle of the table, no longer beside Abbess. Plenty of food, sleep, and prayer is my initial program, and that is good of course. It can be that I get black clothes. But even that is not most important. Abbess said that we need to pray to the Mother of God, so that she would make everything well and would let me stay here.

Later. Our priest joined us at the evening meal, and I bragged about my knowledge of languages. Now, in a genuine monastic way, I have a bad conscience. But I should not expect too much of myself. I am a bragger and find myself to be a little jealous and envious of a young, very pretty sister named Eunike. I myself need to be cautious all the time and keep my other foot on the ground. I must remember that I am the least of all.

Sunday September 3, 1967, in Bytouma
During the day we went to the well of the Virgin Mary. Abbess ran, and so did all the girls. There was thunder and lightning, but nobody showed even a trace of fear. Nature is here like a paradise. Fruits are ripening, waters are flowing, flowers are blooming.

It is lovely to live in obedience. Most Holy Mother of God, save us.

Monday September 4, 1967, in Bytouma
Sister Fevronia and I collected dry spice herbs from the mountainside. It was wonderful. I ended up on a steep hillside from which I could not move up or down. I made an effort, however, to push upwards and asked the holy Mother of God to help, and I made it.

From Mother Euphemia I got a blue-green below-knee-length dress. I also use a black apron. Heart is, however, more important than clothes.

I have now stepped from the road of medicine to the road of faith. I asked to speak with Abbess, and after the meal she asked me to come to her office. I talked about the past times. Abbess says that I have to pray a lot, that the Lord will open the eyes of the Archbishop and my parents. The most Holy Mother of God will not allow me to get ill anymore, she said. The Lord will allow you to stay here, she said. "Pray, Eleni."

Tuesday September 5, 1967, in Bytouma
I don't understand from where the sisters have obtained such limitless love and kindness toward me, a sinner, and toward everybody. They have received it from the Lord. Instead, my heart is constricted. Paraskevi and

Euthymia received black clothes today. They are sixteen years old. For Eleni, it was a hard pill to swallow. Abbess and all the sisters noticed it.

Wednesday September 6, 1967, in Bytouma
Gradually I start to understand what a wonderful paradise the Lord has led me to. I can never thank Him enough.

Abbess gave me a place in the church right in front of the icon of the Virgin Mary. A lot of spiritual benefit and loveliness has been received today. With what care and tenderness she treats me! Sometimes her words to the sisters are quite sharp, but not to me ever, at least not yet. She does not want to scare me in any way.

Anna-Leena returned to Finland to continue her studies. Her father was appointed a supreme court judge, and the whole family moved to Helsinki. Anna-Leena lived with the family in their new home in Helsinki.

STUDENT LIFE

Saturday August 17, 1968
These days I live in a happy and light frame of mind. I find it lovely to be able to walk lightly and even run and study a little, and discuss happily, and live day by day not longing for anything intensively. I somehow have the skill of being glad and joyful, and it feels twice as wonderful after all those hard times.

Tuesday August 20, 1968, in Helsinki
Father and Mother came, but they will leave already tomorrow back to the countryside. It's more fun when there are others here. When alone I easily sink into inertia.

Mother and I went to Linnanmäki. We rode a Ferris wheel and the ghost train and watched a few wild acrobatic performances. I somehow feel pity for those performers.

Wednesday August 21, 1968
"Viva Dubček!" The Soviet Union has occupied Czechoslovakia. Timo Kyntäjä[56] and I participated in a large demonstration in front of the embassy of the Soviet Union on Tehtaankatu.

---

56. Her sister Marja's boyfriend.

Monday September 16, 1968
I am the only student in the advanced course of modern Greek. In other words, I get two hours of private instruction in modern Greek per week. These hours are the most fun that happens to me.

The news of the day is that our eighty-four-year-old grandmother has met her admirer from her youth, who recognized her after sixty years and asked her to marry him. Grandmother does admit that she is a little enamored, but unlikely to say yes to the offer.

Thursday September 19, 1968
I have read the memoirs of Saint Therese of Lisieux. She says that she is "en liten vit blomma,"[57] whereas I, to use English, feel like "a rotten big potato." My respect grew when she confessed that the thought of a nonexistent void instead of a lovely heaven bothered her often. She related to this thought as if it were a merciful affliction, or at least she tried to relate to it in that way. Now she knows already what is the truth. How I wish that it is "the lovely heaven"!

Friday September 27, 1968
Days go by fast, but I suppose usefully. I don't miss company, and therefore I don't force myself to invite people to my home. I understand now that I walk along my own way alone.

Sunday September 29, 1968
Immediately when I am alone and having a "day off," sarcastic thoughts flood my mind, so that mentally and almost physically I start to walk bent down.

Monday September 30, 1968
If one sometimes feels gloomy, there always remain the joy and consolation that one can leave from here. Before leaving, however, I would like to feel lighter and freer. The thoughts from the past make me anxious and weigh me down a lot.

---

57. In Swedish, "a little white flower."

Thursday October 3, 1968
There was a meeting of the Orthodox Student Union. It was fun to meet and chat with old acquaintances. I will participate actively in the work of the Union.

Monday October 28, 1968
I am in Marja's room with rose-illustrated wallpaper, which will become mine, as soon as Marja gets married. I might need to suffer a lot in this room. But on the other hand, nothing probably gives as much joy as suffering secretly. That joy also remains in my life.

Wondrously beautiful snowy landscape expands outside. Always something springs to mind from everything, like from this landscape, both the mountains of Bytouma as well as the alder alley behind Lintula Monastery.

Thursday November 14, 1968
The Orthodox Student Union took a field trip to Lohja. To me, it was wonderful to be with a group of healthy and brisk young people. We grilled sausages in the fireplace and had a lively discussion about the church.

Entrance of the Most Holy Mother of God into the Temple, Thursday November 21, 1968
The spirit of the Student Union is enthusiastic, and we consider the work of the Union very important. Although we criticize some issues in the church, we love the church and the small congregation from the bottom of our hearts. Be that as it may, my love for the church and Orthodox life has wounded my heart. It is dominating my feelings, and my entire world of thought moves in the Orthodox spirit as I now see it, yet wider and brighter. In the Student Union, many members are beginning to be converts.

SUMMER 1969

Friday July 18, 1969
I arrived here [Kuopio] in the morning in a sleeper car of the train. I have met acquaintances, or I could almost say friends: Maria Iltola[58] and

---

58. Future Abbess Marina of Lintula Monastery, who at that time worked as a notary for the Orthodox Clergy-Laity Assembly in Kuopio.

Matti[59] in the Clergy-Laity Assembly, Miss Home in the bookstore[60] at Kaisa market. I went to Saint Nicholas Church, stood and walked around there by myself. It is very dear to me. I have spent countless happy and unhappy moments there.

In the afternoon I will continue my trip to Simonniemi. I wish to be helpful, energetic, and happy. Even little Juho[61] will be in the countryside. When I went to fetch the strawberries I had ordered from the market vendor Kaisa, I met Father Archbishop. He walked across the market square, turned, and came to the same Lauronen's shop, where I was shopping also. "You are here again," he said. I explained that I had just arrived and am about to leave for Vehmersalmi. "Are your parents there?" he asked. "Yes, the whole family is," I said. It feels so good to look Father Archbishop in the eyes. I wanted so much to ask for his blessing, but I did not dare to do it in the middle of the market square.

Saturday July 19–Thursday July 31, 1969, in Simonniemi
It has been a real country day. Elina and I went for a forest trek, I went for a swim several times, in the evening we went to the sauna.

Yesterday evening, just like today, I strolled alone on the peninsula, and even made a little campfire there. Everything is beautiful, peaceful, and even mystical, come to think of it. Now when I can live and think alone without the thought of the monastery constantly hurting my mind, I look at nature and feel closeness to it in a new way.

Riitta and I cycled to Litmalahti.

Contrary to the weather forecast, the day was most beautiful. I tanned myself in the sun. We swam a lot and talked about funny things, so I laughed a lot.

In the evening we played hide and seek. In addition I went to pick bramble berries in Riistalahti and swam four times. It rained; the lake shimmers in the dimness as a haze rises in the further distance.

The whole family went to pick berries and ate kalakukko[62] as the open lake view unfolded in front of us.

I went to sauna. The water was cool, the air soothing, and the sauna steam hot, but not suffocating. It is good to ponder things in the darkness

---

59. Sidoroff, a student in the Orthodox seminary and a summer guide at the museum, who later became the Vicar of Kuopio and a teacher in the seminary.
60. Paula Home, who was a salesclerk in the Orthodox Lampukka-shop in Kuopio.
61. Her sister Marja's first child.
62. A traditional dish, fish pie.

of the sauna, and I concluded that I will not go to Lintula if I don't get a special "guidance" for it.

In the evening I sat on the peninsula and thought of my countless forebears, who during their lifetime have crouched by a fire in contemplation, wondering what they might have been thinking.

In the afternoon the whole family took a trip to the sandy shore, where we children had a swimming competition of "kangaroo." I have almost lost my hope of becoming an adult.

Although I do like it here very much, there are signs indicating that mental work and struggle are beginning to be needed.

The Nissinen family visited us. We went to a high hill to pick berries. In the evening there were also other youth at my campfire. The Manninen family came by and brought strawberries.

This was the last day in Simonniemi. I have had a magnificent holiday. I could not believe that life had in store such lovely days for me. Thank you!

Thursday August 14, 1969
Bishop John visited the museum yesterday with his father. I looked into his eyes, and it was a pleasant surprise. Great love and all around attraction to the church seems to be a quality he and I have in common. I discuss with him as naturally as with any other person.

Yesterday while on my evening stroll I felt how this city is gilded with memories and dreams, a fairytale world, where the heavenly and worldly meet. It would be easy to spend one's whole life here floating between reality and hereafter.

I have come to the conclusion that the only worldview compatible with the worth of human life is to believe in loving guidance and eternal life. I want to align my own life, also in practice, along these principles.

Because I don't like visiting people or talking with visitors, I don't see that I should force myself to have a social life.

Sunday August 17, 1969
Two Greek medical students visited the museum. I got very enthusiastic being able to speak Greek again. One of them had lived four years in Trikala.

Thursday August 28, 1969
Hurrah! Father Archbishop asked us (a group of the workers in the congregation) to his cell for Saturday morning.[63]

Saturday August 30, 1969
We left at 6 am. Maria had arranged for me to ride in the Archbishop's car with Petros,[64] Matti, and the Archbishop's housekeeper, a very nice wholesome woman named Mrs. Nissinen. The cell was a really beautiful place. On the wall of the small cottage hung an iron cross and icon of the Saints of Valamo. First, we had coffee, namely those who drink coffee. Maria was just superb in the way she was conversing. She seemed to relate to the Archbishop as to a former student of hers. Before the meal we strolled around the area, piled alder branches, and chopped an old wooden boat into firewood. The Archbishop showed us how to find a location for a well (with a willow branch). The branch bent down where the ground water was when it was in the Archbishop's hands, as well as in Kaisa's, but not at all when I did it. For a meal we had salad, potatoes, and fish pie. The smoke sauna warmed up and we went for a bath, girls first. Swimming was a great enjoyment. On the boat trip when returning I "studied" the Archbishop's features while he was steering the motorboat, to commit them to memory for times to come. For the first time I noticed how old he actually looked; he was serious, traces of battle and suffering showed on his face.

Sunday August 31, 1969
This was an adventurous day too. I had Holy Communion. The church choir gathered here at Maria's place to watch a film of a Romania trip. The Archbishop joined. The choir sang under the Archbishop's direction. He must be amazingly musical. We watched the film. After that, we sang again hymns that the choir could sing without notes. I asked Maria whether the choir knew the hymn "Oh Gladsome Light" in Byzantine chant. Maria told the Archbishop that I wanted to hear it, and suggested to him that they would chant it. And so the Archbishop directed his own arrangement of it. And when they were singing, it felt as if Abbess in the flesh would have come to me, and as if the entire Bytouma with its mountains would surround me. Tears came into my eyes. I sat on a blanket

63. The Archbishop's summer cottage.
64. Iconographer Petros Sasaki.

on the floor with other youth and lowered my head yet lower. After the chant finished, the Archbishop said seriously: "This should be sung more often."

As the Archbishop was leaving, many asked for his blessing, and I went also and said, "I will leave for Helsinki tomorrow." And he said, "Oh, I see Anna-LIISA will leave tomorrow. Good strength for the studies!" It was the first time he got my name wrong. That has never happened before. And the truth is, that precisely the feeling, that even he does not care about me or remember me, not even my name, generates such a defiant desolation, which in turn is the seed for raging motivation to study.

IN HELSINKI

Tuesday September 2, 1969
It was really refreshing to start the studies. When I got up in the evening and left the seminary library, I was close to crossing myself as if leaving a church. That kind of attitude towards studies is probably the right one. My mind is now more open and freer than before, and I am more ready to be in contact with other students. For this I can thank first the observation that I don't have to try to please everybody, but rather, I have the right to be myself; and maybe even more, I can thank my sincere friendship with Matti Sidoroff and the others from the museum.

I am extremely conformist and get bothered by the most minute things. For example, I would rather listen to music on the stereo than watch a choir or orchestra, and the best is to be able to be alone. The action of the performers and the emotional expressions of the viewers somehow embarrass me; I have the impression that people should not show such emotions publicly.

Monday September 8, 1969
Library life is pleasing.

Thursday September 11, 1969
In front of the professors, I feel extremely unsure and shy. Being self-centered, I am like that by nature—and besides, I feel that I am nothing.

Friday September 12, 1969
Today I passed the cum laude oral exam (the final) in Roman literature and received the certificate of completion. The exam was a nice event. We talked about Stoicism, and I explained how the central principle in it is that one should not care about the twists and turns of fate, because happiness cannot be found in external circumstances. "But what then?" the professor asked. "In the person himself," I answered seriously with a little smile. "Correct," said the professor. Both he and I seem to agree with the Stoics on this.

I spent the evening with the Kyntäjä family, with my sister Maria and Timo in their new home. Little Juho was charming. His aunt's neck cross aroused intense admiration. When Juho will be six months in October, I will take him to the church.

Monday September 15, 1969
I met Maria between the university and Porthania, and she gave me Juho while she was running errands. I pushed Juho along the Esplanade.

Abbess's name day, Tuesday September 16, 1969
Shy, red, and wanting to vanish from sight, I sat with honorable professors, licentiates, and other highly learned people in a laudatur seminar in Greek. I hope I can truly participate. In any case, today again I clearly felt that happy and peaceful state of the soul, when death felt dear and welcomed. Even if I do live thankfully the time given to me, every day I want to wait for death and keep the thought of death, which holds the hope of eternal brightness, as my greatest consolation and secret source of joy.

I am not expecting a lot from human relationships anymore; I am not at home here.

Friday September 19, 1969
I spend long but interesting and varied days at the university. It is a great joy to study under the leadership of smart scientists. The spirit among the students is good. We are a small group, which jointly participates in academic exercises and free-time activities.

Monday September 29, 1969
My patrol guard in Girl Scouts and a friend, who was to graduate from medical school in the spring, is dead. She had killed herself with gas and left a note: "Forgive me, dear parents!" Why did you do it? Why did you

spoil your parents' remaining lifetime, did you shock everyone? Nobody lives here on their own. I thought that she wasn't missing anything, she was greatly loved at home. We had spent countless hours together at earlier times. Last spring, we met in passing and talked about being in touch, but we were not. Why did you do it? It is such a destructive act. She was the only daughter in the family, the joy of her parents. What drove you into such an act? What suffering, what bottomless depth?

Sunday October 5, 1969
I am serving as the chair of the Orthodox Student Union annual meeting. I have been attached to the Union with the same love as to the church, but now I am under the impression that this annual meeting lowered the Union to an ordinary frantic student organization, with nothing to give me anymore. Spiritual goals seem to be secondary in its life. I was not elected to the governing body. Quiet ascesis is not among the activities that organizations pursue these days. I am totally alone here.

Thursday October 23, 1969
I have been asked to become the secretary of Symposion, the student association of Classics. I have agreed. The matter will be decided in the annual meeting.

I was at the "Roman night" evening of the Symposion, which I left early after the program, the Villa Lante film,[65] was finished. I don't want to be a dry moralist, and all sincere joy, even if fueled with wine, makes me happy. It is nice to see young people have joy every now and then in the world, it refreshes the soul. But I myself am joyful in some other way.

Thursday October 30, 1969
I offered the following comment in the Orthodox Student Union after Olavi Merras's[66] talk, where he had emphasized the importance of a fundamental pastoral discussion in confession: "But would it not be possible that in practice, if you get such a confessor, one might get too attached to him and he might, either consciously or subconsciously, become the main focus? Is it not the purpose that people learn to walk on their own feet and the priest will help and support here and there?"

---

65. Villa Lante, location of the Finnish Institute in Rome.
66. Later, the Vicar of Lahti Orthodox Parish.

Wednesday November 5, 1969
I am annoyed by the observation that if I yield, even a little to what I fancy, especially in food, I will gain weight immediately.

It has snowed a lot. Kivihaka is quiet and white. It is good to live in a place where you can see snow.

Monday November 10, 1969
I read the whole day at home. Studying is starting to work even from home.

Father and Mother went to the opera, and I used the opportunity to call Lintula. I started to have that kind of feeling. With their prayers, monasteries bind you so tight to them, that it is impossible to detach. I discussed with Sister Sanni.[67] It was quite a remarkable call. When we had discussed the general welfare of the monastery, I said: "Please remember me also sometimes." "We will remember" said Sister Sanni, and I could hear from her voice that she was smiling. "I will remember too," I said. "Oh, you do remember, have not forgotten yet," said Sister Sanni.

I am happy I called.

Monday November 17, 1969
How good it would feel to get a few words of sympathy! It is such a dry and rough desert without anybody who could understand even a little. Nobody, nowhere; it is pointless to even turn to search. There is none, and probably none will come. Alone, alone. It is hard for a single ember to glow.

Wednesday November 26, 1969
I have been thinking that I will still spend next summer primarily in museum work in Kuopio, letting my character grow being close to the Archbishop. But if Father Archbishop will still not talk with me "normally," or if any kind of warming up will not happen between him and me, I will not go to Kuopio anymore, but rather will use the vacations more usefully from a mental development angle by working abroad. In the museum, time is somehow wasted.

I think that "Olympos" would be a nice informal name for the Center of the Orthodox Church. It was consecrated with the museum and all today.

---

67. Sister Sanni (Jaskanen), later Nun Seraphima (d. 2004).

Thursday December 4, 1969
Father promised to take me to the Independence Day celebration concert, which means that tomorrow I have to endure buying new clothes.

Internally I am very tight now. It feels like there would be so much to read. I will try to pass the cum laude exam in Greek on December 11. I should get a good grip on myself, as they say, and think rationally. I hope the Independence Day will give me a "reading rage."

Independence Day, Saturday December 6, 1969
Meeting Father Archbishop like this is annoying, because there is no chance of speaking with him and I am left with a feeling of incompleteness. He said "Helena,"[68] when sharing Holy Communion, and that at least was positive. The sermon was about independence and spiritually less rewarding.

During the day I was at the concert. Strong music in combination with longing for Greece and other misery filled my eyes with tears for the whole duration of the concert. Prime Minister Koivisto made a very positive impression on me.

In the evening I still went to the vigil in Uspensky Cathedral. The service was celebrated by Bishop John. After the Archbishop, he is easy to approach.

Friday December 12, 1969
I passed the exam. Last night I had a fever of 38.5°C (101.3°F). It probably resulted from the "heating up of the brain," prolonged reading, and some kind of nervousness.

Friday December 19, 1969
I know and have even experienced that I have special abilities of the soul. But now it seems like my external life is mere dawdling with details, pointless and sarcastic discussions, stealing nuts from on top of the cake, scolding because of the wet floor in the bathroom. Living at home does not really encourage the development of so-called supernatural powers of the soul. However, I would like to develop those.

New Year's Day, Thursday January 1, 1970
Tomorrow I will leave for Lintula. One surely must see how they are doing.

---

68. Anna-Leena's baptismal name.

Friday January 2, 1970
My arrival must have been quite a surprise for all. I helped with hauling straw all day. I like physical work. It is only 6:30 pm, but I was overcome with deep fatigue. During the day, monastery enthusiasm was high, and I was about to skip and hop on my way to the barn. I cannot help it, and I don't want to control that flame. It does not matter for such a short visit of a few days. I have talked a lot with Mother Varvara,[69] Maija,[70] Elisabeth,[71] and Irmeli.[72] There surely are many kinds of memories here.

Sunday January 4, 1970, in Kuopio
My Lintula visit finished abruptly. I got a call, and who was it other than Deacon Makkonen,[73] who asked me to come to the museum on Sunday. I agreed, and so I had to leave within an hour after the call and was unable to attend even one divine service. In the morning I chatted with Sister Sanni in the downstairs lobby.

I was in the museum. Many people came there.

Theophany, Tuesday January 6, 1970
The visit to the monastery turned out to be a joy and refreshment for the rest of the winter all the way to Pascha. In one swing it jolted my spiritual life on the right track, gave me courage to try.

The Divine Liturgy of Theophany was heartfelt, solemn, and warm, as it can be in Kuopio. Tomorrow starts the Orthodox Brotherhood's winter days; participants are primarily older priests and me.

Friday January 9, 1970, on the train from Kuopio to Helsinki
In the parish hall I made an intervention explaining the difficulties experienced by someone interested in the Orthodox Church due to lack of basic information about the Orthodox faith. Yesterday Father Erkki[74] came to sit beside me during the day's lecture and asked me to write down my thoughts for *Aamun Koitto*.[75] I have done that already.

69. Nun Varvara (d. 2011).
70. Sister Maija (Holopainen), later Nun Taisia, in great schema Melania.
71. Elisabeth Löfving-Morand, who at that time spent long periods at Lintula.
72. Sister Irmeli (Vuolle), later Nun Elisabet (d. 2017).
73. Heikki Makkonen, the Archbishop's secretary.
74. Father Erkki Piiroinen, Vicar of the Joensuu Orthodox Parish from 1962 to 1983 (d. 1999).
75. Orthodox magazine, *Dawn*.

I give the following instructions based on my experience:

1. Don't ever say anything extraordinary. Even if you understand it very clearly, it is not at all sure that someone else does.
2. Don't act too joyfully and cordially. Don't make your internal change too visible.
3. Do everything thoughtfully and calmly. Don't leave room for confusion. If this is from the Holy Spirit, the Holy Spirit will organize opportunities to meet together. If not, then all the meetings, however beautiful they are, are pointless.
4. Avoid singing except when the community sings as a congregation.
5. Always maintain a deep sense of humility. If this evaporates, receive its absence humbly. If it stays and you stay healthy, become more and more humble to the point that in your spirit you bow to everyone.
6. Continue your earlier work. Read and study diligently. Don't let anything confuse you.
7. Avoid excess perfectionism. Humility above all.
8. Don't ever pay attention to past or future suspicions, but rather treat all people with as much love as possible. If these suspicions come true, it is not your role to judge anybody. Whereas actions, you can criticize and fear.

Saturday March 6, 1971
Large part of my thoughts is dominated by *Logos*, the newsletter of the Orthodox Student Union, where I am an editor. I like editing the paper. Using the public media bears its own responsibility; on one hand there are great possibilities, one can influence both good and bad.

Friday March 12, 1971
I am finalizing the writing of my pro gradu [MA thesis]. I bought a typewriter yesterday. Juho was with us in the beginning of the week. I like him a lot, and he also seems to like "Aunt Annuski." There is a child whose true well-being everyone is watching over.

Monday March 15, 1971
Weight was lifted from my heart when today in the governing group meeting of the Orthodox Student Union I escaped the danger of being

sent to America as a representative to the general assembly of Syndesmos.[76] What do we learn from this? We learn that I am not going to apply for Symposion's trip to Rome in August; rather, if it is up to me, I will spend a peaceful summer at the museum and the seminary. I am already reminiscing about my own stump in the yard of the Orthodox Center. No, I am not really going to fly around the world, when I don't have to. The latest *Logos* has been well received.

Friday April 2, 1971
I become happy just thinking about Kuopio's "Orthodox colony." Everything in some ways circulates around the silent and tender, sometimes inner-light-streaming Archbishop. There is the sweet family Kononen,[77] the Japanese Petros, whom I am very attached to, the Härkönens, Aunt Paula, seminarians, young father Kalevi,[78] and his wife Marja. All of us celebrate Pascha together after living through Holy Week first. And our Paschal joy is transmitted by television to the whole nation . . . One has to accept that, it is not good to just think of oneself.

Palm Sunday, April 4, 1971, on the train on the way to Kuopio
I am a little on the downswing now. Even in the church I felt tired standing. It happens often that if something one has counted the hours for does happen, one is already tired of all the waiting.

HOLY WEEK AND PASCHA IN KUOPIO, 1971 AD

Holy Monday, April 5, 1971
Arriving here in some way lets you detach from the vortex of Helsinki. Inner silence sets in. The self-promotion that a big city tempts you to bursts like a bubble. You can see things from a perspective and understand your own sinfulness.

It was a lovely sunny day. I went to the public swimming center in the morning and from there to the church. In the afternoon I visited Maria's aunt, who was alone in her apartment while Maria was seeing an eye doctor in Helsinki. The overly masculine manner of speech by the

---

76. The International Orthodox Youth Association.
77. The assessor of the Clergy-Laity Assembly Mauri Kononen and his wife Helmi.
78. Father Kalevi Kokkonen, youth pastor of the Kuopio Parish. Vicar of the Joensuu Orthodox Parish from 1983 to 2009.

Karelian elderly woman was fun to listen to. In the evening I had tea with Mrs. Kononen and the girls and their friends. I am immeasurably thankful for their affectionate friendship.

Holy Tuesday, April 6, 1971
The weather was radiant again. In the morning before church, I walked the Kononens' dogs. It is very useful to listen to the long gospel readings in the service of the hours before the Liturgy of Presanctified Gifts. My attention focused again on the fact that the gospels contain something so happily unconventional. The Spirit of God is not chained. Later in the day I visited the Kyntäjä family in the rectory.

Holy Wednesday, April 7, 1971
The dawning of the day was wonderful again. The Archbishop came to the church in the morning after the service had already started. After the service I bought Easter postcards and mailed them.

Holy Thursday, April 8, 1971
The Archbishop celebrated the liturgy, and large crowds of people went to receive Holy Communion. It revitalizes the soul, which a moment before was a desert decorated with bitter herbs. But Holy Communion makes the spring flowers bloom and transforms the soul into a land of springs. I thank you, Lord, for leaving us this wondrous consolation.

Holy Friday, April 9, 1971
During the day when the Icon of Christ's Burial was carried around in the church and the burial was performed, I thought about death. I looked at my candle-holding hands and thought of being in the grave. But I fear not: Christ is a stranger to corruption. It can be, however, that Christ's second coming happens before my departure. I fear not: Both spiritual life and bodily death reveal that a grain of wheat must first die before it can bear much fruit.

Holy Saturday, April 10, 1971
There was liturgy. After that, the caretaker handed me an envelope. Father Archbishop needed help on one more Greek text.

The Lord's Pascha, Sunday, April 11, 1971
Christ is risen! I can add yet another happy Paschal night in Kuopio, in the Cathedral of St. Nicholas in my memories. And with the Kononen family. Tomorrow I will visit the Archbishop and Suhola.[79]

The day after Pascha (on the train), Bright Monday, April 12, 1971
The reception of the Archbishop started at 1 pm, and I got there a little late. I was fatigued, and as soon as it was possible I retired to be with Mrs. Nissinen in the kitchen. We washed and dried dishes.

The Archbishop came to the kitchen after the guests had left. There had been fifty of them. The Archbishop already said goodbye to us, but returned soon after. Maria Iltola had called and asked all of us, Father Archbishop, Mrs. Nissinen, and me, for a visit. Maria promised that I could stay with her for the month of May.

Tuesday April 13, 1971, in Helsinki
Marja told me that another baby is most likely to be expected next December.

Yesterday the Archbishop shared how he had tried to see if he could really drive 160 km/hr[80] with his former car. All the things you have to hear. Luckily he now has a toy with a little less horsepower. Besides, he said he has changed to a more peaceful way of driving.

Sunday April 18, 1971
Pastor Korelin[81] was chosen as the parish vicar of Helsinki from the third place in the election. Many merciful years to Father Alexander! Only two Sundays remaining here, at most.

Monday April 19, 1971
Today many have teased me that surely an Orthodox seminarian or another young man will catch me in Kuopio. And I have replied something like, I am a sworn old maid and that freedom is everything for me. I suppose so.

---

79. Johannes Suhola, rector of the seminary, 1942 to 1972.
80. 100 mph.
81. Father Alexander Korelin, Vicar of Helsinki Parish from 1971 to 1987.

Wednesday April 21, 1971
Sometimes I feel that if I really worked (in the museum) the whole summer from the beginning of May, I might get a little tired. But all this is hard to know beforehand; one's strength could increase surprisingly. I am now somehow fed up and tired of being here in Helsinki.

SUMMER 1971

Saturday May 1, 1971, at the Iltolas in Kuopio
I came from the station to the Iltolas and then to the vigil. I was at the Kononens for tea, and then Maria and I chatted about all the issues of the church.

Sunday May 2, 1971
Maria gets a grateful listener in me when she praises the Archbishop. She said it is impossible to get the Archbishop to talk about other people, even if you try. He just says "so," and that's where it stops.

The guides of the Orthodox Church Museum, Irene Karjomaa, Leo Makkonen (later Archbishop Leo), and Anna-Leena, summer 1972.

Tuesday May 4, 1971, in Kuopio
I decided not to read in the museum anymore, but to devote myself fully to the museum during the five hours I spend there. Naturally even up to now I have only engaged in reading during free moments, but it creates an attitude towards the visitors: "You have come again to disturb me!" The visitors and their comfort are, however, the main thing for the guide.

Friday May 7, 1971
Ulla wrote and asked me to be godmother of her little daughter. This is already my third godchild. As God allows this to happen, for sure He will give strength for this mission too. The child is of course Lutheran.

Wednesday May 12, 1971
In the morning there was a liturgy for cantors in the church. The Archbishop and the boys were singing, Father Niilo[82] celebrated, and I was the only representative of the congregation. Heaven was on the Earth. It was all totally natural. We are not snatched away to any ecstasy, but the living reality of God's kingdom, which in fact is always in existence, is fulfilled. I will not cease to praise God's holy and lifegiving mystery.

Wednesday May 26, 1971
There have been hard days at the museum—too hard for me. Yet another one tomorrow, and then it will ease up. On Friday the Archbishop will leave for Moscow and return on June 6.

Wednesday June 9, 1971
The Ambassador of England and a large group of Swiss visited the museum yesterday.

AT THE SEMINARY

Sunday June 13, 1971
I moved yesterday.[83] I was quite tired. It was to be expected. Until Friday there had been an almost uninterrupted program every day from 8 am to 8:30 pm. Yesterday I was at the Kononens. Kaisa, Irene, and I were

---
82. Father Niilo Karjomaa, Vicar of the Orthodox Parish of Kuopio from 1966 to 1976.
83. From Maria Iltola's to the seminary facilities vacated for the summer.

laughing our heads off for absolutely no reason at all and ate large quantities of pies, sweet buns, and ice cream, which I had brought with me. Such a thing is good for you sometimes. A human being is simply such that he should not push himself too much. Even in spiritual life there can be a kind of woody, dry, artificial feeling at times, and then laughter and joy and simplicity are the best medicine.

Tuesday June 15, 1971
I had a very stimulating intellectual discussion with two white South African boys. First, we talked about Orthodoxy in the Russian Church, and then I asked them about conditions and racism in South Africa. Nothing is as simple as it seems from afar. Kant's principle of living one's whole life in Königsberg, but on the other hand asking everything possible from the people you meet, and nowadays also to read and watch movies to learn more, is quite nice in my opinion.

Thursday July 8, 1971
I was at the Häikiö summer house. It did me good all around. It is somehow so wonderful to have a real discussion. It revives both the mental and, quite remarkably, the spiritual life. When you are just on your own without any stimulating contacts, you can easily drift into a mysterious, deadly, or extremely low-intensity mental state and begin to spin the same thoughts around in your mind. I can now see quite clearly that a person is not meant to be a hermit, whatever the holy fathers think (on second thought, the holy fathers probably do not think that a twenty-six-year-old should live as a hermit). Human beings are created in such a way that interaction with others absolutely stimulates them in very many useful ways. If it is up to me, I would try to continuously keep in touch with Anna Häikiö and others. Getting up and out from oneself does a lot of good every now and then. It is like a fresh wind that airs out the swamps of the soul.

There have been lovely hot days. On Sunday (in Kuopio) Timo and I solved a puzzle: lost wife and a little boy. Timo had, as he said, hurt Marja, and she had taken Juho under her arm and set off to the unknown roads. She was eventually found in Kivihaka in Helsinki.

Saturday July 17, 1971
Mark Twain's book *Letters from the Earth* has been put together in a very clever and cheerful way. Most aspects associated with it can be explained

by his Protestant-Puritan background. But one section has given me—and how many before me!—cause for deep reflection. Because, as a matter of fact, come to think of it, our innocent, happy statement, "In wisdom you have made them all."[84] includes a few difficulties. For example, many diseases are not abstract but caused by living creatures. All the bacteria and viruses, sleeping sickness, rabies—are they also created? Obviously they are, because we cannot assume that the Devil would have created anything. It is really a bit strange that we praise the Lord for the triumph of medicine, which preempts the effects of the organisms created by Him. In ancient times, a sickness was seen as a blow from God; there was no understanding that it was the work of the created, in other words, living beings. It is only good that I am troubled by such problems. I believe, however, that God will lead me to all the truth.

Later in Ilomantsi. Maria and I drove in front, the Archbishop and Petros behind us. We drove through Joensuu and stopped at a gas station for a coffee. The Archbishop invited us for food and drinks.

It is easy to withdraw behind the excuse of all sorts of theological musings, when in fact it is really a matter of guilty conscience. I went to confession and afterwards felt like I had been lifted out of a garbage can.

Feast day of Elijah, Tuesday July 20, 1971
The Archbishop said in the meadow that he wanted to remind himself and others of the true Christian journey. It was all really beautiful: the sun was setting, the campfires were glowing, large cloud formations were sailing in the sky. People were sitting on the lawn and standing further out.

Later. When passing by, Anni Homanen called out to me to come to her home for a meal. There were also other people from the Feast whom the hosts did not know. During the day there was traditional singing, kantele[85] playing, etc.

Later. It is peculiar that always after the feast of a saint, and even at its end, the mind is filled with longing and yearning.

Monday August 9, 1971
The Archbishop explained that at the Orthodox Church's last Board meeting it was decided to offer me two vacancies as a religion teacher: either in

---

84. Ps. 104:24 (New Revised Standard Version).
85. A Karelian plucked string instrument.

Turku or Lahti. I decided to go to Lahti. I can live there either with Aunt Helvi or Aunt Elsa and also take care of my studies. The more I thought about it, the happier I became. I called Aunt Elsa in Lahti. Either one of the aunts will definitely take me in to live with her. Look, Leenuska[86] will become a Lahti resident. "My heart is flooded with beautiful words . . ."[87] I give thanks for this day. I will teach, pay off my student loan, graduate, and go to the monastery. This is a good plan.

Saturday August 14, 1971
Mother visited the museum. What at least is clear is that my life at home in Helsinki would have become impossible. Now she was talking about how Aunt Elsa and I did not get along, how living with relatives usually fails.

Tuesday August 17, 1971
I have been thinking that I cannot go to Lintula after all. I would suffocate there in one week. Even though I like to sanctify my life in everything, I cannot and do not want to go to a monastery. I want to live before God as a free person. I do not want to separate myself externally from others in any way.

WINTER AS A TEACHER OF RELIGION

Thursday August 19, 1971, in Helsinki
I came through Lahti. I went to meet with Reverend Hodju. Hyvinkää is my main employer. The next step in the program is to do the schedule. I can get a peaceful and nice place to stay at Aunt Elsa's. Although it looks like I will also be spending quite a bit of time here in Helsinki.

Saturday August 21, 1971
Winter ascesis started again. Mother and Elina arrived home. Lord Jesus Christ, protect and guard me with Your mercy, and let me always behave as an Orthodox teacher of religion should.

---

86. A term of endearment for "Leena."
87. Ps. 45:1 (New Revised Standard Version).

Saturday August 28, 1971, in Helsinki
After the vigil we went to Helena Nikkanen's house,[88] where we discussed the most diverse topics until almost midnight. With us were, among others, Veikko Purmonen[89] and Pertti Rantala,[90] religion teachers of our church. During the weekend it is good to try to store up Orthodox inspiration. I miss daily divine services.

Friday September 3, 1971
I like work. It is fun to guide the small and even a little older Orthodox believers. I analyze each lesson I teach and think about why some are successful, why there is sometimes a certain rigidity. I think about the personalities of the students.

Monday September 6, 1971, in Helsinki
When I am in Hyvinkää, I feel that nowhere is more fun than there, and when I go to Lahti, I feel that it is the best of everything. I guess you can say that I like my work.

Sunday October 10, 1971, in Kuopio
"I will write your biography one day," I told the Archbishop. "It is not worth wasting paper and ink on it," he responded.

Saturday October 16, 1971
Riitta (sister) suggested on her own initiative that she wants to go to the liturgy tomorrow. I have read "The Way of a Pilgrim." It is comforting to see that there are many different ways; not everybody has to follow the same path in ascesis. Some emphasize one aspect, and others another.

Sunday November 7, 1971, on the train from Kuopio to Helsinki
The Archbishop asked if I wanted to see his new parrot and took me to the holiest of the holy, which is his office behind his room. It is an Amazon parrot that should learn how to speak. And then we talked about Greece, and the Archbishop thought that it is a good plan for me to go there with Riitta. That's what I will do, God willing.

---

88. Daughter of Irinja Nikkanen, later the leading conservator of the Valamo Conservation Institute.

89. Later, among other things, teacher in the seminary, lector of practical theology, and Vicar of the Helsinki Orthodox parish.

90. Later Bishop Alexis of Joensuu (d. 1984).

Wednesday November 10, 1971
If I ever go to a monastery, it will happen for the love of God in the sense that I will go there, because I think that it is the best way to serve and get closer to God. So I do not go there, because I would absolutely want it for my own pleasure. Maybe, however, it is not God's will regarding me.

Sunday November 14, 1971
I wrote to Abbess that Riitta and I will come there in the summer.

Wednesday November 17, 1971
I received issues of *Vechnoe* magazine from Nun Marina,[91] which contained letters by Bishop Theophan—and what letters! There were over fifty letters by Bishop Theophan. I have translated two, so there will be plenty of enjoyable work to do.

Friday November 19, 1971
Bishop Theophan's letters are so wonderful, especially for me at this moment. Probably there will be a very special period in my life that will be called, "The time when I translated Bishop Theophan's letters." People today are completely blind; true happiness is not known; rather, there are countless perverse conceptions.

Saturday December 4, 1971, in Helsinki
I cannot stand to be in this city, constantly an oppressive stress around me.

Bishop John celebrated the vigil. It has been a long time since we last met. When he blessed the people after the vigil, he smiled at me kindly. Bishop John is somehow more human than the Archbishop, with whom you sometimes feel like scratching a rock with your nails, but then, if one comes to a well of water, it is clear and lifegiving.

Monday January 10, 1972
Jaakko's[92] baptism was yesterday. He is a sweet baby. I thought I would seize the opportunity and babysit him. Maybe my life will not have many babies to take care of.

---

91. Nun Marina (Smirnoff), later schema nun Seraphima.
92. The second son of her sister Marja.

Friday January 14, 1972
Nowadays I get along very well on my own in Lahti. I do not miss direct contact with other Orthodox people. It is better to contemplate and pray in peace rather than participate in people's "war between mice and frogs."[93]

Friday January 21, 1972
There is a kind of restless weakness in my inner structure. I have very little energy, and a dream of a bright, peaceful, and harmonious persona will not come to fruition. My hopes for external circumstances are contradictory: periodically I think that peaceful translation work in solitude would be best, but in fact I get bored and lose my enthusiasm very quickly when alone. On the other hand, I do not trust adults. I have no illusions about the behavior of human communities. I do not even trust human love: It is selfish and fickle. My entire hope is by and large focused on the life to come—and on Holy Communion.

Wednesday February 2, 1972
Helena,[94] Riitta's friend and a high school student, is with us. She will play as a soloist with an orchestra from Kuopio here in Helsinki. When I compare that inhibited, rigid, and mentally immature young girl I was in high school and Helena, the difference is quite enormous. I grasped on to only one thing: I want to surrender totally to God.

Lord's Pascha, Sunday April 2, 1972, in Kuopio
Christ has opened the way to the divinization of a human person; He himself is the way. Above all I prayed tonight that I would learn to walk this way. I need to think more about God and about joining God. I would like to walk the road of theosis and illumination. Everyone is meant to follow that road.
    In the evening. Today's highlight was a visit to Karjomaa, the home of the vicar, where Irene[95] had kindly invited Marja[96] and me. The Archbishop and the church choir were there. Father Niilo presented the Archbishop's wish that Marja would talk about icons, and I of Greece. As a gift

---

93. She is referring to a book titled *Batrachomyomachia* by an unknown author. The book is a parody of Homer's *Iliad*.
94. Helena Nissinen.
95. The daughter of Fr. Niilo Karjomaa, the Vicar of the Orthodox Parish of Kuopio.
96. Kristoduli's long-term Orthodox friend Marja Räsänen (later Sasaki).

inherited from my father, I can speak freely without a plan. I explained all kinds of things about Bytouma, and Helmi Kononen said that people liked my talk very much. As I was leaving, the Archbishop looked at me infinitely kindly. I wonder if I am really going to Bytouma in two months?

Sunday April 9, 1972
Sometimes I am disturbed by the thought that I am being taken advantage of economically. Not all of the schools pay me a salary; of course I do not get paid for the translation work . . . But I will hold fast to the Christian attitude of not making trouble about money as long as I have the clothing I need and a roof over my head; let the people exploit me as much as they want. And it is perfectly natural for me, since I get my income from being a teacher of religion, that during other times I will do whatever work is needed for the church for free, without any additional compensation.

I have no special thoughts about this life anymore. Let's see if God will still use me for something. On Holy Thursday during the pre-communion prayer, I prayed privately above all that God would let me travel in His light and then feel the light within me. And be that as it may, the sun started to shine and hit me right then and there. However, this kind of thing does not startle me very much. If God wills, why not—but there is no special happiness in store for me on the earth. The happiness which is in this world is also from heaven. There should be, however, more enthusiasm. Now I see many long, monotonous years of ascesis in front of me, with no special divine consolation. But the one who is patient will win.

Wednesday May 10, 1972
Bishop Theophan's letters do not please me as much as they did at the beginning. He is too systematic; it is as if he is in some way inspired to build all kinds of systems that he then claims are easy to follow. But at least I have come to the conclusion, based on my own experience, that all systems are far from spiritual life. "The wind blows where it chooses . . ."[97]

---

97. John 3:8 (New Revised Standard Version).

Sunday May 14, 1972, in Lahti
Here we had a liturgy celebrated by the Metropolitan. I took Holy Communion. It was so wonderful. The moment the Metropolitan gave me the Holy Communion, it felt so miraculous—the body and blood of Christ was with us and in us. Aunt Elsa came to the church, and we went from there to have lunch. She said that she thought the Metropolitan looked so pleasant and friendly. It cannot be denied that there is a kind of consensus among us converts. This was truly a bright day of the Lord.

TWO VISITS TO BYTOUMA

Wednesday May 24, 1972
A very heartfelt letter came from Metropolitan Seraphim.[98] He thanked me profusely for my interest in Orthodoxy and writes that after consultation with Abbess he is pleased to welcome Riitta and me, and that our stay at the monastery will be free and we will not even need to work (although we will certainly participate in common tasks). This is somehow overwhelming. Over there, faith is at a completely different level of intensity than here. So Abbess, after all that has happened, is ready to receive me again with open arms. I walked around the room enchanted.

Thursday May 25, 1972
I am quite suspicious of the idea that in Bytouma I would all of a sudden realize that my mission in life is to become a nun. For example, something like freedom of movement, which is secured by independence and money, feels very important to me. It is hard to imagine that such vast landscapes would open up within me, that I could restrict the outer movement to nonexistence. At least now it seems to be quite difficult. But I will ask Abbess that the twenty-one days, which I hope to spend there now, I could live in obedience.

Friday May 26, 1972
I have come to the conclusion that absolute obedience would be the only saving grace for me. I am caught in a web of my own thoughts and desires and I do not even know myself what I want. To set one's own ego aside in complete obedience—that would be necessary and wonderful as well.

---

98. Metropolitan of Trikke and Stagoi, 1970 to 1974.

Tuesday May 30, 1972
Fortunately, whether I am in the world or in the monastery, I have learned to surrender to the fact that suffering cannot be avoided. What would it be like to really live ascetically in a monastery? To struggle and suffer and internalize the fact that it is not easy anywhere.

TRIP TO GREECE WITH HER SISTER RIITTA

Monday June 5, 1972
I have a panicky feeling that something special is going to happen, that the old is going to disappear. I can of course also be wrong. "Into your hands, Lord Jesus Christ, I commit my spirit, but You bless me, have mercy on me, and give me eternal life. Amen."

Wednesday June 7, 1972
The departure was appalling. We were about to be late when the taxi we had booked did not come. I said a prayer of thanksgiving to You, Lord, as we finally made it to the ship with dry mouths and drenched in sweat. Now we are traveling anyway. It is wonderful that Riitta came along.

The morning got to me. I wonder what would have happened to my faith if we had been late?

Saturday June 10, 1972, on a train in Yugoslavia
Here on the Yugoslavian plateau, you get glimpses of red poppy fields, swine herds, geese, and people with their hoes. Yesterday evening the train climbed over the Alps. It is an equally great experience every time. We had a bottle of Pepsi-Cola, slices of bread, tomatoes, and fruit to eat. In the evening I took a valerian pill because I had not slept well for many nights. Now I did sleep; it probably helped that we no longer had the stress of changing the means of transportation.

Soon we arrived in the beloved country. Riitta seems enthusiastic. We had finished the food, and because there was no restaurant car on the train, we had French pastilles for dinner. The train track has been following a large river, and the further south we have come, the more welcoming are the people harvesting grain in the field. Tanned children waved at the train as it passed. A quiet, joyful affection overtakes me as we get closer to the region of Thessaly. Surely they are thinking of us in the monastery.

We practiced Finnish folk songs, which undoubtedly we will have to sing in Bytouma.

Monday June 12, 1972, in Bytouma
We arrived in Bytouma already in the evening. The car got stuck on the way. We went to the Compline service in the church. Abbess was on her knees in her old spot. Everybody was happy, and we had fun remembering names. We ate in the reception room with Abbess and Sister Eusevia. Thank You, my God!

Tuesday June 13, 1972, in Bytouma
We climbed to the gardens, started doing handicrafts. Riitta will make a skirt here. The utmost best of all are the church services: in the morning, at noon, and two in the evening.

Thursday June 15, 1972, in Bytouma
Riitta has become very hardworking. To tell the truth, I am really tired of dragging around such a non-believing and stubborn girl. But everyone has their cross, and mine now is "Margarita," as they call her. She is a nice girl, so to speak. Hopefully she will gradually become more independent.

Sunday June 18, 1972, in Bytouma
Last night we had an all-night vigil (12 am to 7:30 am). I have never experienced such deep peace as I did when we stood under the starry sky with a candle in our hand. I also took Holy Communion. Staying here and living the quiet life of an inner person would be the most heavenly thing I know. I cried today about the (upcoming) departure. But from now on, the difficulties of each day will suffice. This is how my twenty-seventh birthday was spent.

Monday June 19, 1972, in Bytouma
I will not leave here, unless Abbess carries me outside the gate with her own hands. I am not as strong a person as she is; the spirit of prayer leaves me immediately as soon as I come to the noise of the world. I will talk to my father confessor, I will pray and ask Abbess and above all Panagia[99] to let me stay. Otherwise, I will die.

---

99. "All-holy," a title for Mary, Mother of God.

Tuesday June 20, 1972, in Bytouma
I spoke like St. John Chrysostom[100] in my confession to Father Chariton, and he said he would talk to Abbess to keep me here.

Saturday June 24, 1972, in Bytouma
Now I am beginning to think that we must go back to Finland. The sisters here are so different from me, their thoughts move in very different directions. It might, after all, be difficult for me to stay here. It will be difficult also in Finland, but maybe the Lord will protect the silence and purity in my soul.

Feast Day of Apostles Peter and Paul, Thursday June 29, 1972
Sometime after 4:30 am Finland can feel like a nice place, because sleeping from 10 pm to 4:30 am plus a two-hour nap during the day does not seem to be enough for this great ascetic. But maybe when one is fully adapted to the climate, that amount of sleep is enough.

Sunday July 2, 1972
Lord, give me the bread I need for my life; in other words, daily divine services, silence. You see that I am tired. No one loves me in Finland, no one needs me there. I cannot bear to be in the midst of people. The hustle and bustle and selfishness and fighting everywhere tires me to exhaustion. Maybe they do not love me here either and do not want me here . . . Where should I go? Lord, take me to you.

Monday July 3, 1972
A letter arrived from the Archbishop. In a way he blesses my stay here, but not to stay right now, but maybe in a year. And it also seems to me that I must go. Ten and a half months is no time at all. If we look at things realistically, it is easy to observe that I have a lot of unfinished business in Finland. Studies need to be completed, part of the student loan needs to be paid off, all the necessary books need to be taken along, and a discussion with Bishop John must be had on the translation work I could do here. The train tickets also arrived. There is a mistake; they are only valid after July 15, even though I specifically wrote that they can be dated for the end of June (they are valid for two months). Also, the departure

---

100. Early church Father (349 to 407) known for his gift for preaching.

station is Athens, although I specifically mentioned that we leave from Thessalonica.

There was a thunderstorm, and the rain poured down from the sky. In the morning I was stacking firewood with the girls. It is very difficult to get them to work together in an organized way. The Greek national character is very individualistic, to the point of being ridiculous.

Saturday July 8, 1972
Abbess is truly a wonderful person. One is overwhelmed when thinking about God's ways. From the mountains of central Greece God gave me a spiritual guide, and to Abbess a daughter from far away in the north, a human being, who might understand her better than anyone else right now.[101] God works in mysterious ways.

Monday July 10, 1972, in Athens
This morning we started to go. First, I went to church as usual. For a final, formal farewell I went to look for Abbess. She was at the washing area scouring wool. I asked if she wanted to come with me to the church, but she just mumbled that she has work to do and told me to get Riitta. Then she wiped her hands on her working coat. We bowed and kissed her hand and both cheeks as we did for other sisters, as well following the common Greek custom. There she stood with sweat like pearls on her forehead. She sent special greetings to Mother and then to the Archbishop.

I was wondering to myself about the outward calmness with which I left the monastery. But what is shocking about doing God's will? We arrived happily in Athens and are staying in Hotel Nestor.

Tuesday July 11, 1972, in Kalamata
We traveled several hours by train and arrived here at the monastery. I am very grateful that God led me to Bytouma. This monastery is in the middle of the city. Riitta and I are dead tired.

Saturday July 15, 1972, in Athens
We went to Aegina and visited Saint Nektarios's monastery. It is a famous pilgrimage site. There were hundreds of people packed into the small monastery. All-holy Mother of God, protect the peace in Bytouma. Yesterday and today we went swimming and biked along the coast. We spent

---

101. Two nuns had left the monastery the day before.

the night in a family [home] together with three other women. The whole island was fully booked. At present we are in Hotel Carlton in Athens by the Omonia Square. Hundreds of people are crowded in the streets; it is a soccer match. I love the Greeks; like children they get enthusiastic about everything!

AFTER THE TRIP TO GREECE

Friday July 21, 1972
I have a deep desire to start my ascetic life in earnest as soon as everything is in order. And the monastery is Bytouma. There, once upon a time, I was given black clothes; I presented my written application to become a novice, and, as I said to Abbess, in a way I already consider myself a member of the sisterhood.

Saturday July 29, 1972, in Simonniemi
I read the minutes of Syndesmos' meeting in Rättvik and thought about many things. Is it right for me to go to a monastery when there are many people who have not heard of Christ? But maybe it is that we all have our own gifts and the church also needs those who pray, and maybe God will show me in time if it is His will that I serve other people in some other way.

Wednesday August 2, 1972, in Helsinki
I do not think that the process of separation from the fatherland, which has already begun in some ways, is going to be simple. But it is something I need to deal with in my heart on my own. When the Holy Spirit guides the mind, there will be no difficulties.

Friday August 4, 1972
Christians do not have the same concept of time as others. Life in Christ is eternal, and it starts here.

Saturday August 5, 1972
I am reading the biography of Saint Nektarios (d. 1920). There we see again how the church treats its holy people; first they are persecuted and tormented, and after their death declared as saints, and everyone wonders how strange it is that such things happen even within the church.

Let's see if I end up getting religion classes to teach. But I trust that God will somehow get me the funds I need to depart to Greece.

Saturday August 12, 1972
I am in a way still overwhelmed by the quiet but real turmoil of thoughts that I had in Bytouma. It is very clear that monastic life is my calling. But the fact that I will once again put on those black "joy generating sorrow" clothes will only be the prelude. God's Spirit has yet to plow and cultivate deep into the field of my heart. I will learn a lot about monastic life. Sister Eusevia's words are true: "Do not put your trust in people." Even in the monastery one needs to strive to please God and not the other sisters.

Wednesday August 16, 1972
The Mother of God, our true Abbess, has become closer to me lately. When I try to concentrate on the life of her soul, the mind is overtaken by a pleasant wonder. How can someone be so unconnected to the life of the soul, that you think that after Christmas Eve she spent her time doing the busy work of a rural woman with many children? In this respect, the Protestants are surprisingly superficial!

Thursday August 24, 1972
It so happened that I will even get the classes of Hyvinkää and Riihimäki, because the hours of instruction for the classes in Helsinki were not enough. I am actually happy about this. First, I can continue to work with familiar students and guide them a little longer, and second, it can be good to leave Helsinki periodically to breathe fresh country air. I try to study as energetically as possible. Money is not a problem, because the number of hours, which includes two schools from Helsinki, will be considerable; i.e., funds will accrue to pay off the student loan.

Sunday August 27, 1972
I was at a wedding in Turku. The occasion was very beautiful and pious, but the sacrament is in some ways very patriarchal, and there is not much encouragement for an exciting and experience-filled life in it. What I mean is that the goal in life set for people is to lead a healthy life following the commandments of God and to be a useful citizen, bringing up children and waiting for grandchildren. This is a noble and good thing and even challenging enough, but not at all suitable for me. The ascesis

by monks and nuns is the struggle of the entire human person for God, throwing everything into the game.

Sunday September 24, 1972
I got rid of [my service on] the Board of the Orthodox Student Union. The quasi-ecclesiastical political action of the Union is unpleasant to me. In the speeches there are sometimes various stupid insinuations against the "dictatorship" of the bishops, which the Union has set itself to break.

Friday September 29, 1972
I took the laudatur exam in Greek and called Henrik (Prof. Zilliacus) in the evening to ask about the result. He said that it went "really well." Undeniably it warms the mind. There is still an oral exam and a written translation exam from Greek to Finnish. The sisters' prayers have given me strength.

Feast day of the Protection of the Mother of God, Sunday October 1, 1972
I like autumn. The scent in the woods, the dry, hard ground, the bright sky—it is easy to run around, the foot rises lightly. I walk and look up high to the tops of the trees. This could be, by the way, the last autumn in Finland.

Tuesday, October 17, 1972
I passed the Greek laudatur exam. The translation exam, which I took alone in Henrik's office, went really well. It was as if someone stood by me and whispered in my ear: translate it in this and this way. So, even that is done!

Saturday October 21, 1972
I have seldom waited for winter in such a dull mood as now. Nasty gray fog, cold to the bone and to the core . . . Warm scented wind, rustling plantains, rippling water—all full of life. Nature has started to mean more to me than before. Well, winter has to be endured, and spring gets closer every day. The thought of winter being unpleasant is also made worse by the fact that I have poor winter clothes. However, I do not want to buy new ones, because if I will stay in Greece, I won't need them.

Wednesday November 8, 1972
Monks, hermits, and ascetics living in solitude can hardly inspire the youth of today, and our church history hardly offers any other kind of idols. There is a painful need for new models even in other areas of life, a new way of Christian life expressed in practice. Something in which a person gives everything, but which would be more in line with today's worldview, with which even the youth could identify. It is probably not meant for them to become monks and nuns in our living conditions. Instead of looking for new ways myself, searching and thinking what could be done, I retreat to the old and proven forms, dress myself in centuries-old clothes, and stop to take advantage of the progress of humanity. Instead of trying to solve the problems of Christian life in the abruptly changed world, constructively using, for example, technology and new knowledge as gifts from God, I move into a centuries-old circle of life, into the Middle Ages and even beyond. Instead of using the psychiatric knowledge of the human person with an open mind, I try to stretch my soul according to the knowledge that the ascetic fathers have gathered on the human soul since five hundred years after Christ. Such thoughts circulate in my mind. But it is difficult to know what is potentially a temptation from the Devil. Am I a coward to go to Bytouma? Can I not learn something new and important there? After all, I believe that there I can learn the science of all sciences and the art of all arts.

Friday November 10, 1972
Professor Zilliacus told me today about a Greek government scholarship which would allow one student to go to Greece for three weeks before the last day of December. But the whole thing was initiated so late, its implementation is questionable. Henrik promised, however, to write to Greece. I expressed my interest in going. The aim would be to get acquainted with modern Greece and its institutions and phenomena. The whole thing was quite surprising; let's see if anything will come of it.

There is one thing of which I am sure. Whatever God's will is for me, I will move out from my parents' home next year.

Sunday November 12, 1972
The situation here at home is getting quite tense. The Protestants have a strange view, that sinners should stop praying and cease going to church, on top of everything else.

Thursday November 16, 1972

The Orthodox Student Union's meeting on Thursday evening ended very unpleasantly. Metropolitan John spoke about the Eighth Ecumenical Council. Veikko Purmonen intervened and emphasized the importance of the entire church in the decision-making, the notion of *sobornost*. The Metropolitan, on the other hand, always stresses the central role of the bishops. After this intervention the Metropolitan explained that the notion of sobornost is not Orthodox, according to the Greeks, and announced abruptly that he needed to leave to work on some writing tasks. Most of all I was surprised and shocked by the quite emotional reaction of the Metropolitan; he was obviously very upset by what Veikko said. Is it certain that he is pursuing an objective interpretation of the canons and for the good of the church? Or should one wonder if power is personally dear to him? Oh, how many great tasks there are! There certainly is room for everyone, but we prefer to argue.

Sunday November 19, 1972

What a wonderful liturgy it was again! The sun was shining in the church, filtering through the incense; there were people, children sitting on the floor. Tender joy filled my mind. After Holy Communion I thanked God again from the bottom of my heart for leading me to the Orthodox Church.

Sunday November 26, 1972

The visit to the Soviet Union was a very enlightening experience, and I am grateful to have been able to do it. I went to the Spiritual Academy—I was there for Vespers and dinner—and this morning in church. The church does not seem to have learned much from the revolution. The rituals of the Tsarist era are followed faithfully. After each trip to Greece the "baroque" services are more and more disturbing in my mind. In the past the church was apparently unable to convince people of the fact that if Christians ruled, there would be justice. And even now it seems that the church is there to satisfy the spiritual needs of the elderly, rather than guide people to living faith and total Christian ideology. Christians must be such that with open and free hearts they are ready to support everything that is true and right, and to deal without fear with everything that is happening. For the one who has a treasure in heaven fears nothing. And a Christian—at least one without a family—is absolutely wiser these days not to own anything which is not an absolute necessity. You need to be internally free even in this respect.

Tuesday November 28, 1972
I got the scholarship to go to Greece! The departure will be, God willing, December 11, in less than two weeks.

Independence Day, Wednesday December 6, 1972
It occurred to me that it would be good to have some kind of recommendation from the Clergy-Laity Assembly to take on the trip to Greece. The Metropolitan promised to give a recommendation with pleasure and invited me for coffee on Friday at 3 pm.

Friday December 8, 1972
Yesterday there was a prayer service for our departure. I visited the Metropolitan. It was very interesting to discuss with him. We talked about monasteries, serving, relationship to material things, etc. I asked about whether it was possible to get translation work for the time in the monastery. He said that it can be arranged. Somehow, everything seemed to fall into place on its own. The Metropolitan and I see many things in a similar way. He gave me a nice letter of recommendation and asked me to come by after my return and share my experiences.
 Glory to You, God!

SCHOLARSHIP TRAVEL TO GREECE

Monday December 11, 1972, on the plane
Up here in the air, things look a little different than down below. You can realize clearly how important love and affection between people is. It begins to feel like an adventure! I look at the word FINNAIR on the wing and know that I can trust that everything humanly possible has been done for the success of the flight. I am proud of the reputation of Finnish work.
 The sun rises above the clouds. What all we modern people can see! Here we sit and can see the sun rise at the altitude of 10 km.

Tuesday December 12, 1972, in Athens
There are three of us here: Maryc from France, Judith from America, and me. We are staying in a very nice hotel. Miss Stippa from the Ministry of Education is taking care of us. This evening we went to the National Theater to see *Don Quixote*. The end moved me. I wonder if I am similar?

Wednesday December 13, 1972, in Athens
In the morning, we went to a university preparatory school where we attended, among other things, an ancient Greek lesson for grade eleven (in our system, grade seven). The boys were very interested and actively participated during the lesson. The teacher was good. We also went to an elementary school where the teaching followed all the latest pedagogical rules. In fact, it was the best school in Greece. Then we were at a sociological research institute, which was extremely interesting. For example, we learned about research on the life of the elderly.

Judy, Maryc, and I get along splendidly. It seems that all the students of ancient Greek are alike. My heart is melting day by day as the time to depart to Bytouma approaches.

Saturday December 16, 1972, in Crete
Again, today we saw the world spanning 4,000 years. We visited the palace of Knossos, the historical museum, and an exhibition of holy church objects, where a young Greek woman explained the things clearly and tediously. We also went shopping, and soon we will go to a taverna, where we hope to see Cretan dances. The handicrafts here are magnificent. When we were in Knossos the sun was shining, it was gently warm, flowers were blooming, and the grass was green. Every evening large flocks of starlings fly over here and crowd all the possible treetops and TV antennas. The chirping is very enthusiastic.

Sunday December 17, 1972, in Athens
Yesterday we went to Taverna Kallithea. We had Cretan cheese, fruit, and between us a bottle of Greek wine (that little amount gave me a headache and a stomachache). They played Cretan music there, and it was interesting when people started to do folk dances, which were a kind of circle dance meant mainly for men. This morning, we had an excursion to the palace of Phaistos, which is about sixty km from Heraklion. The countryside scenery is true Greece and Crete. The landscapes are very beautiful: olive trees, mountains, especially the birthplace of Zeus called

Ida, all green. The weather was pleasant, we saw a flowering almond tree and anemones. On the way we stopped at the Church of the Apostle Titus (sixth century). It was in ruins, but among the ruins two women were walking with burning incense. The place is called Gortyna, and there is a famous boustrophedon calligraphy.[102] I had read about it but had no idea that it is in Crete. We also looked around the villa of Hagia Triada and then had a walk around Phaistos, the location of which is extremely beautiful.

We returned to Athens by plane. When resting here in my room, the phone rang. The caller was General Secretary Habith of Syndesmos. The Board of Syndesmos has a meeting here, and Habith invited me for a dinner organized by the Board. I will meet Purmonen and Alexis.

Later. It was a very rich home full of people, us three from Finland, one from America, one from Australia, and the rest were Greek. We ate, discussed, danced folk dances (not me), and sang church hymns in between. The rooms were full of oriental rugs, antique furniture, and precious paintings. But nothing beats a small, poor monastery in the mountains of Thessaly!

Monday December 18, 1972, in Athens
Things are progressing little by little. I met the Assistant Professor of Byzantine Studies, Constantine Manafisin, which was the most pleasant meeting. He promised to help me in any way with my translation work. In the end he gave me his doctoral thesis. We visited an art school. There the director of the school, whose personality resembled that of Päiviö Oksala,[103] showed us around. Without blinking an eye, he took us to a room where two nude models were standing.

Later. What a day it was! In the afternoon Miss Papamikrouli came to the room with her friend, the director of a Red Cross nursing school. Tomorrow I will go to the nursing school. In the evening we went to some place, a "writers' home," not knowing what we would do there. And what a surprise, the best known writers of modern Greek were there, and we discussed literature. They are very enthusiastic about Finland. One of the younger writers is coming to Finland, and I invited him to our home. Many of them said that they will give us their works. I have already gotten

---

102. In boustrophedon calligraphy, alternating lines of writing are reversed.
103. A famous Finnish professor of Classics.

one package of books, now we are likely to have a whole library to take with us.

A beautiful day is approaching! In Bytouma I will be like at home. There is no need to be tense about anything.

Thursday December 21, 1972, in Thessalonica
We spent the whole day at Panorama Monastery. There are about thirty sisters. Especially Sister Theophano, who chatted with us, is very sweet. The monastery has a practice of holding formal theological talks. Even in other ways, there is somehow a more formal atmosphere than in Bytouma. Sisters were saying that I could go there. But no, Bytouma fits me better. The cozy "bird of heaven" feeling that prevails there is more for me. Everything is natural there without tension, but it is still well organized. And the school provides energy and joy for the whole sisterhood.

Lord, use me there, so that the monastery will benefit, and so will I. Let me forget my own life totally out of love for You and my neighbor. Protect me from becoming an eloquent nun, who always has an answer for everything. But help me to protect the genuine spirit of Bytouma, the quiet, service-oriented love that knows no boundaries. Let me correctly convey those vistas, which you have opened for me, to the sisters so that they would be protected from all dogmatic pride ("we possess the truth"), because the closer we get to the Truth, the humbler we will become. I am ready, Lord.

Saturday December 23, 1972, in Bytouma
Half an hour after my arrival I was already washing windows, and for the next week Abbess gave me trapeza[104] as my obedience. Christmas is being prepared with great enthusiasm. All the girls from the school have gone to their homes or relatives, and I will not meet them anymore.

Right after my arrival Abbess talked with me. She said that we should not ask for anything else except the will of God, and that is what "you Eleni and I Euphemia" will pray for. She talks to me as if I were her equal, which makes me rather confused. Whenever I come here, I first feel like a giant in the land of Lilliput, a head taller than all the others, and, second, feel extremely clumsy and in the way everywhere. This feeling usually disappears little by little.

---

104. The monastery's dining hall. Those with an obedience task of trapeza take care of the meals.

The will of God has not yet become alive. Some kind of mistrust is hiding in my heart, although this trip to Greece is in itself quite a boost to my belief.

Later. Listen, dear sisters! Your sister Eleni was in quite a strange state of mind in the afternoon. I namely thought, what is Bytouma? A handful of Greek country girls, who, for some mystical reason, which they even themselves cannot explain, have dressed in strange black clothes, shivering with the cold through winters in their poor monastery. How could I, a cultured person, ever live here in the midst of them? But then started esperinos[105] and after it was completed and I was kissing icons, all satanic fantasies disappeared, and again, I understood the spirit of monasticism, and for the first time I smiled from the bottom of my heart. Abbess quite likely noticed the change. "I am the Way, the Truth, and the Life."[106] It has been shown that outside the monastery, it is selfishness that rules my life.

Christmas Eve, Sunday December 24, 1972
Oh, how wonderful it was again! After the esperinos we sat in the trapeza and sang Christmas carols. Abbess gave everyone a pair of socks, and then she gave me a crucifix and another pair of socks. A crucifix . . . As I sat there, I thought, how far I have had to come to get a little love. And it is love that makes me not want to exchange our poor dining hall covered with old rugs even for the finest palace in the world.

Abbess spoke about what each of us gives to Christ as a gift. I decided to give my own will. We will start at 3 am with Matins. Father Eugenios will celebrate.

Christmas, Monday December 25, 1972, in Bytouma
Today we talked about the best time to enter a monastery. Abbess was of the opinion that when you are young your mind is still changeable, and that it is harder to go into a monastery when you are older. She herself was twenty-three years old when she entered a monastery. The parents were against it at first, but at last her father took her to the monastery when she was twenty-three years old. Looking back, she thought herself so old that she had already acquired all kinds of stubborn habits. "I am already twenty-seven," I said quietly. Abbess, however, nodded in a Greek

---

105. Vespers.
106. John 14: 6 (New Revised Standard Version).

way, which probably meant that it did not matter. Not in this case. I almost cried with joy.

Second day of Christmas, Tuesday December 26, 1972, in Bytouma
In the evening Abbess told us how Metropolitan Dorotheos had in August come to the church to celebrate liturgy, when the church did not exist and everything was in ruins. He spent the whole night thinking about what to do with the place, should an orphanage, home for the elderly, or men's or women's monastery be founded. In the morning on his way to the church, he heard a woman's voice say, "You decide, I will send you the people." This happened in August; in October the people came. Abbess told us that once they were starving for three days, there was not a crumb of bread in the whole monastery. There were so few shoes, that when someone wanted to go to Trikala to run errands, she used the only good pair of shoes they had. The first room they lived in had no glass in the windows, and there was a five-centimeter gap between the floor and the wall. Judging by all this, Abbess and the other four will live a long time, because they have had to have iron strength and health.

Later. I spent the morning in the trapeza with a book in front of me, but really I was listening to Abbess and Father Eugenios's discussion. It was something quite magnificent—I just wished I could have understood more.

Wednesday December 27, 1972, in Bytouma
Even the sun was shining today. I went with Maria to get the cows. Abbess was afraid that I might be attacked by dogs, but luckily there were none. In the evening, I drew sewing patterns and wrote a letter to a student in Germany with a certificate saying that she had graduated from this school. Then I gave the paper to Abbess to sign. I feel that this situation will repeat itself in the coming years.

The evening was really warm and cozy. Sisters were busy with various tasks, handicrafts, drawing patterns, etc., and Abbess read aloud. It cannot be better even in heaven (except that the Lord is visibly present). Still, five more months in Finland.

Whoever has experienced the mystery of monastic life cannot lead any other kind of life. My calling is indeed very clear to me.

Friday December 29, 1972, in Bytouma
I will leave tomorrow. There is so much snow that the descent will have to start early, and the trip from Trikala to Athens will undoubtedly be difficult. Because of the slippery and snowy roads Abbess urged me to travel by train, which is safer.

The Lord has asked me to join the "angelic life," and it is hard to return to the world yet again. Perhaps this is, however, the last return. I do not know what will happen to me, but somehow, I feel that the Lord will lead me here and make me a partaker of paradise-like monastic life.

Saturday December 30, 1972, in Trikala
Abbess spoke to me about how I must take care of the souls of the children (students) in every way, saying, "I am the abbess, and what would come of it, if I only thought about my own soul and let the sisters do what they want." The salvation of souls is the most important mission. Lord, give me strength, and let me learn from His example!

For Abbess, as for me, it seems to have become clear that if I live, my place is in Bytouma. We talked about what my life will be like there. Abbess said that she would give me all the obediences: the kitchen, the church, the sheep, etc. But similar to other sisters, I will also have my special assignment: books. She talked about how I would help people and serve Christians in Finland through books. "Money," she said, "is not in any way important in this, and we do not think about it." Finally she prayed, and I prayed with her.

Swaying and jumping, we went down the snowy banks on a tractor. I arrived in Trikala from Kalambaka by bus and went to the bishop's house. I had a lot of gifts from the monastery, including a live rooster, but its days ended quite quickly after arriving at the bishop's house. Metropolitan Seraphim invited me to eat at the same table with him and the priests. In the church Abbess gave me advice on how to talk to the bishop. "Explain to him what you want, but if he says that you need to wait another year, respond, 'I would very much like to come, but be it as You will,' because he may be testing you, and if you say 'no,' he will think that you have your own will and would not fit into a monastery." Even at the table I did not want to say "no" to the bishop, and ate until I almost exploded. Every time he handed me something, I looked into his eyes and took it. I hope that he understood why, and he most likely did. After the meal he wished Finland and me all the best, and when he had finished, I continued, "and that I will be back in the summer?" He pretended to be surprised. "What? You want to come back? For how long? Ten days or forty days?" I looked very uncomfortable, and one of the seminarians said, "For good, Father Metropolitan." I explained the translation work, and he still tried to say, "We can send you books from here." I said that I had discussed with Abbess and she was very happy with the idea. "Abbess who? Your own in Finland or this one in Bytouma?" he dared to ask. "Mine is up in Bytouma," I said. "Do you not have an Abbess in Finland?" "No, nobody else," I said. And the bishops and seminarians started to smile—and I felt that the issue had been resolved.

Sunday December 31, 1972, in Athens
The bishop completely charmed me today. He is a good and straightforward person. From the church I went to the bishop's house; like Bytouma's sisters, these days I walk very naturally to the kitchen, where I sit on a stool. The Metropolitan came; I ate and then went to say goodbye to him. He gave a record to the Archbishop, and to the two bishops a wall calendar of Trikke and Stagoi for 1973 (also for me). But what especially warmed my heart was that he kept my cold hand for a long time in his warm embrace. I thanked him for his kindness (among other things, he paid for my trip to Athens), and so I left with the blessings of the bishop of this warm parish, where there are twelve monasteries.

Who would have believed in the beginning of the year that in 1972 I would come twice to Bytouma and Greece! And perhaps it is God's good will that in 1973 I will stay there forever and will welcome the new year as one of the novices.

AGAIN IN FINLAND

Tuesday January 2, 1973, in Finland
I arrived happy. Often my mood is less than happy. I called the Archbishop. He sounded very sweet until suddenly something occurred to him, and he assumed a sudden cool tone. Oh, your unbelief! It seemed somehow very difficult for the Archbishop to believe that Abbess was ready to take me into the monastery. It somehow did not fit his cautious philosophy of life. The Archbishop said that I was missed at New Year's Eve. But I doubt that in any serious way.

Monday January 8, 1973
I called a student who had not shown up in class for a long time. She told me that she had left the church at the beginning of December—and did not tell me anything else. This seventh grade girl[107] is already the third student I have lost. I will not sink or be flooded with feelings of inferiority, because it was not my influence, and it was not a protest against me. But I also see that I cannot work miracles for the students. I just have to go to a monastery.

Sunday January 14, 1973
My brother Antti and his girlfriend Seija came to visit from Leppävirta. In the evening we spent a long time discussing various interesting topics, including religion, and I had a chance to present my own views—although to an audience whose spiritual eyes had completely darkened. But at least I was able to explain a little about the theory of monastic life.

Saturday January 20, 1973
This kind of life enclosed within four walls, where going out is a "happening," is completely unnatural and gets on your nerves. It is different in Bytouma, where the open sky and mountains are a natural part of life. In the summer we are like one in creation, like the birds in the sky—there you really feel like being immersed in the great system of nature—but even during the winter we live in the midst of snowbanks as if on the palm of God. Soon it is possible to think: only four months left. But spring feels longer, in the sense that many new things have to happen before the end of May: green grass and budding leaves and spiritually the whole process of Pascha with its fasting. Lent usually passes quickly, and there are only one and a half months before it begins. And then we are already at Pascha and it is time to start packing. I will book my tickets after passing the approbatur exam for sociology, hopefully in February.

Sunday January 28, 1973
I have somehow become alienated from the events in our church. It started last year, when I was on my own in Lahti, and has continued from there. I am gradually withdrawing.

I am reading a book on demography, which is part of the approbatur in sociology.

---

107. Corresponds to the second year of high school today.

Thursday February 1, 1973
A letter arrived from the Archbishop. "Where did you get the idea that I was surprised at the possibility of you going back to a monastery in Greece? I did not say anything like that. I am just happy for you, because I understand how much one can long to go there."

My relationship with the Archbishop is apparently so complicated that I cannot assume the role of an objective observer.

Sunday February 11, 1973
At the moment my fault is that I assume that things depend too much on the people: we have to do this and that to make the monastery flourish. We need to trust God more and remember that if His influence cannot be seen in the flow of things, the whole effort is in vain. Monasteries stand or fall with the thought whether God is or is not. He is, and we must trust that also in practice.

Tuesday February 13, 1973
There was the annual Miss Finland beauty contest, which was also followed with great interest in this family. I remembered how Abbess one day talked to Fevronia and me about how one should pay attention to one's appearance, namely, that one's face and whole stature would reflect the grace of God.

Sunday February 18, 1973
Yesterday was the last exam, approbatur in sociology. I believe I passed it. It feels quite strange when you are used to studying continuously for the past twenty years, and now the end is here. Real life should begin. But learning is not over; on the contrary, it might just be beginning.

Thursday February 22, 1973
It was a dazzlingly bright spring-winter day. I had passed the approbatur examination in sociology and took my transcript to the office of the Department of History and Linguistics to receive my Bachelor of Arts diploma. On her own initiative, Mother suggested inviting the Archbishop to celebrate the occasion next week, when he would be in Helsinki. At times in the past, I would have been very happy with the suggestion, but now I did not want to do it. I had not met the Archbishop for a long time, and there would not be an opportunity to talk in any case.

I went skiing in the sunlit forest. Today Riitta had her last day of school and penkinpainajaiset[108] party, a tradition for high school seniors before they sit for final exams. In the evening, she came home from the party very disappointed in her schoolmates for their excessive drinking.

I read the book *Rebel Nun* about an Orthodox mother, Maria, who did indeed live the "monastic life" in a rather special way. She dedicated her entire life to serving her poor neighbors and died in a concentration camp. When I read descriptions of concentration camps and other inhuman suffering, I often wonder how I would fare in such circumstances. I have no empty illusions about my own strength; I, who cannot stand even a little cold bite or sleep deprivation without becoming agitated. I am not surprised by all of those who in a [concentration] camp environment fall into boundless selfishness and callousness.

Sunday February 25, 1973
Juho has been here since Friday. I wish he would be protected from all the bitter blows. He must be dearer to God than to me, and He will keep an eye on Juho. Leaving Finland will not be easy in every way.

I thought that I would let Mother invite the Archbishop after all. I need to push aside my own thoughts on the matter and take advantage of the available opportunity. It is impossible to know what all can result from the visit, although it is likely that the Archbishop would not have the time or opportunity to come. Mother will call tomorrow.

Monday February 26, 1973
I decided to depart to Greece with a student flight on May 23. This way, the trip will be very cheap. I will be able to organize the last school week, one way or another. I will book my flight tomorrow.

Tuesday February 27, 1973
Father invited the vicar of Munkkivuori, Eero Saarinen, to our home at the same time as the Archbishop. At first I was not in favor of the idea, but it makes the situation considerably simpler. I can be quiet and watch, and it will ensure there will be no discussion of me or my future.

Today Mother started to tell me in a kind of pseudo-concerned voice that my efforts to go to Greece are "sick." I got so furious that I literally threw her out of my room. She does not understand anything,

---

108. A celebration by high school seniors including a parade and costumes.

yet she still pushes her ready-baked opinions everywhere. This event was followed by some discussion and calming down. My final statement was, "I wish I could leave soon!" Although leaving has its own melancholy, I do not deny it.

Friday March 2, 1973
The Archbishop's visit passed without incident in a pleasant atmosphere. There is a quiet lightness about him, which attracts me very much. That is just the way it is. I accompanied the Archbishop to the tram stop. First, he told me that Mrs. Nissinen takes care of Niklas (the dog), and that Mrs. Nissinen does not live in his house anymore. We talked about the monastery and the works to be done there. Somehow, we came to the conclusion that there is a lot to do here as well. I want to get to know God and to pray, not merely identify with the Archbishop's thinking. That is why it is healthier to go to Greece, though it does hurt my heart. Although even staying here would be painful too.

Saturday March 3, 1973
I went to confession. Father Teppo[109] gave me good advice: "In the long run it is better not to rush. You should always take life one stage at a time."

Tuesday March 6, 1973
Today I received my Bachelor of Arts. In the evening some relatives gathered. Immediately after receiving my diploma, I went to pay the deposit for my trip to Greece on May 23.

Saturday March 17, 1973
On Monday I will meet with Metropolitan John to discuss the translation work I can do in the monastery.[110]

Monday March 19, 1973
The conversation with the Metropolitan was fruitful. It came up that he had celebrated his first Divine Liturgy as a deacon in the Panorama monastery in Thessalonica. We decided that my first translated book will be "On the Priesthood" by St. John Chrysostom. Among others, the

---

109. Father Teppo Siili, priest and youth minister of the Helsinki Orthodox parish, later the vicar of Jyväskylä (1975 to 1978) and Turku parishes (1986 to 1999).

110. One of Kristoduli's obedience tasks was to translate Greek texts into Finnish. She did this throughout her years at Bytouma.

Archbishop called during the discussion. The Metropolitan explained to me some of the church's internal crises in Greece. It is good to know; in Greece it is difficult to get an objective presentation about anything. Objectivity is a foreign concept to the Greek character.

Thursday March 22, 1973
The Archbishop spoke about the "future of monasteries," i.e., the Valamo Monastery, because he did not mention Lintula even once. Of course, after we got to the part of asking questions, I made a remark about this. Usually when I think of Lintula, I am overcome by powerless rage; two poor souls are withering there, abandoned by everyone.[111] I pointed out to the Archbishop that they have not been ordained even as Rasophore nuns,[112] whereas in Valamo a boy is ordained after a period of less than a year. He replied something like the Board of the monastery did not apply for it, knowing very well that it was not any kind of defense. I still have to endure the annual party of the ONL.[113] After that I will withdraw from "public life."

Thursday April 12, 1973
I am living in such a spiritual and every kind of drought, it could not be worse. But hope prevails, because the end of my imprisonment is approaching on May 23rd. In my present state of mind, it feels doubtful if I will be able to stay awake even on Easter night.

Wednesday April 18, 1973
I am in Riihimäki on my way to Kuopio. It is really fun to go there, again to see all the places: the market square, the church road, and the red Church of Saint Nicholas itself. And also the people. I should try to forget myself and think about the joy of others.

---

111. Kristoduli refers to the novices Irmeli and Maija (later nun Elisabeth and schema nun Melania). At that time, Lintula was still largely a Russian community. Church services were conducted in Slavic, and the sisters who arrived in the mid-1960s could not speak Russian.
112. Robe-bearer nun.
113. The Orthodox Youth Association of Finland.

THE ARCHBISHOP FALLS ILL

Holy Friday, April 20, 1973
According to hearsay the Archbishop is ill; that is why he did not celebrate Vespers tonight. We waited and waited, the eagle rugs were in their place, but the Archbishop did not come, so Father Niilo began.

Holy Saturday, April 21, 1973
The Archbishop was not in the church this morning. I asked Maria Iltola how he was doing, and she replied: "He is resting a little, because his heart has not been well lately." Today's Holy Communion strengthened my weakening powers considerably. Sometimes it really happens that Holy Communion acts like refreshing water on a wilting plant. The juices of life begin to circulate again. Soon I will get it once more.

The Lord's Pascha, Sunday April 22, 1973
There were many people in the church until the end, and the Archbishop seemed to be able to celebrate the service. Masses of people crowded to Holy Communion; nothing like that has been seen here before. After church we embraced each other, and it felt just like Pascha.

Outi, Kaisa, Irene, and I walked, or rather ran, after church to the Kononens. Maria Iltola drove by us and gave us a ride. The festive foods tasted good. In the bright morning, we walked towards the city. Strangely enough, I did not feel any kind of nostalgia thinking that this might have been the last time that the Archbishop will give me Holy Communion.

Later. The Archbishop has been taken to the central hospital's intensive care unit after a massive heart attack. They had said in the hospital, "If he survives this, he will be in the hospital for three weeks and on sick leave for two months." He had called Maria during the night, just gasping for breath, and was taken to the hospital completely gray. Nothing can be done, at least not from my side. Maria is the one closest to him. My God, what is the meaning of this?

I heard that Maria had been with the Archbishop for a minute and that he had asked: "How is Niklas (his dog)?" I have cried, and I will continue to cry. I do not quite know why I am crying. The Archbishop had been in great pain. I cry because he has to suffer. I cry because I feel I have added to his burdens. Life would have a strange feeling of emptiness if the Archbishop were to die. He has been the "audience" of my life, in front of whom I have brought all the twists and turns of my life and whom I in my subconscious have seen to have either joy or sorrow with me. Although lately I have realistically seen that it might not be like that after all.

Second day of Easter, Monday April 23, 1973
I had the happy thought of calling Maria and going to her house for a visit. She suggested that I go with her to see the Archbishop in the hospital. I was of course more than willing to do that. We first took Niklas to the Archbishop's residence.

The Archbishop was in intensive care. We dressed in white coats and shoe covers. He had a mask on his face, and various bottles hung from the ceiling. He recognized even me. The Archbishop was in pain, and the nurse said that we should not stay long.

I told Maria that if the Archbishop recovers and needs me for something, I am ready and will not go to Greece.

Tuesday April 24, 1973, in Helsinki
The Archbishop is still alive. A joyful hope begins to live in my heart. Perhaps God will spare him. From my side I am peaceful. If the Archbishop wants me there, I will go, but if not, I will go to Greece as originally planned, and my heart is open to both thoughts. In both cases I could contemplate in silence.

Later. The Archbishop is really feeling better, Maria said. He will make it. I have begun to trust it. But then what? He cannot return to the same torture. And if there is a desire to use me in this situation, why not, although I doubt my own abilities. And I cannot resist sighing inwardly: Bytouma!

Tuesday May 1, 1973
Maria told me that she had asked the Archbishop how he was going to organize his life after the hospital, and had mentioned that I would like to come there during his convalescence. The Archbishop had said, "It can be considered." Maria said I should not confirm my trip to Greece. And she specifically warned that I must treat Niklas as the apple of my eye; otherwise, there is no reason to come at all. I stressed that I will indeed do so. Lord, give me endurance, help and strengthen me. I hope the matter will be settled soon.

Wednesday May 2, 1973
What does God want from me? I am not quite sure yet about going to Kuopio. If it happens, it can be a very beautiful time in my life, a gift before going to the monastery, God willing. When I think of the Archbishop, I conclude that he is one completely exhausted person, both spiritually and physically. And if I go there, I cannot even slightly burden him with anything; for example, by talking about spiritual things. First of all, he needs to be able to completely relax with good conscience, play with Niklas and his birds. And from there the recovery will start. I, Leenuska, am puzzled by all the events ahead. Completely stunned.

Saturday May 5, 1973
My spiritual life is squeaky, like an unoiled machine. What made life joyful has dried up since the Archbishop fell ill. The oil of the joy of life coagulated after the Archbishop fell ill. Nothing decisive has happened regarding my destiny. I spend my time playing cards in solitude and sleeping. Should I stay or should I go?

Sunday May 6, 1973
Siina Taulamo suggested that we form a prayer chain, so someone will be praying for the Archbishop continuously, around the clock. God can heal him. The situation is still very serious. By praying we will at least carry the Archbishop in front of God, whatever happens.
 Later. Maria said that the Archbishop has announced that he wants me there. Tomorrow I will cancel the trip to Greece.

Tuesday May 8, 1973
The Archbishop's heart had stopped last night, but had been massaged to start again. Not much hope was given. Since the prayer circle was organized, my mind has been peaceful. Today I read the Psalter on his behalf and felt very refreshed myself. Death is not a bad thing for a Christian, but perhaps a few more years of life after this shocking experience would be a blessing for the Archbishop and the whole church.
 I did not cancel my trip to Greece. If the situation remains like this, I will not cancel it until the day before, when I will have to pay half. If the time for the Archbishop's departure has come, I want to leave here for Greece as soon as possible, and therefore, as the situation remains critical, it is better to keep open the possibility for departure.

Sunday May 13, 1973
I feel the need to think seriously about the situation. So I have promised to go to Kuopio to take care of the Archbishop. In fact, I had already promised this years ago while I was his spiritual child and admired him above all. Now I made that promise again, with the consequence that my carefully thought out and precisely organized plan, which seemed to have God's blessing to finally go to the monastery, will not come through this time. The Archbishop has accepted my offer against my expectations. What lies ahead now? Instead of traveling to the warm, peaceful, sacred surroundings, to be led by a brave and zealous abbess, I go to Kuopio, to the residence of the Archbishop with the primary concern for the welfare of the little dog Niklas and a few caged birds—how long the Archbishop himself will be at the hospital, nobody can know. And when the Archbishop comes home, there will be a period of conforming to all his wishes. What I wonder most of all is how I can accommodate his infinite attention to detail. It may even be that the Archbishop is not satisfied with me, because I am too impractical and do not agree with him in all matters of principle, and he will send me away. There is also the possibility that he will not get out of the hospital all summer and I will be sitting there using my savings, so that when I should finally go to Greece, I cannot pay off my student loan. But I feel like I am doing my Christian duty and surely there is some kind of God's plan in all of this. Maybe this will be a good practice for monastic life: denying one's own will, enduring people's meanness, serving a neighbor, forgetting at last one's precious self. I have not been able to achieve by far any of these things in the worldly life, a mentality that should belong to a Christian.

Later. The Archbishop is feeling better and had said that he feels that the prayers are supporting him. And Maria said that he is eagerly awaiting my arrival.

Monday May 28, 1973
We are preparing for Riitta's high school graduation. To her own surprise and that of others, she received as many as five laudaturs.

Ascension Day, Thursday May 31, 1973
The telephone lines to Kuopio have been interrupted for a long time, so we have only occasionally received news on the Archbishop. Father

Tapani,[114] who had visited Kuopio, told us that he is already in a regular ward.

It was Riitta's graduation. About thirty visitors came. We took pictures of Juho and Jaakko on the lawn. Elina left in an elated state to go to a pony camp in Puijo, Kuopio.

Sunday June 3, 1973, in the residence of the Archbishop in Kuopio
So here I am in stuffy rooms with an angry parrot. This place has to be thoroughly dusted before AP comes home.

AP = Arkkipiispa; i.e., Archbishop in Finnish. I will use these letters as a shorthand, because I am likely to write a lot about him in the future.

Monday June 4, 1973
At noon I went to see the Archbishop (in the hospital). As soon as I had entered the room, he said: "You had the heart to come and make such a sacrifice." "It is not a sacrifice," I said quickly. "But I think it still is," the Archbishop replied. "At least not very much," I muttered, and it was true. At this moment I would not like to be anywhere else. The Archbishop can get out tomorrow or the next day. He talked about how he was. The Archbishop brought up the letters of Bishop Theophan and said that if he had the strength, we could go through those. I can also mention that during the visit I was overtaken by an enormous shyness, became red and sweaty, and could not think of anything to say.

Niklas the dog is not feeling very well and looks extremely sad. He will surely explode with happiness when he sees the Archbishop again. Little by little I have tried to get to know the parrot Amigo. Which one of us is afraid of the other more is yet to be solved.

Tuesday June 5, 1973
We cleaned. The Archbishop's cleaner, Mrs. Kukkonen, washed the windows with my help.

In the evening I visited the Archbishop. He can go home tomorrow. Did he feel good about it, I asked him. "All the same," he replied seeming quiet and depressed. I was hardly shy anymore.

---

114. Tapani Repo, a member of the clergy of Helsinki Parish.

Wednesday June 6, 1973
It was heartbreaking to see him climb the stairs to his home. He has aged a lot; it is easier to see that in this environment than in the hospital. Heikki Makkonen and Maria brought him in. We had fish soup. The Archbishop did not yet have the strength to move from his room. In the evening, we watched some television. The Archbishop is washing at this moment; I can hear how carefully he is walking. *"You who live in the shelter of the Most High, who abide in the shadow of the Almighty."*[115]

Niklas was a bit of a disappointment; even now he lay down to rest in my room.

Thursday June 7, 1973, in the morning
I have rarely had such a nightmarish night as this one. At midnight Niklas started scratching at the door and tried to get out, where he barked very loudly (no doubt AP woke up). At 1 am Niklas jumped on the floor of my room and let out his blood-curdling howl (AP woke up, if he had been able to sleep at all), then Niklas moved to AP's room and at about 2 am started whining and squealing threateningly (he would have started howling had I not gone to get him), he had to be let out again. AP: "No problem." At 3 am Amigo started to fly back and forth from one doorframe to another. When I got to AP's room, he was just moving a large armchair while closing the other one of the doors. I was about to collapse on the floor in horror. I did not go in but saw through the crack of the door AP going to the bed and there moving his hand.

One thing is clear: both animals will leave from here for tomorrow night and even for the next ones. It is nearly 4 am, another hour to endure before I can get up. Lord, protect the Archbishop!

Later. The morning finally broke, and the Archbishop was alive. We had morning tea, and then the Archbishop asked me to read the morning prayers from the Great Horologion. As far as I could see, he was crying, and I was almost crying too: "The sacrifice acceptable to God is a broken spirit; a broken and contrite heart, O God, you will not despise . . . "[116] Christ was in our midst.

Recently the Archbishop dictated a letter to me, which revealed that by the end of June, he—i.e., we—will be writing an article for a book. I love my varied work here. The Archbishop has not listened to music yet.

---

115. Ps. 91:1 (New Revised Standard Version).
116. Ps. 51:17 (New Revised Standard Version).

Friday June 8, 1973
A so-called gruel case has occurred. Yesterday I cooked some rice-gruel, which tasted terrible, and the Archbishop ate it without blinking an eye. But this morning Maria cooked the gruel. Let's see if I can do it ever again. I am not used to this. Direct criticism would be much easier for me to endure; I am used to that.

Later. The gruel case was solved, because I talked about it. The Archbishop listened with a smile and said that he would trust me to cook the gruel.

My great joy was that the Archbishop walked outside for the first time. At afternoon tea we talked about profound things. The subject of the article he is going to write is, "The Concept of God." I asked if his illness had influenced his concept. "No," he said. "There was no panic at any time." Then he added, "I would not be sad if this voice of mine did not improve. Then I could retire and go to Valamo. I would donate my library there, and Kelja[117] would be sold, and a printing press bought with the money..." He certainly had had time to think about everything.

Thursday June 21, 1973
My parents were here for a visit today. As they were leaving, the Archbishop said, "I would still like to talk about this Anna-Leena." In a tone as if I were a half-crazy teenager, Mother responded, "We will come here mid-July. I suppose she will still be here." "No," said the Archbishop, "her assignment ends the last day of June." He had not mentioned this to me. I replied, "I would like to stay here even longer. I need some kind of sinecure, and this is a good place for it, but if the Archbishop does not want to, then no. Then I will go to Greece." "I do not like her going to Greece," said the Archbishop. "Neither do we, in this we are unanimous," echoed Mother. "I am also very unanimous," I remarked. I cannot quite take the Archbishop's words seriously; if he has any spiritual vision at all, he cannot mean it. But if it were true, which in fact is impossible, then nothing holds me back from leaving for Greece, absolutely nothing.

Saturday June 23, 1973
Keeping a diary is quite impossible during some periods; it would not have been possible to describe these events anew. The first week, the Archbishop was like a baby bird, and I was like a mother hen. And then

---

117. The Archbishop's summer house.

one evening when we were expecting guests, the Archbishop began to tell me about his life when I had casually asked a few questions. What an infinitely beautiful, delicate, and sensitive, but badly tortured soul he is! At this point I started to feel that the departure to Greece could be cancelled, and even the Archbishop said something to that effect. It felt undeniably difficult. The thought that I might never see Abbess, the sisters, and the whole monastery again became overwhelming for me. The Archbishop did not let me leave his room, and so I sat there, tears streaming down my face. "I will not prevent you from going, go ahead," said the Archbishop, among other things. "I cannot, it is not God's will," I replied, and the tears suddenly dried up. The day before yesterday he gave up his dog Niklas.

Birth of John the Baptist, Sunday June 24, 1973
The Archbishop let me go to the church and cooked for the Metropolitan, himself, and me. There were Skolts[118] in the Divine Liturgy, who later came here, over forty people. They were offered coffee. I have seen the Archbishop only briefly after the early morning. He and the Metropolitan were sitting outside in the garden and are now going to visit the Kononens. The Archbishop scribbles notes all day long in his notebook, and today I saw that the topic was, "Letter of a Convalescent."

The Skolts were very charming, and many of them were obviously intoxicated by many impressions. There was someone who had not been even to Rovaniemi,[119] and now they had gone all the way to Helsinki.

Tuesday June 26, 1973
The Archbishop and I have gradually reached the point that was intended: that I would no longer be needed here. And that he, with renewed strength and enthusiasm, would begin to focus more on his duties, even though he is still on leave, and in this I am here to support and encourage him. "He must increase, but I must decrease."[120] I am grateful for these days, these treasures I have gathered being close to this wonderful man who has suffered so much; for the eternal friendship, which undoubtedly will exist between us in this life and the next.

---

118. Indigenous group in the borderland area between Finland, Norway, and Russia.
119. The northernmost city of Finland.
120. John 3:30 (New Revised Standard Version).

Sunday July 8, 1973, in Helsinki
I have spent the whole week doing nothing; just sleeping, eating, and pondering. The tickets are ready; tomorrow I still have to pack. There is surely much to think about: all the things of this time in Kuopio. How might the Archbishop feel when he returns from a walk and there is no one to tell his little observations to, or when he is reading books or watching television and there is no one to discuss with. Well, maybe the Archbishop has such a strong inner life that after getting a few stimuli he can still go on for a long while.

Monday July 9, 1973
Last night in Finland most likely for a long time. But the atmosphere of the soul is more important than the physical environment, even though it depends on it. But, for example, Bytouma and the house of the Archbishop are much closer on the map of my soul than are the Archbishop's house and my parents' home. No one can claim that I have travel fever. I am still very connected to the events of the recent past and have not sacrificed many thoughts about the future. Let it take care of itself. I am deeply grateful for all these experiences and hope and trust that God also in the future will guide the steps of me, a sinner and a wretched being.

Bytouma Monastery. Photo by Nicolas Karellos.

Part II: In Bytouma Monastery

Bytouma Monastery is located on mainland Greece on the slope of Mount Koziakas in the Pindos Mountains. It was originally founded as a monastery for monks but was later abandoned. A new revival started in 1952, when a five-member sisterhood began to inhabit and renovate the monastery under the leadership of Abbess Euphemia. When Kristoduli came to the monastery in 1973, it had been in operation for twenty years. During her time the monastery was built up and expanded.

The monastery is dedicated to the Dormition[1] of the Mother of God (August 15), which is the greatest annual pilgrimage feast of the monastery. Another important feast day is the Friday of Bright Week, the feast of the icon of the Theotokos,[2] the life-giving spring. The monastery has close spiritual ties with the monasteries of the nearby Meteora monastic area, especially with the women's monastery of Saint Stephen.

Bytouma was an agricultural monastery. The sisters had a garden and kept animals: cows, goats, chickens, and rabbits. There was also a sewing room, a workshop where fabrics were woven and church textiles sewn. There was also a school of handicrafts for girls, which gave a special flavor to the monastery's life.

Kristoduli's own obedience task was translation. Her seminal work was the translation of the Philokalia into Finnish.

FIRST YEARS IN THE MONASTERY

Thursday July 12, 1973
I came here yesterday as a "name day gift" for Abbess. The translation work is in full swing. I have my own cell, a place in the church and at the

---

1. The Assumption, in the West.
2. God bearer, i.e., the Mother of God.

dining table, clothes from the monastery (not yet black, of course), so life is in order.

I have been thinking about the liberating fact that in Orthodox monastic life, everyone is an individual. When I first came here, I had an image of an ideal Orthodox nun in my mind, and I thought that as soon as I arrived, I should abandon my own thoughts and feelings and present the views of an "Orthodox nun" in everything. But now I think I understand that it is not the goal; rather, we are all individuals, whose goal is that God would sanctify our being. Therefore, there is no need for vain tension.

Friday July 13, 1973
One should never stare at external rules and become a slave to them. As I understand it, there is that danger in monastic life. The rules are for the people, and they are not eternal. Abbess spoke about this at the morning tea and said that if one cannot rightly use idleness for prayer, reading, and contemplation, it is better to work on Sunday than to use one's time to snoop into other people's affairs. She said that people who can really use all their time for prayer are a great gift from God, but we are not like that, and work is spiritually necessary for us.

Monday July 16, 1973
I told Abbess that I had written to the Archbishop, that I could not find the words to describe how good life is in the monastery. Abbess said, "For everything, my child, we must thank Panagia;[3] she gave us this place and all the good things." Here, whenever we sing prayers for the Mother of God, my heart is overcome with a special warmth and enchantment. But sometimes at the intellectual level, so to speak, there can be a few doubts, but undoubtedly those will evaporate. Panagia is our mother here.

Tuesday July 17, 1973, from Abbess's table speeches
We have to be willing to help other sisters. But often we think: Let Macrina die in the kitchen, let Theoktiste starve in the garden; it is not our obedience task this week; and so everyone just worries about her own task and wounds her soul.

Later. At noon we were planning construction of a new building and walked in the construction site, along brick walls already started. When the tape measure was there, somebody got the idea to measure me,

---

3. Panagia is the name for the Mother of God in Greek.

and the little sisters thought the result to be about two meters, and by just eyeing, the result was 178 cm (the right and real one 171 cm).[4] I was quite hurt, even though my height did not cause a complex for me.

Wednesday July 18, 1973, from Abbess's table speeches
Today's Epistle text was the one that says that nothing can separate us from the love of Christ. "From how many beloved ones we have been separated," said Abbess, "not to a distance of thousands of kilometers as in the case of Eleni, but in any case so that we do not see them, but from the love of Christ nothing can separate us, not pain, not worries, not even death—martyrs were killed just to separate them from God—that can only happen by our own indifference, and therefore, children, in small and large, watch your soul."

Abbess also spoke about murmuring. It is better that we say directly that "this and that bothers me," that we are open, than to practice that destructive thing, namely mumbling unclear remarks. For example, I am not satisfied with Macrina in the kitchen, but instead of telling her directly, I first tell Elisabeth, and she tells Theoktiste, and she tells Theodora, who will finally tell Macrina. Is this well done? No!

Later. Sister Theoktiste concluded: "So it is, in winter we freeze, and in summer we get baked,"[5] to which I said, "Then it is good in spring and fall." Abbess smiled, saying, "Spring and fall we only have in heaven, Eleni." Even I have noticed this in the few years of my life.

Thursday July 19, 1973
My typewriter was damaged during the trip, which is quite annoying. I hope it can be repaired in Trikala. It is very hot, over 30°C [86°F] at noon, but now the wind has started to blow, which may mean that the weather will cool down.

Saturday July 21, 1973
Abbess said, "If someone has love, she also has humility." She spoke as follows on the subject: "Those who are well have no need of a physician, but those who are sick."[6] It is a very comforting sentence for me, because

---

4. Respectively, 5 ft. 10 in. and 5 ft. 7 in.
5. There was no heat in the monastery, and it was cold in the sisters' cells in the winter.
6. Matt. 9:12 (New Revised Standard Version).

all the swellings and tumors of my soul are beginning to show themselves in clearer and clearer light. Lord, have mercy on me, a sinner.

Then Abbess added that we are so ready to condemn our neighbor, even if we are all committing heaven-knows-what sins inside ourselves. "We often think," she said, "I am smarter than the other, I am something special." As if she had spoken directly to me!

I was dozing off in the church during the canon when Abbess suddenly, after it had finished, said: "Eleni, Holy God, Holy Mighty . . . " I perked up very quickly.

Sunday July 22, 1973
Yesterday I received the *Aamun Koitto* magazine and read through it, including all the little announcements. I will write to Rauha[7] and ask her to send me clippings as well. The Finnish texts soak into me as if I were a sponge. And Dad has promised to keep me up-to-date on world events.

Monday July 23, 1973
Today, for the first time, I felt quite homesick for Finland. It is not related so much to a place, but rather to a conversation in Finnish and to a good conversation in general. Even if there were no language problems, discussions between the sisters and me would remain rather one-sided; we have such different backgrounds.

The catch of a long-awaited mail day was a long letter from Marja.[8] I wish there were more mail days in a week!

Through the intercessions of the Archbishop, I have begun to see my soul as it really is. The sight is frightening. For example, I have no real love towards the sisters, nor do I have many virtues. Sometimes I am even afraid to pray, being such a sinner. Mother of God, I lean on you, our Abbess.

Later. In the evening, when I grabbed hold of a pole attached to the top of the cooler to straighten my back, Sister Macrina noticed that I was not wearing a shirt, which resulted in quite a lesson. In the Small Compline in the church, I started, "To thee, Oh Mother of God," at a completely wrong spot, revealing to all the fact that my knowledge of the order of the service was quite shaky. The Greeks, of course, know it by heart from their childhood.

7. Aunt Rauha Lampi.
8. Friend Marja Räsänen, later Sasaki.

It is comforting to look at the starry sky. In any case I thank the Lord for every day I spend here.

Tuesday July 24, 1973
Before Abbess had entered the monastery, a spiritual father had warned her: "There you will be punished, slandered, wronged . . . " "Indeed," said Abbess, "it all came true." But it all also happened to Christ. So I understand that Abbess in particular had to suffer in the midst of small-minded and malicious sisters, and perhaps the abbess as well. But with an abbess like we have, there is nothing to worry about. Be that as it may, with the "golden letters" I have to engrave in my heart, that one has to be willing to endure a little injustice also.

Sunday July 29, 1973
Abbess spoke in the Trapeza how the greeting "Peace to you" from today's Matins gospel reading crystallized for her in a new way. Even if a person had all the virtues, but had no peace, she in fact would have nothing. How precious is inner peace, when all the powers of the soul are in order and in their place, and a deep silence prevails in the soul. I climbed the hill behind the monastery. The plateau of Thessaly stretched before the sun, the holy peace of the Lord's Day reigned.

Monday July 30, 1973
The election was apparently peaceful, and Papadopoulos[9] achieved a great victory. Although the voter turnout was exceptionally low.

For dinner we had crispy pies filled with pumpkin and cheese; there were many of those on my plate. But surprise, surprise: Abbess told sister to put rice on my plate. I did eat a few pies, but not as many as I could have eaten without the rice.

---

9. Georgios Papadopoulos, leader of the military junta of Greece.

Abbess Euphemia.

Wednesday August 1, 1973
The Metropolitan [Seraphim][10] came yesterday and left today. In my life, before the completion of the new building, this means turmoil, because I need to pack my things and move downstairs to sleep in the Trapeza, where the clock faithfully strikes the full and half hour. But this happens quite rarely and is well worth the effort. In the evening, we sat until late in the dining hall of the guesthouse with the Metropolitan asking us for good thoughts, which everyone tried to present to him. He seemed tired and a little nervous; he is probably one of those who gets worn out by continuous public appearances.

---

10. During Kristoduli's stay at the monastery the bishop of the diocese changed three times. For clarification the Metropolitan's name has been added in parentheses in the diary entries.

Today Abbess sent me with others to load wood on the truck. The place was far below the monastery, and the pieces of wood were enormous. Oh, what strength these sisters have! Seemingly lightly they lifted stumps which I could hardly move. We spent about three hours down there. Meanwhile the mail had arrived. Rauha sent a letter and clippings, and I also received *Aamun Koitto*. But not a word from the Archbishop. He should understand that I get worried when there is no news.

Tuesday August 7, 1973
Yesterday we sat for a long time at the table talking about current topics with Father Alexios's lead.[11] He is a person with a very broad outlook, who sees things from many angles, and it is a joy to listen to his talks. Apparently, there is a very sensitive situation in Cyprus right now; the whole island could burst into civil war at any moment. Father Alexios is also very interested in the Russian Church, and we also discussed this topic at length.

Yesterday I was high up on a mountain with Theodora and others getting food for the rabbits. Theodora was cutting huge branches off old oak trees, leaving almost nothing but the trunk. It was an absolutely shocking waste! I remarked about this to the sisters and also to Abbess in a very serious tone. Abbess promised to tell Theodora to take branches from bushes and small trees. I hope that will happen. The head nurse of Trikala provincial hospital and her sister are visiting.

Friday August 10, 1973
Yesterday the girls from the school, three sisters, and I went on a trip to a camping ground located high in the mountains in the middle of spruce forests. There were 120 middle school girls. I talked a lot with many of them, we sang and ate together . . . I made friends with a girl who is finishing her theology studies and wants to enter a monastery (there are quite a few of them here, one could even speak of a "monastic awakening"). At dusk we drove through beautiful landscapes, and our girls were inspired to sing and clap their hands. To my joy I watched their happy faces. At the end of a fun day the common conclusion seemed to be, "Our monastery is still a thousand times more beautiful than the campground." As I watched the girls, I thought several times that most of them probably do not understand that they are now having the happiest time

---

11. Father Alexios is currently Abbot of the Xenophontos Monastery on Mt. Athos.

of their lives. I wonder where each of them will end up! When we arrived at the monastery, it was already dark; Abbess met us at the gate.

The Metropolitan [John] has neither written nor sent any money. For practical reasons it would be most important that he would see to it that the money promised by the Publication Council[12] be sent. No one here can control my work, and I would like to show some concrete results from it.

Later. Father Alexios recounted a few instances when someone had claimed to have seen the "divine light," and the sisters listened with amusement—that even such a thing could happen. Even Abbess remarked that she had encountered such a fantasy. Ok, she did encounter such. I would rather forget the whole thing. It would be interesting to know, however, when the divine light is genuine; it cannot always be only an illusion.

Monday August 13, 1973
Last night we talked until midnight about all the strange events in the monastery's history. The following story had a special effect on me: When Metropolitan Dionysios[13] came to the monastery for the first time and was not yet known to the sisters, after entering through the gate he was so shocked that the sisters thought he had some kind of medical emergency. Later he explained what it was. When he was in a concentration camp in Germany, he had a dream in which the Mother of God told him not to be afraid, he would still return to Greece, to "my house," as Panagia had said. When, fourteen years later, he came to the monastery, he immediately remembered the dream, because he had seen this place—the house of the Mother of God.

---

12. Fee for the translation agreed to by Metropolitan John.

13. Metropolitan Dionysius Charalambous (1907 to 1970). He was a prisoner of the Germans during World War II from 1942 to 1945 before being consecrated a bishop. Later he was the Bishop of the Trikke and Stagoi Diocese. His grave is in the Bytouma monastery.

Bytouma Monastery.

Dormition of the Mother of God, Wednesday August 15, 1973
On Monday I was in Trikala with Abbess and went to get a package of books from Kalambaka. Abbess is an amazing phenomenon. She sees and understands everything. She has an uplifting word ready for everyone. When we returned to the monastery, I was half dead of fatigue, although I had rested quite a while in our little room in the bishop's house. Abbess instead was on the move the whole day; she went shopping, and all the preparations for the big feast were on her shoulders. And when we got to the monastery, everyone began to press her with countless questions. I did not go to the Small Compline, but asked for a blessing to go to sleep; but Abbess went even to that. I admire tremendously the way she treats people. Everything she does, she does with speed and skill. As I drove up to the monastery, I thought again, what will happen to us when she departs from this life, which hopefully will not be a question for a couple of decades. None of us have even half of her gifts of grace. I may have some kind of spiritual vision, but nothing beyond that. And how easily I get tired! And I love silence and carefreeness. Helena, a monastic novice, wishes many years to the abbess.

There were many people here. Lamps were lit outside, where all the services were held. In the evening, I was troubled by the thought that the majority of people who came might not have come to get some comfort for their souls or to be in touch with God, but rather to see and experience some kind of miracle. The enthusiasm of the Greeks for miracles is boundless.

The celebrations are fun, but the ordinary life and the silence of our monastery is yet more magnificent. And I believe that the Theotokos herself agrees.

Later. In my opinion the celebration yesterday went a bit too far. With the church bells ringing, we walked around the church three times just like at Easter, but maybe this is always done on the Feast Day of a church. I think that the Mother of God is surely of the same opinion as I am, that she should not be viewed as the aim itself, but rather the one who shows the way, as even her icons are called.[14]

Holy Queen, Mother of God, lead me to communion with Your Son and our Savior, so that nothing can separate us from the love of Christ, not pain, not anxiety, not oppression, not danger, not sword, not hunger.

Friday August 17, 1973
Abbess said in the morning, "We never benefit spiritually by embittering another person's mind. Impossible!"

I gave Abbess all my money. It is not good to have money in the monastery.

Monday August 20, 1973
Here I notice very clearly how weak my physical strength really is. I am really exhausted after a greater physical exertion, and my head hurts even the next day. But I think that my strength will grow little by little.

I always try to remember that I came to the monastery, above all, to pray and to learn how to pray. As soon as I get the habit of a novice, I will hopefully start to discuss more with Abbess, and I will tell her, "Abbess, I came to the monastery to learn how to pray, but it is so difficult. It seems to me that you can do it, even if you have a thousand other matters to tend to during the day."

Wednesday August 22, 1973
Abbess said today that Metropolitan Dionysios once spoke to her, saying: "We monks and nuns are difficult people. When we have no one else to take care of besides ourselves, we easily pay attention to everything.

---

14. Refers to an iconographic depiction of the Mother of God called Hodegetria, "She who shows the way."

We hurt here, we hurt there, and we have all kinds of aches and pains. But if you go, for example, to Father Nicholas, where he lives with his wife and his five children. At midnight he gets up to read the preparatory prayers before celebration of the liturgy, the little children wake up, the wife, who is a teacher, goes to school, the father takes care of the children, cooks food, celebrates services, prays ... There is no time to worry about aches and pains." Abbess also reminded us to look at the monastery as our home. If we see that something is not right, we should do something about it and not think: aha, something is wrong with that sheep, but it is not my business; it is Margarita's obedience task. And before Margarita comes to help, the sheep is dead.

Everything Abbess says has a strong connection to practical life, and that suits us well. For this reason too I listen to her carefully. The speeches of the visiting priests and of the bishop are a kind of scattershot: sometimes on the mark, sometimes way off.

A cow got lost yesterday, and the sisters searched for it for a couple of hours. It was found. We were sent old pieces of furniture from the old people's home in Trikala. We will upholster them and put them in the "public spaces."

Thursday August 23, 1973
I was deeply involved with my translations, when suddenly I noticed that someone was standing by the door. This time it was Abbess watching me with her bright eyes. She has some particular power and light, it is hard to deny. She looked at me without a curtain on her face, with the eyes of her soul, so to speak, and I looked at her the same way. And my weak and sensitive soul got something like an electrical shock. She is a remarkable person, full of light and power. I am not surprised at all that when I was a child, I had an experience similar to that of a treasure hunter who was accustomed to finding a crumb here and there, and all of a sudden comes to a gold mine. Or the situation could be compared to a sensitive monitoring device, which has been used to react to minute changes and is suddenly exposed to a sphere of strong radiation without any steps in-between. Even less can put you at risk of breaking.

God in any case is the center of my life, but every day I thank Him for Abbess; she is Hodegetria, the one showing the way.

Saturday August 25, 1973
Yesterday I asked Abbess for a blessing to have Holy Communion on Sunday, but she said that novices here usually go to Communion every other week. "Good, I will do that too," I said, although I deeply wished that we could also gradually adopt the practice of going to Holy Communion every time the liturgy is celebrated. "When Father confessor comes to the monastery, we will see," said Abbess. She can relatively easily and for even a small reason say to the sisters, "You will not take Communion for so and so many weeks." Come to think of it more carefully, it would seem very frightening to use this, the most severe punishment the church knows, just like that. Personally, I do not see Communion as a special award, but rather a daily source of strength.

Tuesday August 28, 1973
No doubt Abbess is a bit puzzled with me; because such "highly educated" people have not been here before, and my task is to show that in fact, I am indeed the same simple Eleni as before.

Beheading of Saint John the Baptist, Wednesday August 29, 1973
Today I will finish the *Six Books on the Priesthood* by Saint John Chrysostom.[15] Not a whisper from Metropolitan John to mention the fact that he would have sent the money. If the mail by Monday does not bring anything, I will be surprised. I will not start any new work before I hear something from the Metropolitan. *Aamun Koitto* arrived today. Not a word about the Archbishop's recovery, such silence is typical of the Finnish ways. Fasting here is easy: melons, figs, pears, halva, tomatoes . . .

Thursday August 30, 1973
Sister Dorothea is a little ill, and yesterday a few of us gathered in her cell before the Small Compline. She told us about life in the monastery where she and the abbess were first, and about the iron-clad discipline which the abbess practiced there. Once our abbess had to sit outside the cell for the whole night; the abbess there had told her to come and see her, but did not open the door. It was winter, and there was even snow. Here, too, punishments such as tying a broom to the sisters' backs and forcing them even to go to the church like that, were used in the past, but they have long since been abandoned. I understand very well why Abbess, who

---

15. Saint John Chrysostom, *Kuusi kirjaa pappeudesta* (OKJ, 1981).

herself has had to endure a lot of injustice, is so human—firm yes, but not cruel. I do not really believe in the methods of the monastic formation of the old times. How can you pray if you all the time need to be afraid of the cruelties the abbess might get in her head?

Friday August 31, 1973
The Metropolitan's silence is beginning to get on my nerves. Imagine if he does not send the money at all! What a terrible situation he would put me in! If I do not receive a letter from him by Monday, I will explain the situation in detail to Abbess.

Beginning of the church year, Saturday September 1, 1973
"Oh Lord, bless the cycle of the year with your goodness," and let me learn something.

Abbess was pruning the vine shoots on the upper balcony, and since I was taller and could reach them more easily, I went to help her. As soon as I reached out for the first one, I leaned on a flowerpot and cut a flower seedling. "This is what always happens; whatever I do, it always causes harm," I remarked. And indeed, I am so clumsy in all my actions that I always do something upside down, and someone needs to kindly point it out. It stings my proud heart.

Sunday September 2, 1973
A sign of holiness is that we are always ready to forgive and never to judge. And it is not even difficult, if we think realistically—in other words, remember all that God has forgiven us. I must forgive Metropolitan John and the Archbishop from the bottom of my heart. It is a completely wrong way of thinking and a proof of the rottenness of the soul to think that one has the right to think bitter and evil thoughts of those who are far away. Why should I worry, even if I suffer injustice? Life does not end here, but rather everything will be clear later.

Go forward, therefore, showing love to the people here and to the Finns.

Tuesday September 4, 1973
Yesterday I received a wonderful letter from the Archbishop. It seems that he is gradually starting to soften when he thinks of our monastery. On October 1st he will celebrate his first liturgy (after his illness). But nothing came from the Metropolitan.

Wednesday September 5, 1973
Today six novices from the monastery of Saint Theodore, still in their lay clothes, came for a visit. There are twenty-two of them in all, all high school graduates. For me it is a little alien to the spirit of monastic life that all the "civilized" are gathered in the same place as if they would despise other monasteries.

Sisters weaving.

I felt that—in spite of all the good intentions—they were criticizing our monastery and life here, and in return I thought so many judgmental thoughts about them that it used up the entire Vespers service. It is very difficult for me to tolerate that our monastery should be criticized even in the slightest by anyone other than ourselves. The fact that you think you are in the best monastery of the world is also a form of pride, in its own way. But because of the protection of the Mother of God, Bytouma is, after all, the best monastery in the world . . .

Sunday September 9, 1973
Sometimes it feels a little hard to be the one who cannot do or know anything, and to hear the gentle remarks, "Not like that, Eleni." But it is in vain for me to start weaving a martyr's crown and think that for the love of Christ I gave up my respected position as an academic citizen, easy life, and other things, because coming to the monastery was not a sacrifice on my part. Life in the world simply did not suit me at all.

Wednesday September 12, 1973
A quiet life "in my own chamber," free of worldly cares, suits my character much better, I thought to myself this morning. There are no better things than peace and quiet.

Monday September 17, 1973
What a day! I have a residence permit for a year. In addition, a check[16] arrived from the Metropolitan. Glory to You, O Lord!

Thursday September 20, 1973
One has to fight against disturbing thoughts and try to push aside all the little worries and recollections of things that come to mind that need to be done. After all, one has come to the monastery to pray and not to drown in the worries of this life. If nothing else, one should at least try to turn every thought into a prayer that comes to mind in the church.

Monday September 24, 1973
Yesterday morning Maria and I walked far out in the mountains looking for a lost cow, which we did not find. Otherwise, it was wonderful: quiet valleys in the sunshine full of oaks, chestnuts, and a spring here and there, a hawk circling to find prey. At noon the Metropolitan [Seraphim] arrived. This always means a disturbance to the inner order of life,

---

16. Payment for the translation work promised by the Metropolitan.

because he talks to me a lot and I need to talk too. Now he said that I should make a presentation on Orthodoxy in Finland. He will invite me to present it in a kind of Bible study circle in Trikala. In the evening, we still did some cleaning at the construction site.

I wish that I too before my death could with clean conscience say to generations after me: "Follow my faith, my love, my patience . . . "[17]

Tuesday September 25, 1973
Metropolitan John is coming to Greece today. I wish he could at least call, so I could exchange a few words in Finnish, but it is probably not worth waiting for. He wrote that unfortunately he most likely cannot come here.

In everything I must first turn to God and put all my hope and trust in Him, because if you do not learn to do this and in practice realize that it is worth it, you are in a monastery in vain.

Feast Day of Saint John the Theologian, Wednesday September 26, 1973
Today we temporarily moved the rabbits to another cage and demolished the old rabbit house. Father Demetrios is building a new one out of bricks. We carried stones and boards and bricks. I like physical labor very much. When the body is tired, the thoughts become simpler.

Saturday October 6, 1973
Oh, how I had already missed confession! Father Chariton's words fell like rain on dry ground, and it was wonderful to be able to talk freely and confidentially. God's forgiveness and mercy shines in my soul. What a gift is the mystery of confession!

Sunday October 7, 1973
The whole day was spent high up in the mountains collecting chestnuts. We climbed higher and higher through fragrant fern meadows, sometimes on very challenging paths. The view from the top was magnificent; it was as if half of Greece opened up before us. Far, far away shone the snow-capped peak of Olympus.

Tuesday October 23, 1973
Yesterday, both in the morning and evening, we collected twigs and loaded them into the truck. It was a lovely warm day. The water flowed in the

---

17. 2 Tim. 3:10 (New Revised Standard Version).

brooks. Abbess was with us both times. I asked her about the washing, because I had noticed that the sisters did not wash every Saturday. Understandably this form of ascesis is a little strange and incomprehensible, and for me it will translate into even more hardened washing in cold water. I said to Abbess: "It might seem to you that I wash very often if I do it every Saturday?" "Gradually less and less," she said. For me, once a week is not a lot. In Finland I washed every evening," I said. Abbess looked a little thoughtful.

Monday October 29, 1973
In the morning I walked through the trapeza to the guest room with a broom in my hand. Abbess said that there will not be any more walking through the dining room with a broom in the hand. After sweeping the guest room floor, I went to the front of the woodshed to do some woodwork. Abbess said that I need to wear a work coat over the cardigan. I ran inside to put it on. Abbess said that I should not come to church in such an old work coat. I ran inside to take it off.

Tuesday October 30, 1973
Lord, let me always keep in my mind Your words: "If you say, 'You fool,' you will be liable to the hell of fire."[18]

Thursday November 1, 1973
Today I participated in the slaughtering and plucking of chickens. I protested against the way the chickens are caught, tied by their feet, and thrown on the cement floor to wait for slaughter, and said that even a hawk does not do anything like that, but kills immediately; only a man can think of such a thing. Abbess responded, "Sometimes, Eleni, you do not speak well at all."

Monday November 5, 1973
It should be noted that Jesus said of himself, "I am the way, the truth, and the life." So He does not ask us immediately to believe that He is the truth, but He says first that He is the way; in other words, if we begin to walk the way that He has shown and which He has walked, we will realize that He is the truth and also the life. So, blind faith is not demanded immediately, but we are told to try the way first.

18. Matt. 5:22 (New Revised Standard Version).

In the mountains surrounding Bytouma.

Wednesday November 14, 1973
My heart is like a field in Savo, from which stones emerge endlessly.

Will I ever be able to live a secluded quiet life even for a little while? Most monastics have had such a period in their lives.

Saturday November 17, 1973
Finally, there is someone who wants to raise me. And it will be a hard school. The years at the university and all the degrees were child's play compared to the things I have to learn now. Because Abbess will not pamper me.

Saturday November 24, 1973
I spent my first free afternoon (every nun has one every week, and for me, Abbess chose Saturday) on the mountain above the monastery reading, praying, and thinking.

Saturday December 15, 1973
Abbess changed the obedience tasks, and for the whole Christmas vacation, from tomorrow until Theophany, I got kitchen, together with Evangelitsa. After that the program will include the workshop again. The

whole sisterhood made a visit to the modest home of the monastery's workman to honor his name's day. His home is in the same building as the monastery's barn. We sat there on beds and ate cakes and nuts and wished the host "many years."

Sunday December 16, 1973
For Christ's sake, I am trying to learn endurance against false accusations and remarks. Often they are very small things, but I am immediately on my hind legs when I am accused of something, and I am always ready to defend myself. A true nun is not like that; she accepts criticism peacefully, both small and large, thinking that even if she does not deserve criticism in this matter, she deserves all the chastisement in another context.

Feast Day of Saint Stephen, Wednesday December 26, 1973
My Lord, give me the grace and protect me so that I may always be the one who is wronged, and not the one who does it; the one who is being falsely accused, and not the one who accuses; the one who is judged, and not the one who judges; the one who is despised, not the one who despises; the one that is lied about, and not the one who lies about others, because Lord, You know that I have loved the TRUTH above all else ever since I was a small child. Let that love manifest in me until the end.

New Year's Eve, Monday December 31, 1973
In the fog we move into the new year. Out in the world it is getting darker and darker. Lord, let the light in my heart and in the hearts of my sisters shine brighter and brighter. I do not know why, maybe because of the dark fog or being tired from the kitchen work, I feel fatigued somehow. On Saturday the obedience tasks will change. Evangelitsa and I asked each other for forgiveness for all that had happened during our work together. My new obedience is to bake with Aphrodite.

Thursday January 10, 1974
I go with Sister Theodoule to feed the goats, of which there are about ten in the rabbit house. We fill ten bottles of milk in the kitchen, pack them in a bag, and go in the morning and evening to greet the enthusiastic goats (there are also two lambs among them).

Sunday January 13, 1974
In the monastery we are always on the front line; therefore caution is needed, especially in the beginning. Someone who lives in the world can periodically fast more than we do, work more than we do, stay awake, pray, but the possibility of rest is always there, even if it is never used; just the awareness of it gives life a different tone. But for us in the monastery there is no home front, we cannot pick up Donald Duck in our hand, turn on the television, and sleep until 10 AM. We move forward continuously, every day, without a break. I am grateful for this life because I do not like compromises.

Monday January 21, 1974
Restlessness is always to be expected among people. And even the sisterhood I can best serve by trying to strive to learn the spirit of silence and peace. My origin already shows me this way, for the Finns are peaceful and quiet people compared to the Greeks. How good it is to sit quietly in the midst of nature, to listen to the sound of the water, to look at the grass, and to listen to God speaking.

Monday February 4, 1974
On the 4th day of February, AD 1974, when Metropolitan Seraphim was the Bishop of Trikke and Stagoi and Abbess Euphemia the Leader of the Monastery, the Sisters of Bytouma under the leadership of the priest of Paraskevi, Father Demetrios, and the abbess planted an olive tree grove, which is hereby recorded in the chronicles. We spent the whole day planting olive trees, and we also fenced the area. We ate down by the big tree.

Tuesday February 12, 1974
Yesterday and today we were down in the olive tree grove (the trees, though, are only one meter high), where we planted two fields of onions. The weather was lovely; the sun was shining; the waters were running. Hoeing is my favorite work, although I cannot even do that properly. It is becoming a serious issue, that I cannot do anything properly.

This morning we talked about death, which Abbess always presents as a very frightening thing. I, however, have been accustomed to think of death first and foremost as a rather comforting thing. In all hardships the thought of dying is a great comfort. Right now, I do not have any interest in dying, and I do not think that God will take me away prematurely, before I have developed to the point He has meant, and I have realized the arc of life that is within the limits of my possibilities. Of course there is hell. But if a person is constantly praying and wishes with all his strength to fulfill the will of God, whatever it may be, in great or small ways, even if he were to fall constantly, God would hardly allow him to be destroyed because of Christ.

Wednesday February 13, 1974
Today's headline could be, "Bytouma nuns build a road." In the morning Abbess went to Trikala, and at noon she called us to go and repair the road, which was damaged by the river during the rains. So we left. Sister Theodoule sat on the back of a mule called Kitso, and we went down almost to the crossroads of Kaloneri. The road was badly damaged, but we got into the swing of things, carried large rocks, sand, and gravel, and lastly, we leveled the road with a heavy cement pipe. To increase the weight, Sister Theodora climbed into the pipe and rolled around in it while we were rolling the pipe. The road became a real Abbess Euphemia highway. In the dark of the evening, we climbed back up to the monastery.

Friday February 15, 1974
The truth about one's soul begins to unravel. The wild beasts in me have awakened: stubbornness, talking back, disobedience . . . and quite a sorrow has come over my soul when I look inside. The ego would have to be killed entirely, and I am thinking that I do not have strength for that.

Sunday of the Last Judgment, February 17, 1974
As I read the Pilgrim's Tale, the absolute necessity of prayer became clear to me yet again in some new way. Whether we understand it or not, we are dependent on God in every way. He gives us life and strength, and without Him we can do nothing. With every breath, with every heartbeat we are connected to Him, whether we wanted it or not—we just have to be aware of it and rest lovingly in His hands, and then paradise will open up to the human person. Heart and breath are the two rosaries given to us by nature.

Tuesday February 19, 1974
The road washed out again because of heavy rains. We sold this year's lambs, forty-six in all, and transported them all the way down to the plateau. It was raining and foggy. Abbess dressed each one with a plastic bag under the work coat and cut holes for the head and hands. With five

ewes leading the lambs, we hurried down the mountain and through the rivers, one of which was especially gushing and broad. We stepped in the middle of the stream and in its roar pushed the lambs from hand to hand; we had to be careful so the current would not take any of them. Rubber boots were of no use. In the end I still waded across the stream the second time, and Sophia and I, with the help of Sister Macrina, carried Sister Fevronia to the other side. She continued with the lambs to Kalambaka, and we tried to keep her feet dry. We managed well, in any case. And from the lambs we made quite a bit of money. I doubt if any Finn would have experienced or will ever experience something like that.

First week of the Great Lent, February 25 to March 2, 1974
I almost fell asleep while standing in the church. I was hungry, but when I went to the workshop after the service to light a fire in the small wood stoves, I concentrated on that task so much that I completely forgot both hunger and fatigue. I did concentrate on getting the fire lit, but on praying to God, He who is the consuming fire, I cannot focus.

It is clear that the Greek mentality is in some ways very different from the cool, multifaceted assessment of things that I am used to. In this sense I will always remain a stranger. I cannot freely explain my thoughts even to my father-confessor, because they would surely be misunderstood. When I think about it, it is possible that God might want me to return to Finland one day.

Tuesday March 19, 1974
Only yesterday I thought that the fast seemed to affect me hardly at all, but then Sister Dorothea said that I had become pale and that it is better to eat, "because if anything happens to us, we will have to leave the monastery." And right away my head began to feel strangely odd, and my whole being anemic.

Yesterday I was with Sister Theodoule, who has accepted me as an assistant in the many interesting tasks she does, such as grafting wild plum trees and feeding bees with sugar solution.

The Lord's Pascha, Sunday April 14, 1974
Forgiveness has risen from the tomb. On no other occasion is there such comprehensive joy as at Pascha.

Christ has risen from the dead, Father Archbishop and all the other Finns! Perhaps the mail will next time bring me an Easter greeting.

Wednesday April 24, 1974
I had a few conversations with Abbess today. Among other things she remarked that I had confused Joanna and some others with my talks. She was referring to the fact that I do not hide my doubt, that there could be a natural reason for the movement of the curtain of the Holy Doors (namely, the stove warms the air). Others, Abbess included, unconditionally believe that it is a miracle. I am ready to believe everything that is true. These are the sufferings of the first "civilized" sister.

Tuesday April 30, 1974
Sister Macrina had told Abbess this afternoon all the bad things and indiscretions she has observed in me—and what a good memory she has indeed! And Abbess told me in a strict tone how disrespectful I was, full of stubbornness and the spirit of talking back. And it is true what she said. Unfortunately, I am quite a disappointment to her. Reproaches, rebukes, and trials I need.

Wednesday June 19, 1974
At the moment I have no work. I am waiting to receive the original text of the biography of Saint Anthony.[19]

On the Day of Commemoration of the Holy Great Martyr Euphemia, Thursday July 11, 1974
In the morning, Bishop Polycarp of Corfu called and announced that the Synod had dismissed Metropolitan Seraphim today.[20] Personally, I do not feel it as a heavy blow, at least not yet. The Metropolitan has always been like goodness itself to me, but he does not have the depth or spiritual seriousness such that I would have received spiritual nourishment from him.

Friday July 12, 1974
Personally, I think that the spirit which condemns everything and accuses opponents of immorality, and freemasonry, and spiritualism, etc.,

---

19. Athanasios the Great, *The Life of Saint Anthony the Great*, transl. Kristoduli (Friends of Valamo, 1978).

20. After this, Seraphim served as the Metropolitan of Oreos (in name only) from 1974 to 1991, but returned later to be the Metropolitan of Stagoi and Meteora (from 1991 to 2017).

does not represent Orthodox tradition and therefore needs to go. The sisters cannot see this and therefore cannot understand me either.[21]

Sunday July 21, 1974
The Greek radio is talking about losses of the Turks in Cyprus, in between spewing out typical war propaganda. In these military matters I have decided to be more of a woman journalist who reports her findings, people's moods, attitudes of the officials, etc., rather than to express my personal opinions to the sisters, although sometimes it can be a little difficult to endure the clearly one-sided announcements of a country at war, or at least one planning a war.

Monday July 22, 1974
This morning Abbess took the radio out from the hands of the sisterhood and forbade late listening in the evenings. "What is to come, it will come!" And she was very wise in what she did. Life must go on, and while the rest of the world prepares for war, for us, as paradoxical as it may seem, a time of deepening concentration and silence has come.

Tuesday July 23, 1974
I am filled with real admiration when I think of the peacekeepers. Are not these men also human beings, who have children, a wife, a mother, and yet they voluntarily charge ahead to the fire to prevent the opposing parties from killing each other? Each fallen peacekeeper is a martyr. "Blessed are the peacemakers . . . " Abbess just said that two hundred Finnish peacekeepers have arrived in Cyprus. I cry with pride.

Wednesday July 31, 1974
For myself, I am trying to grab myself by the neck, because it is not okay for the head to be only full of bishops and politics. Our task is to praise the Lord. I look around and thank, and thank again, for a flower in the garden, for the sun, the water, the plums, of all these wonderful, good deeds of God towards us. I give thanks for life, whether there are hardships or not, because in any case it is wonderful to be alive.

---

21. Metropolitan Seraphim's dismissal caused turmoil in the monastery.

Sunday August 4, 1974
In general, I do not like to divide people into purely good and purely bad, because in every person there are both good and bad. Abbess said, let's think about Saint Nektarios: was there anything bad in him? I replied—and I believe I did it with the full blessing of Saint Nektarios—that it is not impossible at all, that he could have had a small weakness and that even in the greatest evildoer there is something good. I also said that in some way I always feel the need to defend the people who are accused by everyone else, and later I said to Abbess that I believed that Christ also did this, when he defended harlots and tax collectors.

The Transfiguration of Jesus, Tuesday August 6, 1974
I will never ever join any religious political party; talking about "our" people and of those others is out of place in the Church of Christ.

Thursday August 8, 1974
Personal hardships sometimes feel heavy. The reason is that I have no humility. If I had true humility, I would not feel bitter in the face of arrogant treatment or reproach.

Sunday August 11, 1974
Obviously, the time has come for me to abandon the attitude of a little crying baby into which I so easily sink, and as an adult boldly trust in God to fight for what is good and right, and to dismiss small evils and pressures.

    I received Holy Communion to gain strength. With the help of God! He did not lead me here in vain.

Monday August 12, 1974
In the church, I was thinking, why did I come to the monastery in the first place? It feels like things have actually aligned in that way on their own. It is a bit of an exaggeration to say that I would have come for the love of Christ, because I am not even close to loving Him or even knowing Him, and even my faith is like a silk thread which feels thinner and thinner. But my sincere hope is that I learn to know Him, not just by hypnotizing myself into a state, but rather as an objective reality.

Saturday August 17, 1974
The excessive communist propaganda, according to which America is the beginning and root of all evil, which these days is soaking into the Greeks as into a sponge—it is always more pleasant to accuse someone else than oneself—is tiresome to listen to. And these little fools naturally believe everything. They are hurtling with high speed towards communism. If that is the will of the people, so be it—the freedom of my spirit cannot be curtailed by anyone.

Wednesday August 28, 1974
The Archbishop will be sixty years old today, and my thoughts are there with him, where there is likely to be quite a multitude of people.

Friday August 30, 1974
Yesterday afternoon, Sophia and I were guarding the maize crop and breaking nuts and had a really great conversation. Similarly, the discussion with Sister Macaria this morning was edifying. Once again, I was made to realize that God has His angels. I wrote down the main points of the discussion with Sophia to send to *Aamun Koitto*. However, while writing, it is difficult to retain the sensitivity and the fragrance of the discussion. In the morning, I was sitting again and guarding the maize. The jays were about to eat it right in front of our noses.

Tuesday September 10, 1974
Fevronia, Aphrodite, Sophia, and I were the happy expedition team that set off for Kalogeromandri. First we walked down to the Kaloneri junction, where we continued on the morning bus to Trikala. There we waited for a little while until the Bytouma village bus arrived, with the driver we had hired to take us to Kalogeromandri. We got lost a few times, but finally arrived at the Cheese House of Saint Vissarion, a small brick house with its red shutters in the middle of a Finnish meadow. There Alekos and little Niko and my old enemy Tsep-dog were waiting for us. We asked for news, rolled the cheese barrels to the car, and ate our packed lunches and the pie baked by Alekos's wife.

Feast Day of the Great Martyr Euphemia, Monday September 16, 1974
Under Father George's lead we celebrated an all-night vigil in honor of Abbess's feast day. I have seldom been so sleepy during vigil as I was then.

Staying awake is absolutely my weakest point, and I do not see myself gaining a lot of benefit from it. I will never become an ascetic nun.

Bytouma Monastery, upstairs walkway.

Tuesday September 24, 1974
Today's program included, among other things, a fire. The garbage dump, where we throw papers and other waste, caught fire. It was first noticed from the school, and just as we were finishing our meal, Sister Eusevia shouted: "Fire!" We all ran to the place. We took two hoses and all kinds of buckets and other containers to put out the fire. In the beginning, the flames were high, and there was a danger that the fire would spread to the trees and from there to the school. With hoses in hand, the sisters courageously jumped into the smoke and flames. The flow of the river was led to the laundry area, and from there we took water and soon had the fire under control. This was the fourth dangerous fire in the history of the monastery.

Friday September 27, 1974
Yesterday I got a bundle of letters, including one from the Archbishop. How deep is the compassion I feel towards him, thinking that he could only spend less than two years in the monastery, and after that he had

to go to the world "as a stranger and an outsider"! It is one of the hardest experiences a person can encounter. Only another monastic soul can profoundly grasp it. To Abbess the Archbishop wishes "strength for guiding her flock."

Friday October 11, 1974
Even my own eyes have been opened to see that just here is the difficulty and the worst fault and sin of my character: I do not have even an iota of love in me. Yes, I do help others and pray for them, and if need be, I am ready to sacrifice; but "I am a noisy gong or a clanging cymbal"[22] if I do not really feel the pain of my neighbor in my heart.

Friday October 25, 1974
Father Dimitri blessed the new house, and we had a modest celebration. May the blessing of the Lord be always with us! At noon, eating for the first time in the new house—it felt as if we were on a visit—Abbess solemnly from her own place, which for me, the last of the novices, seemed to be very far away, spoke the following: "I hope from the bottom of my humble and sinful soul, that everyone who is now looking for her place in this new building and at the table would also look for her place in the spiritual life in fulfilling her goal and purpose."

Monday October 28, 1974
Theodora and I collected acorns for the rabbits in the morning and afternoon. In the afternoon the sheep came down there, and all three dogs came to bark and growl at us, especially at me, because they do not bother the ones dressed in black. God only knows what horror and fear fills my mind when these beasts begin to bark. I cannot help but be embittered that I have not been given black clothes, but I am being sent for tasks outside the safety of the monastery courtyard.

Saturday November 16, 1974
We were talking at the table, and I asked the bishop[23] about a question that had occupied my mind in the past few days: How can we reconcile spiritual joy and the sorrow for the suffering people of the world? Is it right for me to be joyful when at the same time I know that thousands

---

22. 1 Cor. 13:1 (New Revised Standard Version).
23. The new Metropolitan, Stephanos, of the Diocese of Trikke and Stagoi.

and thousands of others are in extreme spiritual and physical pain? And what did this wonderful man say: We do not think that we are breathing. In a similar way, just as breathing is natural, so is joy in Christ.

O Lord, I can rejoice in You with good conscience! Let the whole world go mad, let as many people commit suicide, let people suffer injustice, but nothing can take away my joy in Christ. Nothing! To my last breath I will rejoice in the Lord.

Entrance of the Virgin Mary to the Temple, Thursday November 21, 1974
So, black clothes were given yesterday. After the midday meal I read the Paraklesis[24] and then I went to the "confessional," where Abbess and Sister Eusevia were waiting with a pile of clothes. I took off the top layer of my "worldly" clothes, and with the help of Sister Eusevia I put on black. I made a full prostration to Abbess, who had watched the dressing in deep prayer—from time to time I could hear her sigh.

This and that will still happen in life, but one significant leap has been taken, and there is no return. I have thrown myself on the fact that Christ is the way, the truth, and the life.

Thursday November 28, 1974
I was thinking today, how beautiful the name "sister" is. This is the way the world relates to us and waits for us to relate to it in the same way. We are the sisters of Christ, and through Him the sisters of everyone. We relate to other people as if they were our sisters, or at least we should.

Saturday December 7, 1974
Abbess's advice to cling tightly to the cross saved me and drove away a strange excitement in my brain. I came to the monastery to endure everything and even to die, if it is necessary, and so I will NEVER LEAVE ON MY OWN. It is another thing if I am chased away.

Wednesday December 11, 1974
A typical day in Bytouma: After Matins, to the kitchen. After the morning meal, a group of sisters went to look for a cow. I walked around and about in the mountains. The cow was not found, but it was fun to walk in the midst of the frosted maple tree leaves glistening in the sun (the cow was found in the afternoon, peacefully grazing). From the mountains back

---

24. Prayer service.

to the kitchen, to the garden to cut onions, and when we were washing them, Abbess came: "Eleni, please go with the others to load wood on the truck." Again, a walk to the mountains, and with joy we threw a few tons of sturdy logs on the truck. Carrying wood to the kitchen, Abbess: "Look how messy you are, completely covered with debris from the branches. Shake the pieces of wood before you take them in your arms." A meal. Cleaning the onions. Prayer rule and rest. I ask Abbess if we have liturgy tomorrow. "Yes, if you will celebrate. Get out of here." Kitchen work. Pickling cauliflower in the store together with Sister Dorothea. Back to the kitchen. Vespers. A short moment in the cell. Reading in the winter room. And in the evening it is Evangelitsa's and my turn to do the dishes. And I am very satisfied with the day, because there is a relative calm and peace in my soul.

Saturday December 14, 1974
My salvation lies in the Jesus prayer. When it is constantly in my mind, nothing disturbs me, but as soon as I stop using it and let my thoughts wander and start thinking about different situations, I feel confused and unhappy.

Saturday January 4, 1975
I am living through a difficult crisis. In a way, life does not satisfy me. In the morning in church, I usually think about how I will leave for Finland and go to Lintula, and what I will do there; and on the other hand, that I will miss being here a lot.

Friday March 7, 1975
The most amazing moments repeated over and over again are those when the sun begins to shine in the soul after a period full of challenges and heavy thoughts. And it always happens somehow unexpectedly. Just as it is difficult to believe in the arrival of beautiful weather, while the rain is pouring down from the gray sky, so it is in the life of the soul during periods of hardship—and yet one day the clouds disperse, first moving apart and then disappearing without a trace, and the sun fills everything with joy and brightness.

Forgiveness Sunday, March 16, 1975
Abbess does not understand this kind of silence-loving characters. These Greeks are heartwarmingly moving for enjoying the interaction with

other people so much, and in a way, I feel miserable and guilty for not being able to chat. Silence has a fragrance for me.

Thursday March 27, 1975
Yesterday I went to Trikala again to get a filling in my tooth (I was there also on Monday). There were six of us altogether, who rode with Father Chariton, and we all went there for different things. I was with Sister Syncletica at her home, where her elderly parents live in their beautiful house. As I walked around in the town in front of one house, I chatted with a little boy named Georgey, who was bragging to me about his toys. I told him that I also had toys up at the monastery: live kid goats and lambs.

Fourth Week of Lent, Sunday April 6, 1975
Thinking about envy and jealousy, I have come to the conclusion that now is the time for a decisive battle against those forces, which have poisoned my life since childhood. And what is the method for the fight? To go forward in humility, to think and take for granted, that I do not deserve the love of God or of people, and to be humbly satisfied with that. But if something like that happens, you must receive it, not like someone who demands it, and who thinks that it is obviously his, but with deep gratitude and awareness of your own worthlessness.

Friday April 18, 1975
Periodically I feel the urge in my heart to embrace all the suffering, sad, bored, disappointed people, to comfort them in some way. And of course, I always have prayer.

Holy Friday, May 2, 1975
Forgive me, Lord, that I have so little understood and even less put into practice Your spirit, Your state of mind. Lord, press Your pure image into my heart, so that I may gradually become like that image.

Saturday May 24, 1975
In monastic life, it is necessary always to keep Holy Friday firmly in mind. The joy of Holy Pascha is the foretaste of heaven; Holy Friday is the experience of ordinary life. As long as we are in this life, Holy Friday will not leave us.

Saturday May 31, 1975
Yesterday we spent the whole day up in the woods fetching wooden sticks to be used as trellises for bean plants. The previous evening Abbess said that I would not join, but in the morning she said, "You go too!" This week I had a flu and felt myself tired. But yet again I saw how little one can trust one's own human feelings. I climbed up there, and at noon we descended with Aphrodite and a mule and a donkey loaded with wooden sticks down to the monastery, where we left the load—and up again! Usually young, energetic, and open-hearted people go on such trips and leave all the murmuring and complaining far behind. Heart and soul are aired.

Saturday June 7, 1975
There must not be any place for force or pressure in spiritual life. If that happens, it is no longer spiritual life, which refers to a free union between God and people.

Wednesday June 18, 1975
Thirty years of this earthly journey will be fulfilled. In the recent past, I have been involved with such heavy physical work that I have had hardly any time to reflect on the years that have passed. On the contrary, it is somehow comforting to think that there will be an end to this torture. My purpose is to discuss with the abbess about the work. It has been mainly carrying and digging in my case. I am particularly bothered by the uncertainty. One day I can hardly stand on my feet because of the workload; another day there is hardly any meaningful work to be done. My intention is to ask the abbess if she has any idea of letting me learn some handicraft. I would rather work outdoors, but the fact remains that I do not have Margarita's strength.

Sunday July 6, 1975
My parents arrived on Monday evening (by taxi all the way from Ionnina) and stayed here until Thursday morning, when we went together to visit Kalambaka and I took care of my residency papers. My parents turned out to be very nice; we took some trips to the surroundings and talked about everything under the sky, which was not too healthy for the inner peace of a monastic. They were totally fascinated by Meteora, and they received a great welcome in all the three great monasteries, Meteora, Varlaam, and St. Stephen. The friendliness of the sisters and the

schoolgirls here overwhelmed them in a hurry, and in turn the sisterhood seemed to like them.

Sunday September 7, 1975
Yesterday we had visitors. A sympathetic German family came: mother, son, and daughter. Foreigners are my very own guests. After I complained to Abbess that they are sometimes treated as enemies of the state, the service has improved remarkably. Abbess herself usually does not appear at all, but Sister Eusevia and Sister Macrina do their best. Generally, as at this time, the foreigners also buy handicrafts, and even I feel like contributing something to the monastery.

Later in the afternoon, Father Alexios arrived with his spiritual children, and they celebrated Vespers. They sing in a magnificent way—one's heart opens.

Friday September 19, 1975
Almost every day I can steal a few minutes from Abbess to tell her something that has happened or is on my mind. I benefit greatly from these conversations.

Tuesday October 28, 1975
What bothered me most about Abbess's words was that she told me I was disobedient. Without obedience, there is no monastic life.

Wednesday November 5, 1975
For two days we were washing the wool, which we then started to pick apart at high speed. The only interruption, apart from meals, was when we unloaded eight tons of cotton seed (for the sheep) into a warehouse. Washing the wool was tough; we washers were doubled up by the rinsing basins all day.

Saturday November 8, 1975
I must begin to fight my weaknesses and sins systematically. They must be attacked one by one, because trying to fight them all at once is like punching the air randomly. Most of all, the grace of the Holy Spirit is needed, not only to cover and bury the weaknesses and evil deeds of the human being, but to work together with the efforts of him or her to bring about a deep transformation, a lasting transformation, because we are called to deification.

Saturday November 22, 1975
If you overcome yourself in one thing, it is easier to do that in another. Similarly, if you fall in one thing, it is easy to fall in another, because it is like an unwinding ball of thread. But there is also another reason caused by the Devil: In one's mind you fall from great heights, where you have raised yourself in your blindness, and then do not care anymore, if you fall in another instance, it is because you can no longer see the halo around your head.

Tuesday December 2, 1975
I apparently need to boldly face the fact that I have not and will never find a spiritual leader. How bitter a complaint this has been for many nuns and monks over the years! Such blessed "elders" must have been few and far between.

Saturday December 20, 1975
In any case, one must go on and try to repent, because in some respects, with all my dreams of a life as a hermit, I was losing the right way. Abbess noticed it. I need to show more understanding and compassion to the sisters, to Abbess herself. You have to see what is best for others, not for yourself. And if I do that, I do not believe that God will deny me the grace of the Holy Spirit, the light of an unceasing prayer, because it is fulfilling His will in this situation.

Christmas, Thursday December 25, 1975
Many people from Finland remembered me again this year. Father Archbishop sent me the Jesus Prayer booklets and a letter that benefited me spiritually. I am beginning to open my ears more and more to the few but weighty words of the Archbishop.

Saturday January 10, 1976
I live with quite conflicted feelings. Somehow my eyes have opened to see that staying here may become difficult as time goes by. There can be a kind of danger in becoming numb: I can just stay here but will not progress in the things I came to learn in a monastery.

Who knows, maybe I will return to Finland in the end.

Abbess seems to keep me in her memory. Today, during the change of the obedience tasks, in addition to the usual "animals," I also got the dining room with its entrance and terrace—as if carrying manure would be one of the lighter tasks. However, this observation made me perk up, because from it I can conclude that Abbess, in her strange way, is challenging me. And it is always fun to be challenged, especially if one proves to be able to meet the challenge.

Translation work is not included in the term "work" here.

Tuesday March 2, 1976
I received a letter from the Archbishop, and from the few words in it, it was as if the eyes of my soul were lit up, and I understood how dangerous a path I was about to slide into: pride, murmuring, and blaming others. I was also willfully separating myself from the rare blessing of having a spiritual father. I had lost the end of a thread and was fumbling in pain and darkness. Now, however, I found the end of the thread, the only one, that allows the ball to run free again—it is humility. I went to Abbess's cell and confessed to her all of this.

Tuesday April 13, 1976
If it were up to Abbess, she would cut off all my connections with Finland. What might be the reason? I would like so much to show her blind obedience in everything, but many others are also entangled with this question. I have begun the translation of the Philokalia; can I abandon it now and thus betray the Valamo Association?

Holy Thursday, April 22, 1976
I hope and pray for one thing: to experience the secret transformation that the Holy Spirit can bring about in a human being. If, when I die, I have not experienced it nor seen the Holy Light, then life and ascesis have been in vain.

Holy Friday, April 23, 1976, unsent letter to the Archbishop
I have deeply and seriously considered writing the following letter to the Archbishop:

> Your Eminence Father Archbishop,
> We have already reached Holy Friday. The Pascha of the Greeks and the days of Holy Week are so full of different traditions, that one sometimes thinks that the Devil himself invented all of them, so that people would not have a moment to think about the actual content of the events.

I am writing because of a question that periodically and especially now occupies me. Nothing special has happened, and I am not writing this from a momentary impulse, as I did once before. Soon I will reach three years here, and I am beginning to feel more and more clearly that staying in a foreign country is not going to benefit me anymore. In the midst of a certain Greek superficiality and many prejudices, I am beginning to feel a kind of spiritual numbness. Two ways of thinking about this are tearing me apart: On the one hand, one lives in blind obedience to Abbess, come what may, in spite of her periodic tyranny, until her death, and then reconsider again; on the other hand, when I see that the program of the monastery causes restlessness for someone like me and that the priorities in it are not the inner goals that I have set for myself, and because I feel myself somehow rootless, to return to Finland (Lintula) and continue my translation work there. How is the situation in Lintula these days? I certainly do not expect a carefree life there; I am used to hardship. I also do not believe that I can do something special there—I do not know anything about spiritual life—but if it is God's will that something develops from that place, I would also be there and available for the Finnish Church. The main problem, however—and I am asking for an answer from You especially for it—is that after three years in the monastery I do not feel that I have progressed in my inner growth. Thoughts are as scattered as before, the warmth of the prayer, which I could taste every now and then when in the world, I do not experience. Rarely does a day go by—or even an hour—without a constant struggle against thoughts. And when I look at the older sisters, "vestigia terrent."[25] There are none who would have achieved inner peace.

Would it be better, then, in Lintula? First and foremost, I would lose the opportunity to live in this obedience, which is a blessing of our monastery—Abbess does not let even the smallest thing alone; she even gets involved with my translations. Relations with Abbess Antonina[26] would be cool and polite at best. The advantage would be staying in Finland—I could even meet You from time to time—the possibility of interacting with people of similar backgrounds, speaking Finnish. Because in the midst of all these Greek prejudices and astonishing thoughts—among other things, the sisterhood thinks it is a tragedy that torture is banned in the jails—I surely got used to practicing the

---

25. Latin for "the tracks frighten."
26. Abbess of Lintula Monastery from 1975 to 1998.

struggle of silence prematurely. Of course there are also human emotional reasons; for example, lakes and forests are beautiful mirages in my mind.

How to bring clarity to this chaos? There is yet a third alternative: Change monasteries in Greece; I am especially attracted to the idea of the women's monastery, a sub-monastery of Mount Athos, whose sisterhood has a very different origin than ours; I even know a few of them. Changing monasteries would of course be felt as a deep insult here. I have asked Abbess if I could visit other monasteries, mainly those in this diocese, and she said, "in the spring," so after Pascha I could take up the issue again. Most likely she will make it difficult, if not impossible. There is an atmosphere of envy and suspicion between the women's monasteries. I would very much like to talk with some educated sisters, who are everywhere but here. I feel somehow withered among these cows and chickens.

I expect that you, after you have read this with the eyes of your soul enlightened, will be able to send me some advice as to what can be done, if anything, and I trust that you above all will keep an eye on what is best for my soul.

Respectfully, Helena

Holy Saturday, April 24, 1976
I wrote this letter in my diaries, but at least for the time being, I will not write it to the Archbishop. If it is God's will for me at some point to go to Finland, He has His ways of fulfilling it without any effort on my part.

Thursday May 6, 1976
"Remain in yourself and you will be free from your temptations, but if you come out, endure the consequences," write the Holy Fathers. To gather the mind into the heart and from there to call out to the Lord—there is our work, there is our joy.

Friday May 7, 1976
Abbess said: "You must give up writing. Others work themselves to death, and you sit in your cell and write." "The brain gets tired in that work," I remarked mildly. "Yes, but it is not productive," answered Abbess. Later, when an opportunity presented itself, I said slowly to Abbess that if I have become a nuisance with my writing work, it might be best for me to change monasteries, and that I can no longer bear these continuous

quarrels about the writing. Nobody in Finland has any idea that these works have been translated with blood ...

For me the issue is clear, however deeply heavy it would be. If I am not given a chance to do translation work, I will change monasteries. It is obvious and strange that Abbess, who is a clever person, does not get it. Translation is my duty to Finland.

Thursday May 20, 1976
At the height of my misery my typewriter broke—the part that holds the color ribbon was cut. When I told Abbess the news, she responded, "That is good news, you will go to wind thread." Apparently, it is not God's will to enlighten her in this matter, which means that it is my responsibility to leave from here. Oh my God, I do not want to.

Later. I had a long talk with Abbess out on the terrace. In broad strokes, I told her the following: "I leave this matter for you to decide: If you really think it is impossible for me to continue the writing work, tell me so directly. Say, 'you may not write anymore; either you stop, or go elsewhere,' and then I will leave, because I cannot leave the work of writing. And in that case, you help me to find another monastery where this kind of work can be done. If you think it is possible for me to continue as I have been doing up to now, do not bother me with these questions, because I cannot stand it any longer." At least she knows exactly what I think.

Abbess said that in her view I am like a pressure cooker with the lid tightly closed, but when you heat it up, the pressure finally blows it open. So, one fine day I won't be able to take it anymore and will leave. Hmm, Abbess's pressure cooker has a valve with which she can reduce the pressure. So do I; prayer and inner spiritual work are my channels to let the pressure out.

Saturday May 22, 1976
Today we climbed a high mountain to collect herbs to dry for the winter. Early in the morning, as we walked under huge spruce trees, we began as if from one mouth to sing "Praise the Lord ... " and after that, *Paschal troparia*. The birds were singing brightly, and among the dark green spruces grew white lilies and other exotic mountain flowers. Above, ice cold water flowed from a spring. The solemn beauty and the feeling of an uninhabited wilderness mesmerized me.

Saturday June 5, 1976
I have noticed one thing: When you give yourself to the ascetic life with all the strength of your soul and body, then the grace of God also comes to help.

I thank You, my Lord and my Savior, for giving me this life, for giving me the opportunity to be connected to You. I thank you for work and the ability to work, I thank you for the earth and the fruits of the earth. I thank You for the great trees and for the white flowering lily. I thank You for the life here in the monastery. Remember, Lord, the souls of our fathers, who have struggled and labored here, and let us make right use of the wonderfulness of this place. I thank You for the light, You, the Light and Giver of light. I thank you for the darkness, You unknown. I thank You for the night and for the day and the rhythm of life.

Wednesday June 9, 1976
The typewriter arrived today at the monastery (repaired).

I wish the fate of the lost manuscript[27] would become clear; then I would have no other worries. If it is really lost, I will retype the writings of Mark the Ascetic in a few days, if I have the opportunity. Typing cannot unfortunately be done during the night because of the typewriter's rattle.

Saturday June 19, 1976
Yesterday ended thirty-one years of this earthly wandering. Today I received Holy Communion. Reflecting on everything at that moment, I decided to dedicate the thirty-second year of my life to the attainment of peace. It is a gift that the Lord specifically promised to give to us and that He gave to the disciples even before they asked Him for it. "Peace be with you!"[28] I too want to reach for this peace that passes all understanding, even though the world of today seems to think that it is the duty of a human being to be constantly more or less worried for an infinite number of reasons. I, however, want to attain that great luxury, peace. May the Lord grant it to me!

Sunday July 11, 1976
Three years have passed in the monastery.

---

27. The manuscript Kristoduli sent to Irinja Nikkanen was delayed in the mail longer than usual because of a strike.
28. John 20:19 (New Revised Standard Version).

This past week has been so full of events that someone who is outwardly used to a stable life has become quite dizzy. The fact is that I had already begun to miss a little diversity. The Heavenly Father saw this and arranged this eventful week in my life. On Monday I went down to Kalambaka to take care of the residence permit, which got done without difficulties. Abbess's cousin was visiting, and we went to show her the monasteries of Meteora. So I was able to accompany Sisters Dorothea and Syncletica and kira-Spyridoula from Kalambaka to Meteora, where we visited the Holy Monastery of Transfiguration, Varlaam, and the Holy Monastery of Saint Nicholas of Anapausas. In the Monastery of the Great Meteoron we were brought relics to venerate.

On Wednesday Father Alexios arrived here with a few of his "monk children" and spoke evocative words to us.

On Thursday morning I stopped by Abbess's cell to tell her that lately, especially after Abbess herself had mentioned such a possibility, I had been troubled by the thought that it would be nice to visit Finland. I told her that since to my understanding the thought came from the tempter, I would not myself begin to do anything to promote it; but if God sent an opportunity, I would not deny it. "Let God act!" said Abbess. And God indeed acted and fast! In the afternoon of the same day the sisters woke me from my afternoon nap shouting: "Anna has come!" And indeed, the joyful personality of Annele Baljaskin[29] had arrived at our monastery.

Afterwards we spoke Finnish and exchanged detailed news. After hearing Anna's experiences, I began to see Finland's situation more realistically again, and the "temptation" to visit has evaporated.

Monday July 19, 1976

This may be my last night in the Holy Monastery of Bytouma. Abbess has begun her harassment of my writing again, insisting on a promise that I will not write anything in a "foreign language." Even the translations are to be sent to Finland in Greek! It may be that God is letting this happen on purpose so that I, forced by circumstances, will have better opportunities to advance in my ascetic life in another monastery founded by more educated sisters.

The above series of events began with my request for a blessing to write to *Aamun Koitto* about the holy relics.

---

29. Annele Baljaskin was on a one-year fellowship in Athens.

Dormition of the Mother of God, Sunday August 15, 1976
When a person feels grace inside, she has to fight and struggle to keep it. Because grace does not just leave a person. When it does, it is a sign that I have grieved the Holy Spirit. That is probably why the reign of grace in my life is so short. God's grace also visits my soul, but I am not hospitable. Above all, one must take care of the spark of grace in the soul and guard it.

Saturday August 28, 1976
For those who may be reading this, I would suggest that you exercise extreme caution in choosing whom you open your heart to. For retreat in this matter is a painful process.

Sunday August 29, 1976
You have received Holy Communion. You have received mercy, but how do you guard this gift? I remembered a song I learned as a child with its profound teachings: "Don't let the little eye see everything, don't let the little ear hear everything . . . " To guard the inner flame, one must strictly guard access to one's heart.

Elevation of the Lifegiving Cross, Tuesday September 14, 1976
Last week I received a letter from Father Archbishop. There was a kind of quiet tenderness in it that moved my heart. He wrote about the translation of Abba Dorotheos's homilies; that is, steps have finally been taken to acquire the book here.

Saturday September 18, 1976
Yesterday I finished the text of Saint Hesychios the Presbyter's in the Philokalia and will take a break in translation work until early October. In other words, until (a) the previous translations have been paid for; and (b) I have received the introduction of Abba Dorotheos's homilies. I replied to the Archbishop's letter for the first time explaining the difficulties I have had with the translation work. With the help of God, those difficulties are now over; hopefully, I can share some of them with the Archbishop.

The struggle to guard one's mind generates joy and peace. Why think of something evil, when I can resist such thoughts? Who will be hurt more by such evil thoughts than myself?

Saturday November 13, 1976
Today a certain little nun could sing the Te Deum. Yesterday I received a letter from *Aamun Koitto* in which Editor Laine wondered why it had been so long since I had written anything for the magazine. I translated it for Abbess today and asked her what to do. She said: "Write!" In the summer, Abbess strictly forbade me to help *Aamun Koitto*, but here we are, things have developed favorably.

Sunday November 14, 1976
Tomorrow begins the Nativity Fast. I wish I could get spiritual zeal! There is a lot of personal experience in the fact that if you pray deeply and patiently for something, God will answer your prayer. And yet sometimes, one does not even bother to pray.

Christmas Eve, Friday December 24, 1976
This is one of those nights when for once, peace and goodwill permeate from the atmosphere of the globe, at least in this hemisphere. It would be wonderful if this event of extreme humility that took place in the manger, great in its holy simplicity, could become real life for all of us Christians and first for me! The Son of God became man in a stable and was put on the straw of the manger to rest. Far away is all the pomp of life, all that is outside the extreme necessity. Human life is most beautiful when it is simplified.

Thursday January 13, 1977
Lately I have had interesting and enriching conversations with Mother Abbess almost every day. She spins yarn in her cell and is easily accessible there. A few days ago, I told her about a tense conversation I had with Sister Christonymphe, about the words I had said to her. Mother Abbess raised her head from the spinning work and said with bright eyes, "Would it not have been simpler to say: 'Forgive me, Sister' . . . "

Friday January 14, 1977
If I believe and am sure that God and his kingdom exist, and that on the other hand there is eternal punishment and separation from Him, would I not do everything possible in this short life on earth to get into that kingdom, whatever it takes? That is the goal of the whole earthly life, and if you keep that in sight, this life will also be happy.

Saturday February 5, 1977
Sister Eusevia returned my passport today, which had been with Abbess when she had cashed my last translation check. It turned out that all the money from my translation work so far is kept in an envelope in the monastery! The amount is about eighty thousand drachmas. I went to speak with Abbess directly. "When you have not even been tonsured as a nun yet," she said. "These funds come from the work done in the monastery," I responded, "and belong to the monastery." With a very bitter spirit I thought about the whole thing and how inflation is eating away at the proceeds of my work. Later when I saw Abbess, I said again: "I have seldom felt so bad as I do now with this money. I pour spiritual sweat into these books, and these funds are not so easy to get from the people in Finland, and now they are wasted here and reduced in value. And then we cannot get sewing machines for the schoolgirls, and overall a large number of people are living in misery in the world." Abbess raised her eyes, saddened because of her sister's illness, and looked at me: "And what has that got to do with you?" Then suddenly I remembered those two monastic virtues: lack of possession and obedience. Even if Abbess would throw "my" money in the river, it should not bother me. And immediately I prostrated in front of her and said again, "Forgive me, Abbess." She added, "At some point I meant to ask for your opinion, but since things are as they are, I will not." "Do not ask," I said. And now: forget the whole thing and continue your carefree life in non-possession and obedience.

Wednesday February 16, 1977
The old man can never calm down. He is envious, ambitious, full of evil thoughts, his eyes see crookedly, his ears hear suspiciously. Lord, free me from the old man. Let the new person grow inside me. He is humble, quiet, bright—to him You give Your peace.

Sunday March 6, 1977
Soon after thirty years, aging begins. That also often occupies my mind. Some people completely lose their mind and personality in old age . . . But it is said that the path of righteousness is like the light of dawn that gets brighter and brighter until noon. Is it justified to infer something about a person's relationship to the grace of God based on the way he grows older and what kind of death he has? I have been observing that if God's grace lives strongly in a person, his death is like taking off his clothes, and what kind of clothes: used but still wearable. In other words,

the superiority of the soul's grip lasts until the end, and the weakness of the body cannot influence it. What might happen to me, when already today when this body of mine gets more tired than usual I immediately also feel some kind of irritation in the soul?

This afternoon, Father George and the girls from the grammar school dormitory, who had made a spiritual "rush" to a remote village for the joy and refreshment of the inhabitants, paid a brief visit here. Yesterday we loaded wood in the olive grove, and in the afternoon we dug and carried earth in the courtyard, where the flowerbeds are being renewed by pouring cement paths. After this work I still feel like I am filled with lead.

Veneration of the Holy Cross, Sunday March 13, 1977
Metropolitan [Stephen] arrived, and the service of becoming a Rasophore was performed. Sister Kristoduli continues the monastic ascesis of the novice Eleni in the Holy Monastery of Bytouma. Let me be, Lord, as the name demands. Nothing else needs to be asked for throughout one's whole life.

Monday March 14, 1977
Before the tonsure, I stopped in Abbess's cell, made a full prostration asking for forgiveness for all the worries I had caused her these past years. And I added: " . . . and I thank You, that you did not let go of the reins when I was wandering here and there. I came to the monastery with a worldly mindset and false self-confidence, and it certainly took a lot of work to weed them out."

The new name makes me shy. I feel like I have been sold into slavery.[30] That is why I came to the monastery, so that all of me would belong to Christ. The new name seals it in a way.

WORK-FILLED ASCESIS

Holy Thursday, April 7, 1977
Once again, I return to the harbor after a trip of painful inner thoughts. Mind must be kept in the heart. For as long as the thoughts are buzzing around in the head, there is no peace, all the time Satan is mixing his poison into them. But when they are enclosed in the heart and sealed with

---

30. The name *Kristoduli* means the servant of Christ, or the slave of Christ.

the name of Christ, they are safe, even if they want to break out again by force and start to circulate on their endless track again.

Wednesday May 18, 1977
While I wait for the second call of the talando[31] to Vespers, I think to myself, what might I need to say at the moment of death? That I have loved neither God nor people? That the only thing that I can offer to God is a bundle of forced, dry "good deeds"? Because if the baptism of God's grace does not moisten the soul, nothing will sprout in it. Far away from my heart are the rivers of the living water, of which the Lord talked to the Samaritan woman.[32]

Striving for a continuously happy and carefree state does not benefit a human being. It simply has to be accepted that both mental and physical suffering belong to life, to this great gift given to us by God.

Saturday July 2, 1977
Last week I finished Abba Dorotheos and started translating the Martyrs[33] by Metropolitan Dionysios. I am living in the atmosphere of a war-time prison. After all that he endured, the Metropolitan must have had great courage in front of God. This body, which has gone through such hard things, now rests here behind the altar. While translating, I somehow feel like cooperating with the author.

Monday July 11, 1977
Last night Father Isidore of the Varlaam monastery celebrated an all-night vigil, almost seven hours. These all-night divine services are, at least for me, more physical than spiritual ascesis. I am tired, and every now and then my attention wanders.

I have spent four blessed years in the monastery. I thank the Lord and pray with the pain of my heart that I will never lose sight of the goal for which I came to the monastery. In the world one has the opportunity to do such good deeds that cannot be done in a monastery. And we will have to face a terrible judgment before God if we leave the good we could have done in the world and do not fulfill the higher good that we could have influenced by prayer in the monastery. Then, enclosure in the

---

31. Talando, a wooden board, which is rhythmically hit by a wooden hammer instead of church bells to announce the beginning of services.
32. John 4:14 (New Revised Standard Version).
33. Dionysius Kharalampous, *Marttyyrit* (Kirjaneliö, 1978).

monastery becomes a selfish justification for leaving others to their own devices.

Tuesday July 12, 1977
Two terrible wars—the result of the aspirations of a few prior generations. And we still do not see any signs of learning from them. The same lust for prey, the same hardness and coldness, the same false love of others based on humanism. Instead of humanity as a whole falling down before God, lamenting and repenting: "Lord, we see what happened when we trusted in our own powers; come and help us, we want to obey your laws"—instead of this happening, the result is an even more complete abandonment of God. And what will follow from that? It is hard to even think of those atrocities.

Help me, a worthless nun on this remote mountain, in the midst of these lively country girls, to first live the way I recommend to others, and by prayers prevent catastrophes.

Wednesday July 13, 1977
Today an uplifting event happened: In the middle of the busy work of translating the Martyrs, the typewriter broke. Tomorrow a bus will come up here to fetch Kir-Lefter, who will go down to Trikala to do errands. Mother Abbess will send me along with my machine—alone, how else. How I will manage to come back up, God only knows. I will probably climb up on foot as usual from somewhere, totally fried and brain boiling. Trikala is probably a real inferno.

Wednesday July 20, 1977
Yesterday and today we finished a big job, cleaning the sheep pen of all the winter's manure. It took a hoe to break through the dry surface; there was wet manure underneath. The smell was something else, but we got used to it quickly. I shoveled the manure into the wheelbarrow.

Friday July 22, 1977
Many times during my stay here it has been clearly evident how God is protecting my life and health. If He is taking care of this temporal, He undoubtedly also takes care of the soul, which is eternal. This thought gives me courage.

Saturday September 10, 1977
I had forgotten a bundle of clothes that I had collected from the clothesline in the lower entrance, and Abbess gave me fifteen parakleses for it. I will probably not be able to read all the parakleses of punishment before my death.[34]

Tuesday September 13, 1977
What a blessed life! I was down in the olive grove watering olive trees, and my only worry was how to keep repeating, "Lord Jesus Christ, Son of God, have mercy on me," as I moved the hose from one tree to another.

I received Holy Communion on Sunday. Light, joy, love—I am unworthy to receive these gifts, which the Lord sends only out of His mercy to me, a wretch who cannot keep them.

Sunday October 23, 1977
Today in the liturgy I again became troubled by the thought that I am not given the church as an obedience task. What an undeserved joy it would be to serve at the altar when Holy Communion was offered! I received Holy Communion and after that saw things in a different light. I looked at the crucifixion on the altar, and a voice within me said, "For a nun, crucifixion is crucifying one's will on the cross." There should be no will of one's own. Obedience, the workshop—bless Mother Abbess; obedience, the church—bless Mother Abbess.

Before Holy Communion I stood in front of the icon of Christ. I thought about this unique ascesis that God has given me and that I feel, in spite of all the difficulties, to be the only right one for me. This is good for me. I was always ambitious, I always wanted to shine, and now I came to a foreign country, where my "skills" and so-called talents are not visible, in the midst of a culture with a different language, where even reading fluently gives me trouble among people who do not understand intellectual work. And yet I love these uneducated country girls whom God has sent me to. There is roughness, hardness, unbridled desire to put oneself first. I see it as my task to fight this, first in myself and then in the sisterhood, so that the spirit would gradually become gentler, more peaceful.

---

34. Parakleses were given to the sisters as penitence for various misdeeds.

Saturday November 5, 1977
What I had feared, happened. In the morning Mother Abbess asked at the table to whom she should give the church and to whom the kitchen. When there seemed to be some confusion on the church, I also said that I could go and help Sister Dorothea. Then Mother Abbess started a terrible sermon about how I would never get the church, because I am so careless, nor the kitchen, because I am so messy.

Tuesday November 15, 1977
I began to read Saint Isaac the Syrian, and it has greatly helped in reducing the importance of the obedience tasks. Every task is just a task—we have been asked to focus our attention elsewhere.

Wednesday November 30, 1977
Sunday afternoon I went to Abbess's cell, and we discussed for about an hour very seriously, and I told her all the possible thoughts that had been on my mind. The end result was that I finally calmed down. Mother Abbess said that I should give myself entirely into the hands of God; then I will be like one wing in the air. I will try to do that.

Yesterday I got a letter from Siina Taulamo, writing from Kenya, where she at the age of over seventy had gone together with Maria Iltola for mission work. There are many difficulties confronting them there.

Friday December 9, 1977
In monastic life one proceeds through challenges.

For the first time in my monastic life, I feel silence inside. Let us see what new plans Satan has for shaking the foundation. But everything has its limits. The Lord says to the enemy of the soul: "Thus far shall you come, and no farther."[35] And if one can endure the hardship, even deeper and more genuine peace follows.

Thursday December 15, 1977
Today, after Vespers, Metropolitan Stephen ordained Sister Fevronia and Sister Thekla to small schema. This time I was struck by a statement in the text of the ordination, which says that slander, humiliation, and suffering are an obvious part of monastic life—a part of its program. One

---

35. Job 38:11 (New Revised Standard Version).

is encouraged to have joy in facing them; to experience them is a sign of being on the right path, the one that saints of all ages have walked.

For me, everything that happened tonight was a good reminder of the right attitude of monks and nuns. As Christmas is approaching, thoughts wander a little too often to Finland.

Friday December 23, 1977
It was mail day. The heart is full of warmth for those people who once again remembered even me. Father Archbishop wrote and sent a pamphlet called "Last Temptations." And how he began his letter! "Beloved Sister Kristoduli in Christ." I do not quite know how to express the joy of this heartfelt greeting. He did not forget . . . This might seem like a little unexpected burst of joy from a nun, but we should not forget the word "in Christ." Without Him there would not be the bond between Father Archbishop and me that exists now. Love in Christ is the most beautiful thing there can be in the world—and it continues and is perfected in the eternal light, where the Lord will one day take me, too, for the prayers of Father Archbishop. How good it is to live as a Christian!

Thursday January 5, 1978
The night before last, we had an all-night vigil from 9 pm to 3:30 am. It was the memorial liturgy for Metropolitan Dionysios.

We did not have enough time to rest after the night vigil—only a few hours—when a new program had already begun. We began to pack bags, carry various items, and then someone said that it was about a trip to Fanassi to meet Metropolitan Seraphim. After a while Mother Abbess announced it to me officially: "Be ready! And I want you to be serious and dignified."

Wednesday February 1, 1978
Today was quite a tearful day, but in the evening, I again got new strength and courage. Even if all the enraged abbesses of the world were to rise up against me, I would have nothing to fear.

Thursday April 6, 1978
In fact, I have to confess that I need challenges. Then I pray more devoutly. When there is nothing special, my thoughts wander—mostly in the direction of Finland and especially Kuopio. When I am overwhelmed

with worries, I think that as soon as I get through this hardship, I will be able to think about divine things in peace. But unfortunately, it does not happen that way. There should be a way to anchor one's thoughts more and more in God. This matter really occupies my mind.

Friday April 7, 1978
I received a letter from Irinja Nikkanen, in which she expresses an anxious wish that I might sometime come for a visit to Finland to finalize the translations of the Philokalia. I discussed this with Mother Abbess and answered Irinja that I can come—but not for more than two months. Let us see where this leads. Even just the thought of such a big trip makes my stomach turn, but if things demand it and such an effort is necessary, then it has God's blessing, and the trip might have meaning both for me and for others, who through me get involved with the tradition I represent. As such, I have sometimes felt that I should visit Finland. Right now there is reason to calm down and entrust the continuation of the matter to God.

Sunday April 9, 1978
Today, on the Sunday of Saint John Climacus, Mother Abbess made me for the first time read a chapter of a canon in the Triodion,[36] which is hereby gratefully noted. Now I have no worries. May the Lord help me to always keep my thoughts on Him.

The Lord's Pascha, Sunday April 30, 1978
It was a radiantly beautiful day. In the afternoon we went for a walk to the meadow. It is blooming, golden yellow. The trees have young, light green leaves. My God, if even this visible world is so beautiful, what must the "new creation" be like! Today grace almost shone through nature—when, for a brief moment, one could see to the core of all things, to the bright truth hidden in everything.

My obedience task this week was the kitchen.

Friday May 26, 1978
The whole week has gone by in the hassle of making hay, and the worst still remains: the meadow below the monastery, where the hay must be carried up the steep path on one's back. But we will manage, as always, by working together. We get tired together, we rest together, we get nervous

---

36. Lenten texts and prayers.

together, every now and then, because of exhaustion and because the sun hits our heads . . . The cooperative spirit of the sisterhood grows in these chores. And in any case, compared to the rest of the world we are in a good situation: In the monastery cooked food awaits us, along with a cool cell in which to rest, and the compassion of the other sisters for the hard-working laborers.

Wednesday June 28, 1978
This week I will have the first obedience that requires more responsibility: taking care of the visitors, a task that contains many surprises. My first visitor was a girl who came to the monastery with a goat and a kid. The animals were promised to the Mother of God; they were taken around the church and then joined our flock.

Friday July 28, 1978
Last night we had an unforgettable vigil! Thank you, Lord, to You, for making me a nun, for giving me this angelic life. Truly these recent times I have lived in paradise-like feelings. Thank You, my Savior! In fact, the secret is very simple: humility, being childlike, elevating the mind to the Lord—and then you are as happy as you can be. One evening while we were sitting on Mother Abbess's balcony, I thought that it must be like this in the Kingdom of Heaven.

Tuesday September 12, 1978
I received two letters, one from Father Archbishop, who finally replied to my question of a possible visit to Finland, by saying that (a) a distinguished committee is needed for the translation of the Philokalia, similar to the translation of the Bible; and (b) my translations are nearly worthless, and others need to work for months to improve them. He put the last point a little more politely, but the meaning was the same. Anyway, inside I feel ready to give up translation if it comes to that.

Saturday November 4, 1978
This week the program included slide presentations. Father Athanasios from Meteora showed them on two evenings, first from Mount Athos and yesterday from the monastery of Saint Nektarios. The slide sets also included commentaries mixed with music.

Monday November 13, 1978
Today we worked on an area designated as a cemetery. Forced by the circumstances, such an area must also be prepared. It will be in a beautiful place at the foot of the rock as you enter the monastery on the left, outside the gate.

Saturday November 18, 1978
This week I received in print the *Life of Saint Anthony*[37] from Finland, the first of the texts I translated. It gave me new enthusiasm. The Friends of Valamo Association does not want me to give up the translation work. Nowadays I translate in the evenings in my spare time, so that I can pay off my student loan paid by the association.

Feast of the Entrance into the Temple of Our Most Holy Lady the Theotokos and Ever-Virgin Mary, Tuesday November 21, 1978
It would be wonderful to die right now. It is early morning after an all-night vigil. It is as if the skies are opening up in these vigils. I do not want to go back from here, but one must continue this daily ascesis.

Wednesday December 20, 1978
Glory to You, God, we have come to the evening, and the day has passed peacefully without a guilty conscience. I often think like this in the evening with a grateful mind. I do not know—perhaps I take things even too brightly and should weep more over this sinful state. In their foundation, these two attitudes—of gratefulness to God for guiding the peace of my soul, and the knowledge of one's own weakness—are not contradictory.

Sunday December 31, 1978
I was about to begin the new year without Holy Communion. A few days ago, I told Abbess what I happened to say to Sister Theoktiste about Sister Eusevia, and she said that I cannot receive Holy Communion before Pascha. I did not take it too seriously, but when I asked for her blessing for tomorrow, she refused. I sat all day in my cell with awful thoughts circling me from everywhere. The refusal to grant Holy Communion simply knocked me to the floor. It is as if the medication is taken from the sick person with the statement, "Get well first, and then you will also get the

---

37. Athanasios Suuri, *Antonios Suuren elämä* (Valamon Ystävät ry., 1978).

medicine." But to my surprise, Abbess asked me to go to her after Vespers and said, "Go to the church and pray half an hour in front of the Mother of God, so that you will not behave like that a second time . . . " I went, prayed with tears, tired from the battles of the day, and after that Mother Abbess gave me permission to approach the Holy Sacrament tomorrow.

Friday January 12, 1979
In children's stories it is told that someone was looking for a happy person. They would have found one today here on Mount Koziakas. Sometimes I feel right-out ashamed to be so happy in the midst of all the misery and suffering in the world. But this happiness does not depend on the state of this world.

Irinja Nikkanen wrote that Professor Zilliacus had reviewed my translations and found them reliable. Mother Abbess urged me to write today when I asked her for some work.

Sunday January 14, 1979
Today I was given a new task: to teach English to the girls three times a week. I am happy to teach the girls if it is of some use to them.

Saturday February 3, 1979
Being a teacher is hard for me. It is a question of English, but at the same time, one way or another, I have to take responsibility for these souls. And I am very afraid of that. For myself, I would rather hide in the depths of the earth . . . There is nothing more difficult and consuming than guiding souls. I would not want to take responsibility for anyone for any cost. But sometimes you have to teach, to pass on worldly or spiritual knowledge. If no one had bothered to teach me anything, what would have happened? This thought obliges me to work with the girls.

Wednesday February 14, 1979
We began our daily work in the hunting area. The distinguished board had planned that I would plant trees and dig with others for seven hours and then rush to the monastery to give the girls an English lesson. According to Abbess, teaching English is nothing more than a light conversation. I remarked about this plan, that it would not quite work that way. They gave in, but the prevailing opinion must be that I found a good excuse from English to be lazy! Anyway, from this intellectual work, writing and teaching, which are the most strenuous for me, I might one day

receive some kind of martyr's wreath. For the others, you see, they are not considered work at all.

Saturday March 31, 1979
I received a letter from Father Archbishop. He told me that he had been five days in the hospital before the Clergy-Laity Assembly. Then there was a sentence that made my tender heart bleed: "When I think of my heart, I always remember with gratitude how well you helped me to recover." I was moved to tears. Does he really miss me?

It could be that this was written as a kind of consolation, because then came the announcement that the translations I had made of the teachings of Abba Dorotheos could not be used—poor quality. Kyllikki Härkäpää has made a new translation of them into Finnish.

Saturday April 14, 1979
Personally, I am in a state where I would not like to see people at all, but who would ask that of a sister in a cenobitic monastery . . . [38]

Most of all, I would like to get some kind of heavenly "hint" that I am on the path and in the place where I should be. I miss being able to think, to pour out my heart before the Lord in peace. I seem to be entering the middle-age of the spiritual life, which is hard work without many consolations, without the enthusiasm of the beginning, and without the serenity of the end (hopefully I will meet that too!), the time when God challenges and then withdraws into hiding. Then you have to be, above all, firm and courageous. There are many who have never survived this time period. Sometimes I am overcome by the fear that I will sink into indifference, into routine, so that I will never achieve what I want.

Maybe my life will be spent without a major achievement, without inner formation, because my person is a little lazy and wants to get everything complete and ready from God.

Holy Wednesday, April 18, 1979
I thought about my own soul, which receives the dew of grace, but exactly measured, so that it can live and get by, but without anything extra. Perhaps one day the Lord will send a superfluous rain to make it blossom and sprout, to open the streams of living water.

---

38. A monastic tradition that stresses community life rather than being a hermit.

In Holy Communion on Palm Sunday my soul calmed down and began to lighten. Often in these last days, I have thought of the Lord's commandment—it is a commandment, not only a guideline: "So do not worry about tomorrow, for tomorrow will bring worries of its own. Today's trouble is enough for today."[39] I am gladly one of those "fools" who close their eyes and with a trusting heart, entrust themselves and others to the care of God.

The Lord's Pascha, Sunday April 22, 1979
Χριστός ανέστη, χαρά μεγάλη! Christ is risen, great joy!
   Water is pouring down from the sky, but still, everything is full of light, the sky, and the earth, and those under the earth. Christ is risen from the dead! There is no greater joy on the earth or in heaven. Especially when it is proclaimed by Christ himself, who has entered our hearts in the Holy Communion. These days it is hard for me to pray, "Lord, have mercy!" because it is so clear that He has already given us mercy.

Feast of the Lifegiving Spring, Friday April 27, 1979
At the meal I asked the Metropolitan [Stephen] to explain these words: "The wind blows wherever it pleases. You hear its sound, but you cannot tell where it comes from or where it is going. So it is with everyone born of the Spirit."[40] That segment in the Bible has always fascinated me. Wind is the symbol of the Holy Spirit, its sound is the clearly felt impacts of the Holy Spirit on us, Metropolitan explained. But something deeper is hidden in those words, said the Metropolitan, but did not say in more detail what. To the extent that a person becomes familiar with the Holy Spirit, he begins to understand how "the wind blows where it wills."

Tuesday May 22, 1979
Lately, at my prayer altar I often think that God wants me to remain insignificant and unknown after all. And this thought ignites a sweetness in my mind. What could be sweeter and safer than to be able to be small, insignificant, and unknown one's whole life to people, but to be close to Christ the Savior?

---

39. Matt. 6:34 (New Revised Standard Version).
40. John 3:8 (New Revised Standard Version).

Friday August 17, 1979
The Finns are somehow cold people. I wrote—childishly enough—to the Archbishop already when I was in Trikala, explaining the "story of my appendix." It is somehow part of human nature to want to share such experiences by telling others.[41] Subconsciously, of course, I expected the Archbishop to write me and wish me good recovery, ask how I was doing, etc. But I have heard nothing. It does not make me particularly sad—we monks and nuns are a little strange even in the way that we feel a kind of secret happiness when people neglect us. But in any case, a little is needed to lighten another person's mind.

Friday September 28, 1979
"Ask, and it will be given to you; seek, and you will find; knock, and the door will be opened to you." This evening, I read these words from the Gospel, which I first read upstairs at Mäntyniemi when I was an eleven-twelve-year-old girl, and in whose promises I then decided to believe. I am filled with joyful amazement when I see God's answers to the one who asks, seeks, and knocks: Orthodoxy, monastic life, guidance to this dear monastery after so many years of longing. Imagine that I really am and have already been in Bytouma for over six years!

Tuesday October 9, 1979
Be that as it may, it is very difficult for the modern-day nun to follow Hesychastic tradition . . . Today I was officially asked if I would like to be a driver. I said yes because there was no other alternative, and Mother Abbess had earlier warned me privately not to refuse.

Saturday December 15, 1979
The churchwarden, kept awake by the great responsibility, has happily completed her assignment. Yesterday I served alone at the altar for the first time, and today for the second time. I have learned a lot during the week; Sister Dorothea was bedridden for two days with the flu and did not participate much in these tasks, except to bake the church bread. I thank you, Mother of God, that you helped me with these tasks and that all went without any incident. The moments at the altar when the gifts are lifted up are festive.

---

41. Kristoduli had her appendix removed in July.

PART II: IN BYTOUMA MONASTERY

Thursday January 10, 1980
Today I received Holy Communion, and I thought, how a monk and a nun must completely stop expecting joy from external events and only pay attention to the inner life, inner joy or sorrow. I have been freed from the expectation that fills the lives of many people from beginning to end: I wish something joyful would happen! I derive joy from inner events—and there is plenty of that.

Monday January 14, 1980
I always feel secure when the second antiphon is sung in church, and I remember the words, "God loves the proselyte."[42] I am in the same position as were the proselytes once upon a time in Israel; in other words, the factor that unites me with others is religion, not nationality, and in many ways I am defenseless. But what could be safer than to know that God Himself has taken my things under His protection, so that instead of people, God Himself is on the side of the proselyte.

Sunday February 3, 1980
I am still living with the car crisis. Tomorrow we will go to Trikala and Kalambaka again in connection with those matters. I have not yet been able to fully fit the car into my internal patterns.

Tuesday February 5, 1980
Yesterday, together with Sister Eusevia, we got the papers in order, rushed to the monastery to gather various things, and then Sister Fevronia and I went back to Trikala again that same evening. And now we are students in a driving school! This morning, we had our first lesson. I felt like someone repeating a grade, because almost everything was more or less familiar.

Friday February 22, 1980
The driver's license has been passed happily. Yesterday I answered questions about traffic regulations, and today was the driving test. In front of me was a rather young woman taking the test. Right at the beginning she was taken up a hill, where she stopped, and two inspectors urged her to make a hill start. The rest of us followed her in another car. Poor Mrs. Eleni made a few futile attempts: the car did not move an inch, or rather it

---

42. Deut. 4:18 (New Revised Standard Version).

slid backwards. That was the end of her attempt, and I was next. I moved from one car to the test car. Hill start has always been one of my best skills, and I got the car moving on the first try. I drove a little on the small roads, stopped in front of a stop sign, and finally backed up between two parked cars. The inspector asked me a few questions and said that it was fine. Next week I will get my driver's license, and the responsible job of driving the monastery car will begin.

Sunday March 2, 1980
The soul rests here in the monastery. It is hard to watch the hustle and bustle of the world. It also makes one feel pity. People are busy with and worried about material and temporal things; there is hardly any time for eternal things. Envy and all kinds of petty anger reign.

The first stylized chapter of the Philokalia was waiting in the monastery. The stylization was very thorough. In some places you can hardly see the original text. Next week, the review of how well the stylists have succeeded in their work will begin.

Thursday March 6, 1980
Today I had the adventure of my life. I would rather not remember it at all. We went to Trikala with our car, Sisters Dorothea, Macaria, and Kostala, one of the schoolgirls. Everything went well, although it started to rain in Trikala. When we left there at about 2 pm, Fotula Salma remarked, "Oh yes, Abbess called and said that you have to leave quickly, because it is snowing up there." My face turned pale, but I thought it was just a question of melting snow crystals. That terrible road is treacherous even in normal weather, let alone in snow. We struggled up, I made it through a dangerous curve. The snow was getting thicker, the car felt like it was slipping. With tears in my eyes, I tried to move forward. In a bend above the olive grove, trying to avoid the potholes, I landed on the rocks, and, bang, a big stone hit the car under the engine. Of course, I stopped. We went down to see what had happened. I moved the car back, and the sisters dug the stone out. I tried to drive forward. The wheels were spinning. The sisters threw branches under the wheels, and that is how we solved the problem. To continue the trip turned out to be impossible, there was even more snow. We decided to put chains on the tires. But I had never seen it done before. One way or another, crawling around the car, we got the chains on. Then we drove on. There was a strange knocking noise, and I asked the sisters to see how the chains were doing. The other one had

opened and was wrapped around the tire. Once again, I stretched myself out on the snow under the car, and together we tried to free it. Then came Kir-Lefteris Alekos, who had been sent from the monastery to investigate things. Rarely have I been so happy to see someone. In any case, we made it up, and the car hopefully did not suffer too much damage.

Sister Kristoduli in Bytouma courtyard.

Saturday March 29, 1980
Life has been pretty car-dominated this week. I have gone down to Trikala four times and will go again tomorrow. Now we are getting Sister Fevronia trained, so I went down again today and will go again tomorrow. A driving instructor we know is coming with us. He was very pleased with my driving; I did not know before that I had any skills in this area.

Sunday of the Holy Fathers, May 18, 1980
Here in the monastery, I am trying to gather myself for that great test of strength (the trip to Finland). It is true that even though it can be good for the sake of change to go somewhere, the soul is empty outside the

monastery. You must talk a lot, hear different things, there is no opportunity for silence in solitude; the service life of the church is disrupted. In the coming week there will be work in the garden and the opportunity to pray in nature.

Feast of the Holy Spirit, Monday May 26, 1980
A kind of restlessness begins to overtake me more and more as the departure for Finland approaches. My whole state of being is less and less spiritual: I do not stop to pray, my thoughts are scattered, my nerves are tense, and I want to argue with everyone. I eat more than usual . . . If something positive happens in Finland, it must be the work of God's grace, not of my insignificance.

Saturday May 31, 1980, in Helsinki
Matti Jeskanen[43] is coming on Monday, but we already started with Irinja to browse through the translations. There will be a lot of work, really a lot; all extra appointments must be eliminated.

Monday June 2, 1980, in Helsinki
Today has been a hard-working day. Matti Jeskanen arrived in Helsinki, and we slogged for fourteen hours on the Philokalia in the Valamo Information Office. Matti is smart and it is really productive to work with him. Such will be the days in the program until Friday.

Thursday June 5, 1980, in Helsinki
The pace of work remains intense. We spend more than twelve hours in the Valamo Information Office . . . Eyes are tired, back and feet ache. But that is OK, the main thing is the joy of the work. The assignment is progressing nicely. The strength is there, thank God, as long as there is enough time. The collaboration with Matti ends tomorrow for the time being, and there is still a lot of text left. We have only studied Mark the Ascetic together so far, and there indeed was a lot to study in it. We are hoping that the other texts will be a bit easier.

Sunday June 8, 1980, in Kuopio
I met Father Archbishop. I went to see him at 7 pm. When the door opened, another guest, a young man, was leaving. Father Archbishop was

---

43. Master of Arts Matti Jeskanen was the main editor and curator of the text of the Philokalia for most of the translation project.

standing behind him. "Well!" he said, as he was giving his blessing and looked at me, and I looked at him. He has not changed at all, except that his hair has become a little lighter. We sat in the living room, and the Archbishop asked many things, told of his recent travels. The Archbishop looked at me in a very lovely way when I said how great a joy it is for a person to be able to live out what he feels is his vocation.

There was also talk about the autocephaly question. The Archbishop said that everything would be very easy, if there was not one bishop who is opposed. And his voice sounded tired.

Thursday June 12, 1980, in Kuopio
The evening was already approaching when there was a knock at my door.[44] And who was at the door but the Archbishop. He invited me to share a meal with him in his apartment. We had cabbage soup and bean stew—the true national food of Greece. And again, we talked about many things: The situation in Africa, alternate ways of translating different terms. The Archbishop showed me pictures of monasteries he had visited in America. He walked me back through the corridors. I began to feel much better, although the Archbishop made me write in his guestbook and gave me some small gifts, which could mean that he will not invite me there again. But never mind—this time he did invite me, and "God remembered me"[45] by his mediation.

Sunday June 22, 1980, in Kuopio
We have come this far. Last Monday Irinja and Matti came back, and we continued to work hard. Life became brighter when other people also came. We visited the Purmonens and met with Bishop Alexis[46] and Father Veikko almost every day. Despite all the hard work, progress was slow. There were still sixty sheets to be mailed. Irinja and Matti left on Thursday evening. That same day we were at the Archbishop's for afternoon coffee. He said that in Russia, when the Philokalia was translated, the most experienced monastery elders were invited to explain the most difficult parts. But we do not have such experienced elders. "You have become quite a Greek," the Archbishop blurted out at one point. It felt

---

44. Kristoduli stayed in the main building of the church in Kuopio, in the facilities of the theological seminary.
45. Ps. 106:4 (New Revised Standard Version).
46. The Assistant Bishop of Joensuu from 1980 to 1984.

really good to have someone to scold me a little . . . it felt like home, like the monastery.

Monday June 23, 1980, in Kuopio
I was with His Eminence Archbishop Paul this evening—maybe for the last time, perhaps more for the last time than I could comprehend. I did not really realize that it might have been the last time, and nothing was said to indicate that. I brought him a translation of a letter and thought I would just leave it at the door because it was already 8 pm. But the Archbishop asked me in, sat behind his desk, and asked me to sit across from him. I told the Archbishop about my difficulty, not having as deep a repentance as I should, and asked him to pray for that for me. "Is it possible to be both happy and sorrowful at the same time?" I asked. "Yes, indeed it is possible," said the Archbishop to that. I also told him that this trip to Finland has humiliated me in some way; I do not feel anything close to what I felt in the monastery. "The Fathers do say that no one returns to the monastery the same as he left it," said Father Archbishop to that. "It is good for the one who never needs to leave the monastery." At that moment I sensed that in some way I heard the voice of God this evening.

Thursday June 26, 1980, in Kuopio
It was quite a farewell visit with Father Archbishop. I asked him when he would come to Greece, but he said that there were no plans for that. "This may be the last time I meet You," I said. I thought that we had to be clear about things. "Yes, it could be," the Archbishop said to that. "The thought of dying for us monks and nuns should not be repulsive in any way," I said, "although it has its own wistfulness. I hope you will write a letter for me to receive after Your death." "It seems so vain to me to make such an issue of one's own death," said Father Archbishop. "I guess so," I said, "but you also need to think of those who are left behind . . . "

"By the way, I feel," said the Archbishop, "that the last book[47] is written as if I already were deceased. There is that type of vain adorations in it." "You never talk badly about the dead," I said, and we had a heartfelt laugh.

---

47. Isä Kristuksessa. Arkkipiispa Paavalin juhlakirja 28.8.1979. OPL (Ortodoksisten Pappien Liitto) ja Valamon luostari 1979. *Father in Christ*. A festschrift in honor of Archbishop Paul 8.28.1979. Union of Orthodox Priests and Valamo Monastery 1979 (transl.).

Then he got up and went to his study. I got up also. He gave me a pendant with a crucifix. "I will give you this as a memory of your visit here," he said, and that gift went directly into my heart. "Please write sometime," he continued with a smile. "Yes, indeed, I will write two letters, and then, if I do not get a reply, I will not write again," I said, and the Archbishop smiled again. "Go with God," he said then, and I left.

Saturday August 16, 1980
The trip to Finland weighs heavily on the state of my soul. The formality, the indifference, the rigidity, the lack of caring and interest, the cold hearts . . . Until now, Finland was a kind of background support for my monastic struggle. I thought that somehow people would follow my phases with interest, think of me as one of their own, as their representative in the monastic life. But it is not so. I have been forgotten. What does the writing on the wall say? A real nun is happy when no one remembers or is interested in her.

Saturday October 11, 1980, in Bytouma
According to Irinja, part I of the Philokalia can be completed in December, according to the program. For the prayers of our Holy Fathers, this gigantic work will finally bear fruit. I am moved by the self-sacrifice of many in this work. First and foremost, of course, Irinja, but now Matti has again used one of his vacation weeks for this work. Then there are the background forces, volunteer proofreaders, fundraisers, etc. I am very satisfied with the text now that Matti has corrected it.

Tuesday October 21, 1980
The magnificent winter evenings have begun. We have Vespers early, and it leaves more time to pray and read in the cell. Then you feel like a real princess, the daughter of the Heavenly King! And the humble cell is like a palace that you would not change for anything. Prayer, and through prayer, hope. You only feel bad when your conscience blames you for something.

Sister Kristoduli in Bytouma.

Wednesday December 3, 1980[48]
I am thinking of Saint Kristoduli, who in her time was sitting this evening in a prison, waiting to be beheaded. She was also a human being like us. Hope for the time to come probably spurred her thoughts. We are fighting under the same flag. She glorified our name with her martyrdom, and now she prays for me so that I would not disgrace her name on my own ascetic racetrack. Holy Kristoduli, you brave fighter, pray for me!

Monday December 8, 1980
Today is the historic day when heating has been installed in all the cells. Thank You, most beloved Mother of God. You looked at us, who were cold. For me, too, the cold was the hardest physical challenge. This far, but not any further, so has our Lord seen to be good.

Christmas Eve, Wednesday December 24, 1980
This week I had to go down to Trikala several times, most recently today in the Christmas rush to get packages of yarn. I am also beginning to see my new cross. The car has made me an "important" person in the monastery, and I have to take care of various things. I myself try to approach this with an attitude of utmost obedience: what is entrusted to me to do, I do, and I avoid getting involved in anything else. However, I notice that this

---

48. Kristoduli was named after a martyr commemorated on December 4th.

state of affairs does not please everyone, and the reception when I come from Trikala becomes cooler and cooler. It is even difficult to find people to carry the shopping from the car. My mind has been embittered many times, but from now on I will take things differently. I will rejoice with this cross and thank God even for all the meanness I encounter.

Theophany, Tuesday January 6, 1981
Last night it snowed, and now the sun is shining, everything glows and radiates. I always wait for snowfall in the winter. In Finland I was used to snow-covered landscapes. In Finland, it is actually more beautiful in the winter than in the summer. Snow-covered tree branches, frosted birch trees when the sunset colors the sky reddish. Those are the most beautiful memories of those landscapes. Lonely skiing trips in childhood and early youth in the forests of Puijo have left permanent tracks in my soul. There in the silence of the snowy forests was formed a longing in the soul for something more beautiful than the life there could offer. There, without myself even knowing it, simmered the decision—or, in fact, one should not talk about a decision, because I cannot remember ever deciding to become a nun; rather, it was as a self-evident outcome, the natural end result of development—to become a nun.

Feast Day of Saint John the Baptist, Wednesday January 7, 1981
Life in the monastery can be very rich, if you want to make it so. There are plenty of opportunities to get closer to heaven.

Wednesday January 21, 1981
I am mainly translating, i.e., reviewing the translations of Philokalia part II. It is heavy work that demands spiritual strength. Luckily it is possible to shovel snow and do other things to get a break.

Saturday January 31, 1981
When you learn to know your own weaknesses, you also become kinder to others, and as you want to be forgiven, you also forgive others.

Lately we have been holding services regularly in the dining room. The moment of the hexapsalm is also very beautiful there. One candle casts a dim light, flames of the fire show through the cracks of the stove door, and you can hear a warming rattle. Mother Abbess or one of the sisters reads the hexapsalm with a steady voice, and we listen with our heads bowed to the floor. (That posture is not so much an expression of piety as a kind of resting moment, although it probably should not be!) Anyone who feels insecure in their life should be with us at Matins during the hexapsalm in our monastery.

Sunday February 22, 1981
In the monastery, a person becomes transparent. You get used to expressing your thoughts without hiding anything. You are worried about something, you do not like something, something confuses you—in a flash to Mother Abbess to tell her about the state of your soul. The parts of pretending and the ability to hide emotions, essential for the life in the world, disappear.

Friday February 27, 1981
My testament to the next generations of monastic brothers and sisters is: Learn to express your thoughts, and you will live in great peace.

Tuesday March 17, 1981
God led many gifted teachers along my path, for which I am very grateful. I remember them with warm feelings, from Aune Antikainen, my first primary school teacher, to Professor Zilliacus. Aune Antikainen and Senni Kuvaja, both of my devoted Christian primary school teachers, laid a strong foundation in my child's soul: absolute honesty and hunger for truth, respect, and love of God. Then came Vieno Määttänen, Raakel Muhonen, the enthusiastic history teacher Virtanen, and others; at university such true humanists as Zilliacus and Thesleff.[49] I am grateful to them all. I hope such teacher personalities will also be found for the children of today. A good teacher can do a lot.

Sunday March 22, 1981
Now, during the Great Lent, we stand in church for hours and hours. And it could be even more. There is a feeling that in the church we live the real life, and outside of it, life is less valuable. Sometimes one hears the question, "Aren't these long services tiring and boring to you?" To that, one can only smile. A human person is a liturgical being; in the worship of God, he finds a deep inner satisfaction.

Friday April 10, 1981
Philokalia I is finally published. A letter came from Irinja full of good news. On Palm Sunday in Finland, i.e., the day after tomorrow, Moleben

---

49. Holger Thesleff, professor of Greek Classics.

of Thanksgiving will be celebrated in Kuopio, Helsinki, and Valamo, for the Philokalia. The Archbishop has already been given a hand-set copy of the book at the annual meeting of the Friends of Valamo. In her speech, when handing over the copy, Irinja said, among other things, "Your own spiritual child has made it possible for us now to have the Philokalia."

Lazarus Saturday, April 18, 1981
The tired, very tired, but happy and content caretaker of the church hands over her task today to her successor. There were four liturgies during the week—two liturgies of the presanctified gifts, a Liturgy of Basil the Great, and a Liturgy of St. John Chrysostom, which meant that I received a varied formation. When you work as a caretaker of the church, you feel like a little servant of the Mother of God. Prayer, unfortunately, receives less attention, when the mind is always focused on candles and censers, processions, boiling water, and other practical tasks.

Philokalia I finally arrived. For the first time I am reading it with real understanding. Finally, you do not need to worry about the translation. For me the final result is quite good; I, for one, could not do more.

Friday May 1, 1981
The Feast of the Life-Giving Spring and "Vappu"[50] on the same day in 1981. Nature radiates in its summer splendor. In procession we went down to the Chapel of Panagia, singing as always. The cross led the way, relics came with us, the clergy, the monastics, and the people. I wish we would proceed like this altogether towards Paradise! The monastery was crowded with people, and until late in the evening, groups of people came, children with garlands of flowers on their heads, all looking joyful and content. And so passed this sunny day.

Saturday May 30, 1981
In general, the Philokalia has generated enthusiasm. In Kuopio there was a three-hour celebration in honor of its publication. Both the Archbishop and Bishop Alexis spoke there. Deep gratitude fills my mind.

Monday June 8, 1981
Why am I translating and writing this diary in Finnish, when I could just as well write it in Greek? I am writing it because someone in the land of a thousand lakes might benefit from my little experiences, and so that the

---

50. First of May celebration.

Finnish sphere of life would expand with another story. It is doubtful that another person there would have lived as a nun in a Greek monastery.

Friday June 19, 1981, running errands in Athens
What a restless life here in the big city! I understand very well why the fathers chose the desert. It is hard to see one's soul in all the noise and commotion, let alone focus on God in any way. Maybe someone can, but I certainly cannot. I wonder how God will judge these city dwellers whose lives are full of busyness and worry. If they ever get a chance to stop, they cannot take advantage of it—so accustomed are they to endless running, noise, and commotion.

Monday July 27, 1981
I received a letter from Father Archbishop. He is somehow lukewarm to the idea of me doing an interview with Suomen Kuvalehti. I have thought about it some more and have decided to refuse. I cannot open my soul to be examined by people's curious eyes—especially since most of them are full of suspicion and I would undoubtedly be misunderstood.

This letter from the Archbishop was, in a way, the first that mysteriously warmed my heart. In it he talks about himself and his health and in many ways tries to guide me to humility.

Sunday October 11, 1981
This week has been a real "crazy week." The last three days of it I spent mostly at the steering wheel of the car. I would like to get the power to be the witness of Christ when moving around in the world, and why not also in the monastery? But so far, I do not feel that I would have received power for it from on high. What remains is just to wait in the church and in the cell, that at some moment an ember of the Holy Spirit would burst into flames inside me. Before that, there is no reason to attempt deeds that override the mandate, if one can say that. One should not try to witness something of which there is no personal experience.

Thursday October 22, 1981
On Sunday I had an argument with Sister Eusevia. My mind felt heavy, but I could not bring myself to ask for forgiveness. But today I asked for forgiveness so that my own writings would not be a judgment on me. How can you advise others if you cannot fulfill what you write yourself? The

most important thing is the peace of conscience. And you get that peace when you become humble and put yourself in the lowest place of all.

Tuesday November 3, 1981
Having seen all kinds of things in my monastic life, I have learned that the only right way to be a monastic sister is to always be ready to accommodate the will of others; i.e., the will of God expressed through others. Let us leave the powerful of the world to their battle of wills. We little ones must trust that there is an all good and all mighty Will that in love guides our life. It is totally unfitting for us, who by entering the monastery have thrown ourselves on the invisible ones, to push our will to the forefront in other matters.

Saturday November 14, 1981
I have really dedicated myself to writing. I am waiting for Philokalia part II in English to compare my translation with it. Otherwise, more than half of the texts of Philokalia II are ready.

Friday November 27, 1981
After sunny weather we woke up to snow this morning, and by now in the evening the snowbanks have piled high. I am helping with the cows this week. I have been sloshing around in the snow with the wheelbarrow to empty the manure piles.

Thursday December 17, 1981
I was back in Trikala after a long while. Since we got the car, I have not even once spent such a long time—over a month—continuously, in the monastery. It was a real rest for my nerves to stay here. Sister Fevronia did the driving, but today it was my turn; we transported the schoolgirls to their vacation.

Saturday January 9, 1982
I like to think about heaven and heavenly life, how it will be. There we will be free from all the pains and obstacles that this earthly body of ours produces. And we will not have to resort to our limited ability to speak, but the beauty and richness of our inner world will be conveyed directly to God and to each other. There is no need to be afraid of misunderstanding, only love reigns.

Sunday March 14, 1982
In remembrance of Saint Gregory Palamas, I thought of spending this Sunday practicing inner prayer with "the mind in the heart." But our human plans are other than those of God's. Just as I was concentrating on this in church, two schoolgirls ran in panting. One of the girls had fainted, and I had to leave to give first aid, missing the canon of Saint Gregory. I felt sorry for the girls anyway, who had to stay indoors for days because of the bad weather, and after the liturgy I offered to take them for a walk in the mountains. Thus, the whole morning was spent. In the afternoon Metropolitan Alexios[51] came, and we cleaned herbs both for him and the sisterhood. Even amid these tasks, I tried to keep my inner concentration.

Friday April 2, 1982
Mother Abbess has used me as her "little brush" to paint souls, as Saint Therese would say. She gave me the task of talking to two people, one of the youngest and one of the oldest sisters. The poor paintbrush felt uncomfortable doing such tasks—she would rather paint her own soul in peace—but out of obedience and after much prayer, she tried to do her best. Perhaps God blessed the task.

Sister Kristoduli taking care of the chickens in Bytouma.

---

51. Metropolitan Alexios was the bishop of the diocese after October 1981.

Holy Friday, April 16, 1982
New kinds of temptations have started to bother me lately. The thought says: You have been in the monastery for almost ten years. You have not been able to see God, nor have you made any progress in the virtues. Do you really think that in the future you will have such an experience or make such progress? How many people have entered a monastery with high hopes and failed? Would you really be an exception? These thoughts do not tempt me to leave the monastery, but rather to abandon the great goal and live contentedly, let us say, at the fringes of closeness to God, without trying to get to the core. My answer is: Why, tempter, do you want me to look at those who have failed and not at those who have succeeded? There are many of them. They have pulled heaven down to earth already in their lifetime.

Let it be mentioned that I received Paschal greetings from Archbishop Paul, Metropolitan Leo, and Auxiliary Bishop Alexis. I cannot deny that sometimes I feel sad that the Archbishop has completely forgotten me and does not write here anymore. At the beginning of Great Lent, I wrote to him, asking for forgiveness if I had saddened him in any way with my writings to *Aamun Koitto*. But no reply, just the printed card. A profound and spiritually edifying correspondence could have developed between the Archbishop and me, if only he had wanted it. I will not write there either unless it is necessary.

Saturday May 15, 1982
The way I want my life to be for the benefit of my neighbors has crystallized more clearly in my mind. I would like to become a supporter of the doubters. The godless people have given up searching, but the doubters—those beloved doubters, who probably make up the majority of the population in civilized countries—are searching, they want to find, they would be ready to believe if, but . . . I would like to make a difference by removing the "ifs" and "buts," and I am beginning to feel that I would be ready to endure anything if it were necessary to further that goal.

Tuesday May 25, 1982
The job of the winter is finished: Today I sent the last part of proofread translations of Philokalia II to Irinja. My summer job will be to translate Father Cherubim's *Recollections of Mount Athos*.[52] I feel like a schoolgirl

---

52. Cherubim Karambelas, *Recollections of Mount Athos*, English and Ancient Greek Edition (Holy Cross Press, 1987). Sister Kristoduli translated this work from the original ancient Greek text into Finnish.

who has just started her summer vacation, even though the summer will bring physical strain for me. But never mind, as long as I am healthy. Thanks to a cold, I was able to finish the last pages of Abba Philemon, because Mother Abbess forbade me yesterday to participate in the common work. I seized the opportunity and finished that translation. Now I feel very well again.

Tuesday June 22, 1982
It has been such a busy time that I have not even been able to write. And yet, I have been severely accused of being lazy and doing nothing! Sometimes I have a moment to write a few lines, and that is viewed as the height of laziness. This is strange, because, after all, these assignments are paid for.

Sunday August 1, 1982
I will probably never forget this past week. I lived as if in a whirlwind. Thank God, the trip to Athens went well. We left S. in the hospital with Sister Dorothea and returned to Trikala on Tuesday. Before coming to the monastery, Sister Eusevia and I went to greet the Metropolitan. At that time, Archbishop Seraphim of all Greece came to see him. Sister Eusevia and I took his blessing and stayed to help with meal preparation. We returned to the monastery late in the evening. On Thursday we took the schoolgirls to the camp of Pyrra high in the mountains—a three-hour drive one way. At noon, I was getting ready to rest a little, when two older camp girls asked to talk to me. We discussed during the whole break. I even gave a talk there. On Friday I took Abbess back to the monastery of Saint Stephen. On Saturday, Kir-Vasilis from the village of Megara died, and we went to the funeral. Shocking sadness.

And the biggest news last: Last night the abbess of the Saint Stephen Monastery died. We went there in the morning, and I came back with the first carload in the afternoon. Now I have no more strength to write.

Sunday August 8, 1982
This week I received a letter from Archbishop Paul. He writes that he has become stronger and that it seems that the will of God is for him to continue in his responsibilities. Our Metropolitan Alexios is eager to invite him here. Somehow, I have a feeling that he will come one day.

Friday September 24, 1982
I wish we could find more drivers somewhere! This constant running in the world is wounding to one's inner life. Mother Abbess says that serving as a mule driver did not prevent Saint Theodora from being sanctified. I have not, however, planned to be sanctified in the monastery as a driver! In fact, I was thinking more about a hesychastic path. But for a sister of obedience, one's own plans do not count.

Tuesday November 30, 1982
In recent times, when I have been praying, I have felt the need to be silent and wait. In such quiet moments, the will of God can be heard in the little corners of the heart. Prayer is meant to be a conversation, not a monologue.

Friday December 17, 1982
A large thick envelope waited for me in my cell. It was from Father Archbishop, and it contained a wonderful book of icons, the text of which was in his handwriting. I had asked him to send it to me, but I assumed that it would be a small booklet without photos . . . Father Archbishop was quick to make such a sacrifice to gift me such a precious book. And the greatest joy was that with the book there were also a letter and a Christmas card. After Independence Day, the Archbishop always remembers me because he usually meets my parents at the Independence Ball at the Presidential Palace.

Thursday January 13, 1983
The longer I stay in the monastic life, the more clearly one single thing stands out before my eyes, the only thing that is worth a man's interest—God's kingdom, eternity. Oh, the terrible secret of death! If we cannot solve it and be sure that it is not the end of everything, then even the rest of life has no meaning. Only eternal life gives value and meaning to temporal life.

Saturday February 5, 1983
I am presently translating documents from the Ecumenical Patriarchate that the Archbishop sent me. Before that, I had time to start a little with the Philokalia. The Archbishop has sent me friendly letters. *Athoksen*

munkki isä Athanasios[53] has been published in Finland, and I also got a few copies of it here. *Neitsyt Marian puutarha*[54] has also been well received by the Friends of Valamo, and they will most likely publish it. Such literature interests people nowadays—interests while comfortably sitting in an armchair, but seldom arouses the desire for a practical experiment.

Friday March 18, 1983
A letter and new translations from Father Archbishop were waiting for me in the monastery. For once he has overdone it, if one can say so, and, contrary to his habit, he begins his letter: "Beloved Sister Kristoduli in Christ," which naturally warms my heart. With people who do not use exaggerations, such heartfelt expressions are all the more moving. May God grant that the love of Christ will truly inseparably unite the soul of that person who in solitude has fought and suffered—and won!—with my soul, the soul of a little nun.

Pentecost, Sunday June 26, 1983
This week I was in Thessalonica. We were Mother Abbess, Sisters Dorothea, Macaria, Justina, and me. We visited the Lydia sisters. On Wednesday we visited a large women's monastery, Souroti, which is very close to Thessalonica. Father Paisios from Mount Athos was visiting there at the same time. We have heard a lot about Father Paisios. He is one of the starets-fathers [elders], perhaps the best known here in Greece. He agreed to meet us in a hermit's hut above the other buildings of Souroti Monastery, where he lives when he visits. I think I will never forget the moment when his eyes met mine as we climbed up to the hut. Light, warmth, and joy flowed from his eyes into my soul. Lately I have been living in a spiritual drought, but now the gaze of grace has been cast into my soul.

Friday September 30, 1983
For the past two weeks we have had a Finnish lady from Kouvola with us. She was altogether a charming acquaintance, a crying and laughing Karelian. For the first time I had to practice spiritual guidance in a more serious way, even when I need it the most! And I saw different sides to it.

---

53. Published by the Friends of Valamo Association in 1982.

54. Published under the name of Jumalanäidin puutarha (the Garden of the Mother of God) by the Friends of Valamo Association in 1985.

I understand that helping others in their spiritual life is a difficult and heavy task. No wonder Mother Abbess sometimes seems to hide from us!

Wednesday October 19, 1983
This is a historic day for our monastery because today the last schoolgirls left. The school has been operating already for twenty years. I wish that the Mother of God, through this event, will lead us to an even deeper and more hesychastic monastic life.

Tuesday October 25, 1983
A great joy fills my mind when I realize that I too can belong to a group of humans whose goal in life is to approach the Only Reality. How many such souls there have been, and now even I, in my tentative attempts, am one of them. My Lord and my God, new things are mystically unfolding before my eyes. Yet I have begun to understand the beauty of this path more deeply.

Monday October 31, 1983
Father Paisi Velichkovsky's biography is an inspiring reading for me as he was indeed engaged in the same works as I. However, in one respect his work was easier than mine: The Slavic language is much closer to Greek than Finnish is.

I also began to think seriously about the fact that all those who have worked with the Philokalia so far are saints. The Greek Saint Nicodemos and Saint Makarios have even been officially canonized, while during the revolution in Russia there was probably not enough time to canonize the Russians, but, in any case, they—Father Paisi and Bishop Theophan—have the reputation of being holy.[55] I truly feel shy in such company. But it is wonderful to have such holy intercessors helping in the work. Through their prayers, may the Lord also help me so that I would not personally shame the holy group of translators and publishers of the Philokalia. And if we include the writers of the texts, the flock of the surrounding witnesses becomes truly great. How deeply grateful I must be that, in all my worthlessness, I may be involved in work like this.

---

55. Both were canonized in 1988.

Saturday November 12, 1983
The ten-year anniversary of the Friends of Valamo was celebrated last Saturday. I got a fresh description of it from my father. Father Archbishop had been there. According to my father, he was in rather bad shape. His time seems to be coming to an end—at least here on earth. In the depths of my heart, I wish that I could still meet him sometime. The Archbishop has been the "light on my path,"[56] although he will undoubtedly continue to be that even after his departure from here.

Sunday January 15, 1984
Last week I spent celebratory moments with the translations of Philokalia II. Half of it, already stylized, was sent from Finland. The magic wand of Matti Jeskanen & company had done miracles. One has to say, though, that sometimes they get enthused to be a bit too poetic, which can be expected. In any case, I am happy for the good outcome and feel that the work is on firm ground. Even I feel that I can manage things. With the permission of Mother Abbess, I approached Father Theoklitos from Mt. Athos by letter to ask for his opinion on some of the difficult sections. It of course brings more credibility to the translation.

Saturday February 18, 1984
We are already living the preparatory weeks of the Great Lent. All kinds of things have happened. Some time ago we were in Thessalonica for almost a week, the sisters at a dentist and I as a driver. Again, we went to the Monastery of Panorama for the Sunday liturgy.

It has been snowing this week. My day starts (after Matins of course) with shoveling snow at the chicken coop. There is almost a meter of snow already, and more is coming. The roads are of course cut off.

Forgiveness Sunday, March 4, 1984
I truly cannot say now whether I am far or near to God. I feel that I have no special requests for God for myself, and it is as if I am not praying. But on the other hand, I feel that He never leaves my mind.

And so it is, spread the sails, Kristoduli, the journey of Lent has begun. It is quite an interesting voyage. You can see how the enemy is trying with all his might to wreck it. The city of resurrection awaits on the other side of the open sea.

---

56. Ps. 119:105 (New Revised Standard Version).

Tuesday March 13, 1984
The life of a sister in obedience is full of unexpected adventures—it does not matter whether they are pleasant or unpleasant. I was sent to Thessalonica to take care of Sister J. No one knows how long she needs to stay in the hospital.

Saturday March 24, 1984
I spent one week in Thessalonica.

I want to throw myself before the Lord and just simply put myself and this whole world and all the people with their pains and worries under His protection. He loves all people much more than I do.

Holy Saturday, April 21, 1984
We have sailed through the sea of Lent again. This year's sailing turned out to be quite different from what I had expected—I sailed half of it in the sewage of a big city. How fortunate are we, who can live in the countryside amid pure nature!

Wednesday July 25, 1984
Today and yesterday we spent cleaning the monastery of the Great Meteora. We spent the night in the monastery of Saint Stephen. We had to clean the big church, two smaller churches, and a number of other spaces, all of which were in a condition that can be expected of a men's monastery. A surprising event happened yesterday; the prime minister of Holland visited the monastery with his family, who was on vacation. Father Athanasios invited me to be the interpreter, just as I was, in my working clothes. And so, I guided the very sympathetic, modest prime minister and his family around the Great Meteora. He said that he would be coming to Greece in the fall for an official visit, but then added with a slight sigh, "That is another matter."

The Transfiguration of Christ, Monday August 6, 1984
Last Tuesday, Metropolitan Alexios took the nuns of the diocese on a sailing trip along the coast of Mt. Athos. We were sixty nuns in all, eighteen from our monastery. Until the last minute, it was hard for me to believe that I could go. We were at sea for a total of six and a half hours. We saw the monasteries on the west coast. Holy relics from three monasteries were brought for us to venerate by prostration.

ARCHBISHOP PAUL'S VISIT TO BYTOUMA

Sunday August 26, 1984
I received a letter from the Archbishop. His plans have changed because he has been invited to Athens on November 19. His book *Miten Uskomme*[57] is being published in Greek. He told me that he has asked the Archbishop of Athens to include a visit here in his itinerary. If he has the strength and if the weather permits—both in the hands of God—he will certainly come.

Monday November 19, 1984
The atmosphere is getting thicker. Tomorrow is the day when my father and my shepherd [Archbishop Paul] will arrive in Trikala. Some of us will even go down to help the Metropolitan with the preparations. Self-evidently I will be among them. The Archbishop will come on an official visit with two deacons and the Ambassador of Finland, Eva-Christina Mäkeläinen. It is hardly likely that there will be an opportunity to speak with him alone. But between the Archbishop and me, words are hardly needed. The Archbishop will celebrate Vespers and the Liturgy in Trikala. On Wednesday he will go to the Korpovo Monastery, and on Thursday he will come here. It seems from everything that I will be with him from the beginning. May God give him strength. Already in advance I thank You for everything.

Tuesday November 20, 1984, in Trikala
Father Archbishop arrived.

Entrance of the Theotokos into the Temple, Wednesday November 21, 1984
Liturgy was something out of this world. I was in a state that is impossible to describe, as if away from this world. The humble white figure of the Archbishop, the Finnish deacons, all moved me deeply. Could I have ever imagined that my Archbishop would celebrate liturgy in Trikala!

---

57. *The Faith We Hold.*

Archbishop Paul in Bytouma, November 1984.

The deep spirit of prayer that surrounds the white-haired figure of the Archbishop has a strong effect on me. How grateful I can be to him!

Yesterday, after Vespers, there was an official reception attended by important people from Trikala. The Archbishop gave a wonderful little talk, which I translated into Greek.

Thursday November 22, 1984
The Archbishop arrived in the evening (in Bytouma). How can I repay the Lord for all His good deeds towards me? The Archbishop will stay here till Sunday.

Friday November 23, 1984
It was a wonderful sunny day. It was almost as if even the weather reflected the brightest of the bright atmospheres of this day. Ambassador Mäkeläinen left at noon. In the morning we went up the road, and in the afternoon we went to the Chapel of Panagia. In the evening, the Archbishop and the deacons shared a meal with the sisters, and the Archbishop gave them his gifts. To me he brought an icon of Christ. The Archbishop is the Archbishop, whom I knew when I was staying with

him. The official person, who sometimes has come to the fore, has completely disappeared. The sisters are also very enchanted with him.

Friday November 30, 1984
It has been a week since our pure and bright Archbishop sanctified this humble cell with his presence. There has been some time to digest the impressions. The Archbishop and I were both in our element here, and that is why this encounter left such a rare, sweet fragrance in the soul. My soul became calmer and stronger when I was near him. The Archbishop radiates a gentle, quiet light.

Thursday December 6, 1984
One thing that caught my attention about the Archbishop was the way he continuously tries to see the benefit for his flock in everything. I myself try to always take care of my own peace, which is not the right attitude. Every time I settle to pray, I try to give thanks for the great joy that the Archbishop's visit was for me. As fervently as I had prayed for it, as fervently I need to thank the Giver of all good things.

Friday December 28, 1984
It occurred to me that the only real dividing factor between people is sin. It separates us first from God and then from each other. All other separations are temporary; only sin can lead to eternal separation.

Saturday January 19, 1985
I especially turn to the Lord with the request that my inner world be quieted. Periodically you see that there is such a crowd of thoughts that there is no comparison. And the Lord in His goodness has taught me. Here, more than anywhere else, the word is true: "Unless the Lord builds the house, those who build it labor in vain."[58]

Thursday January 31, 1985
The days go by intensely with Philokalia II. From time to time the mind is overcome by a kind of supernatural joy at being able to serve in such work. I glance at the icon of Christ smiling, and it seems to me that He is smiling back. Today I finished going through the "On Love" sections. Before moving on to the "On Theology" sections of Saint Maximus, my mind was overcome with fatigue—as if with a bodily weakness—when

---

58. Ps. 127:1 (New Revised Standard Version).

I went through the thick pile of papers, which I knew contained many difficult problems, beginning with the headings. In the afternoon I got right into it—and look! Enthusiasm—and should I say, a kind of spirit to fight—returned. Already some sections with their problems have been solved. Saint Maximus, enlighten my mind!

Saturday February 9, 1985
Two kinds of awakenings are needed in the Finnish Orthodox Church: dogmatic and ascetic. In fact, they go hand in hand. You cannot think deeply about God—or see even the most minute reflection of the Uncreated Light—if your life is not in such an order that it is easy to see what a person considers most important. Simple life, ascetic life, is a springboard for higher truths. The Holy Trinity—Father, Son, and Holy Spirit.

There have really been terrible frosts in Finland. Nothing has been heard from the Archbishop. The attitude has to change. Had I already become quite demanding? I consider it my right to receive a letter from him. Now I must think that I do not deserve such a thing, and if I sometimes receive a letter, I can consider it an undeserved joy: God has also remembered me.

Forgiveness Sunday, February 24, 1985
This year during the Great Lent I want to think mostly about purity of the heart and all that is attached to it. Sometimes the whole human being with all its functions looks like an ugly phenomenon; human life in general, dull. But this must be the tempter's point of view. God has "in wisdom made them all."[59] Purity of heart undoubtedly leads you to see everything in the right light.

Wednesday March 20, 1985
Now I am just waiting for the book itself to come into my hands. I cannot remember when for the first time I heard the word *Philokalia*, but I do remember that at the very beginning of getting to know the church, perhaps even before actually joining, the Philokalia fascinated my mind. I envied the Russian speakers who had access to it, and I kept on sighing, "I wish I could get to know it too!" And now I can see to it that no Finn has to sigh like that anymore! Is that not a great reason to be thankful?

---

59. Ps. 104:24 (New Revised Standard Version).

Sunday March 24, 1985
How beautiful are Sundays and feast days in the monastery! In the morning there is a three-hour service that ends with the Divine Liturgy. Afterwards, I usually write letters. Then we have a festive meal and a daytime rest. On Sunday there is no hurry to get up, and we sleep longer than usual. Then I feed the chickens and walk outside, if the weather is nice. You can read and pray in peace. There is a quiet peace everywhere. A guest might come, and if I want, I can exchange a few words. Then follows a pious, short Vespers service, and then free time again to get closer to God in whatever way feels right at that moment.

Archbishop Paul celebrating liturgy in Bytouma, May 1985.

Thursday March 28, 1985
The first truly sunny and lovely spring day brought truly sunny and lovely news. The Archbishop wrote—finally! He is coming here on May 4th together with Mitro Repo. Oh, what joy! I cannot concentrate on translations at all after this news, so I will go and clean the chicken coop from an overgrown raspberry bush.

Saturday April 20, 1985
God is simple. How comforting, how peace-giving it is to think that behind all the diversity and complexity of life there is an infinite, radiant Simplicity. And it is to this simplicity we are also called.

Sunday May 5, 1985
It is really remarkable that people who have had such different phases of life as the Archbishop and I can have such a similar inner life. Of course, compared to the Archbishop, I am at the foot of the mountain—but of the same mountain.

Monday May 6, 1985
The Archbishop arrived happily a little before midnight and was in quite good form! He even talked to us in the church, thanking us for waiting awake like the wise virgins.[60]

Thursday May 9, 1985
Here we live as in paradise. This morning the Archbishop celebrated the liturgy together with Father Nicholas. And what a liturgy! Mitro knows Byzantine chant and chanted the whole liturgy. The Archbishop seems very satisfied with his stay here. I have a chance to talk with him alone in the afternoon when I take tea to his cell.

In the evening we walked along the riverbank. Glory to You, Lord, for these bright days. For both my life and Mitro's life, this time will surely remain a bright memory.

Sunday May 12, 1985
Today was yet another beautiful day. We descended to Trikala, the Archbishop, Mitro, and I, and three sisters. The Feast of Saint Vissarion, the main feast of the diocese, is celebrated on the Sunday of the Samaritan Woman. The Archbishop celebrated the liturgy and participated also in the litany. With my heart in my throat, I stood at the edge of the central square as he stood on a podium in the sunshine with a miter on his head. From the square he was driven by car back to the church.

---

60. See Matt. 25:1-13 (New Revised Standard Version).

Sunday May 19, 1985
Today the Archbishop participated in the celebration of the liturgy. There were many people in the church. He gave a sermon on how our life should be a journey from liturgy to liturgy. In the evening, we went down to the village of Paraskeva and had Vespers in the small remote church of Saint Nicholas, located in a beautiful natural setting. There, in the midst of the people, he visibly enjoyed his time, had loukoumi,[61] and drank water from a plastic cup. Much could be said about these paradise-like days.

Monday May 27, 1985
From the Archbishop's farewell address: "I have been a bishop already for thirty years, and I have never taken my official thirty-six-day vacation. Therefore, I thought, as the end of my term is approaching, to try for once what a summer vacation is like. The only other time I have spent in the way that my stay here has been, was in my youth, before the wars, in the Skete of Saint John.

"The first Abbot of Valamo, Father Chariton, said that a monk and a nun must protect their heart from attachments. It is very natural that the human heart tries to get attached to other people, but we came to the monastery to live a supernatural life. Our prayer cannot be pure if we are attached to anything. But it is also said that our duty is to love our neighbor. How is that possible when we should not be attached? It is possible in Jesus Christ. For Him we love and serve others."

THE DEATH OF ABBESS EUPHEMIA

Saturday June 22, 1985
Abbess has been a little ill lately.

Spiritual guidance is a difficult and deep thing. The goal is not to make the sister in obedience an obedient robot, but to show her the way that leads her to union with God. How wonderful it would be if I could get a spiritual guide who could work with this goal consciously before her eyes!

Thursday July 4, 1985
On Tuesday we went down to Trikala and Kalambaka, where I mailed the deacon's vestments ordered by the Archbishop. There was a small package

---

61. Turkish delights.

from him in the post office. It included a big bundle of photographs, an audio cassette of the midnight service, and a beautiful letter, which starts: "Thanking and praising God, we returned home from Greece . . . " The photographs were very lovely.

Friday July 12, 1985
It is true that in spite of everything, I am somehow surprisingly deeply rooted in Abbess, and the thought that she will be missing from here forever pains the depths of my heart. "I am only the scaffolding," Mother Abbess said a long time ago. Now when this scaffolding is being removed, the building feels as if it is swaying, but I think it will stay standing after all. The Great Construction Inspector has taken care of it; otherwise, He would not take away "the scaffolding" to be near Him.

Saturday August 10, 1985
As an intercessor, I am deeply involved in the suffering of others. This evening on the balcony, my heart was constricted: There are more and more difficult problems everywhere. Abbess is getting worse and worse. One should be transformed into a continuous cry that goes up to God day and night.

In Finland the Archbishop is battling with the difficult question of theological education. The responsibility undoubtedly weighs heavily on him; the Clergy-Laity Assembly meets in the coming week. He wakes up a couple of times at night to heart pain, his sight is weakening slowly but surely. Lord, please give the right solution![62]

Thursday August 22, 1985
I sit in my cell in complete silence with Irinja's letter on my lap. It gives a brief description of the Clergy-Laity Assembly meeting. The Archbishop was of the firm opinion that a functioning spiritual academy should be established under the leadership of the church. However, the Clergy-Laity Assembly decided that the education of the clergy would be organized as a part of the University of Joensuu. At the end of the meeting the Archbishop had refused to preside, and Metropolitan John continued as the chair. The Archbishop had added that he would not be the chairman of the Assembly when the matter is dealt with in the future. Perhaps the Archbishop sees this as a sign that he needed to serve as the Archbishop

---

62. The Clergy-Laity Assembly decided, against the wishes of the Archbishop, to move the clergy education from Kuopio to the University of Joensuu.

up to now, not any further. Already thirty years as a bishop, and even before that active in the church, showing the way to fulfill the will of God. Those who wanted it have accepted it. If he retires, he will have more time for us spiritual children near and far.

Monday September 23, 1985
One thing I wish: Whatever may happen to me in my life, I, until my last breath, would like to be able to live in a place where liturgies are often celebrated. I believe that the Divine Liturgy, and, as its climax, sharing the body and blood of Christ, is more than enough to comfort a person, whatever might happen to him or her.

Sunday September 29, 1985
I believe firmly that the work done by Archbishop Paul for the Orthodox Church in Finland is just beginning and will continue as long as the church exists.[63]

Monday October 7, 1985
Abbess Euphemia slept in the Lord at 11:45 am. I do not have the strength to write more now. I thank God that I was given the task to stay with her during her last night.

Wednesday October 9, 1985
Mother Abbess's funeral was yesterday. During the liturgy I had a vivid feeling of her presence, and it continues. It is as if she follows my life and my thoughts. Now the mystery of Kristoduli, which probably occupied her a lot, has been solved for her as well. Now she can see how much I loved her and how sad the events of the past years were, how often I had to suffer in vain. And I, for my part, have become convinced of the golden core in her heart. And so all is well between us, and there is no fear of new misunderstandings. Is that not so, Abbess?

Saturday November 2, 1985
Now I can think in peace. When I look around me, everything, even beautiful nature, cries out to me: Perishable! All of us people will be ground down in the teeth of death. I am overwhelmed with an even stronger desire to simplify the external side of life to the most essential and to focus

---

63. Here one can hear Sister Kristoduli's wish that Archbishop Paul would be canonized and that he would continue to be active even after his death.

on the eternal. The majority of people allow themselves to be betrayed in the most ridiculous way. Until their last breath they gather their strength trying to improve the conditions of this life. And this cannot even be called life! I do not want to be among those who, on their deathbed, realize the vanity of earthly matters. I am not saying that such things should not be reasonably taken care of. But the most important thing is not to attach one's heart to them, not to worry about them, because it is not worth it. Nothingness, futility, transience. It is a familiar saying that we are strangers on earth. But how many really understand it?

Thursday November 14, 1985
First and foremost, I should think about what God's plan for me is. When you feel like you are in the sphere of God's plan, you are happy and enjoy doing the tasks before you.

Saturday November 30, 1985
The will of God does not mean a dictatorship from above to which everyone should submit. What is meant is that everyone should find God's will within and be ready, with all willingness, to do it. In this way, God's will can be done in everyone's life, similarly as it happens in the heavens among the angelic forces.

Monday December 2, 1985
Fewer and fewer can understand the vision that the Archbishop has of Orthodoxy, a vision of pure-hearted people who, together with their pure-hearted bishop, are steadily advancing toward the eternal Light, Christ. But perhaps there are still some who keep in their hearts the Archbishop's "spark theology," a teaching that caring for the spark of grace and its kindling is the most important thing in Christian ascesis.

Thursday December 5, 1985
I had already begun to think that life was quite leisurely these days. There are no more "cold showers" with which Mother Abbess so generously rinsed me. But today I understood that new, much more difficult, and fancier temptations will begin. Those showers had their own purpose, and Mother Abbess must have seen things that I cannot see.

Friday December 6, 1985
The whole sisterhood is upside down. The Metropolitan came by and talked to those with whom he had not talked during his last visit, among others, me, and then in the end he invited the entire sisterhood and announced that on Sunday night we would have an all-night vigil, after which we would vote for a new abbess. Only those who have been ordained to little schema for at least three years will have the right to vote; i.e., nine people in our monastery. So far, he had not even whispered about such a thing. I immediately asked how this had been handled in the Saint Stephen Monastery, because I knew that everyone had voted there. According to hearsay, they had quickly drawn up an internal statute, had it approved by the Holy Synod, and acted accordingly. And the Holy Synod had "by mistake" approved an additional article giving the Rasophore nuns the right to vote as well. But the whole story is a farce.

Saturday December 14, 1985
This even quieter and more secluded life, which I have begun to practice now during the reign of the new abbess, fills my soul with peace and gives me the opportunity to see my own sins. How wonderful are these winter evenings in my own warm cell with the sound of the rain falling outside.

Christmas Eve, December 24, 1985
Today we have the Divine Liturgy of Saint Basil the Great. I wished that it would never end. In the Lamb of God we embrace the whole world in prayer. With pain born of love, we lift up to the Lord children and the elderly, monastics and married couples, the lost and heretics, the sick, the abandoned, the imprisoned—all, all, without forgetting anyone, to the Lord. With love we reach out to God for everyone. With love He bows down to us to return our love with love, because no one loves people more than He does. What could resist the sum of all this love!

Saturday December 28, 1985
I am beginning to become a very single-minded person. In fact, I am only interested in one thing: Eternal Life. For that, I have become a kind of fool: I have forgotten my knowledge, lost my interest in the events of this world. Eternal Life! I would like to get to know it and then, God willing, witness it to others.

Thursday January 16, 1986
It is pouring rain outside. I sit in my own beloved cell by the light of a table lamp. Tomorrow I am supposed to go to Athens. This time the whole idea is exceptionally repulsive to me. The daily liturgies continue in the monastery, but I must be in the noise of Athens for who knows how long. To begin with, I wish to get the car driven there safely. I do not want to go at all, but what can I do?

THOUGHTS BEFORE CHANGES— HOMELAND ON MY MIND

Friday February 7, 1986
Metropolitan Alexios has firmly decided to go to Finland next July, and he will take me with him as his interpreter. I am beginning to believe that it may come true.

Monday March 3, 1986
This morning, after Matins in my cell, I suddenly felt a kind of certainty of life beyond the other side of the grave beginning to develop within me. It is namely one thing to believe in it and another to feel it in one's being. Of course, I have believed it before. I know two people who have this certainty very clearly: one is the Archbishop, and the other is my father.

Forgiveness Sunday, March 16, 1986
If you want to practice complete silence, you must be completely detached from the things of this world, as if you had already crossed over to another world. This is what I want to try now. God and soul—soul and God. It is an encounter that can almost separate the soul from the body. Courage, Kristoduli. Perhaps this is too early for me, but, on the other hand, Father Confessor gave me his blessing willingly, so I should trust this blessing.

Clean Monday, March 17, 1986
The Lenten spring has begun. The absence of Mother Abbess is very much felt. I used to go to her on Clean Monday to get her blessing and ask for some words of guidance for Lent, and to share my plans with her.

Wednesday March 19, 1986
It is quite easy to close one's mouth, but to stop one's thoughts—that is another matter. But silence is also beneficial. It reduces external impressions and strengthens the inner life. One quiets down to hear what is flowing inside.

Thursday March 20, 1986
This evening the gospel text that was read in a way is the cornerstone of my life: "Ask, and it will be given to you; seek, and you will find; knock, and the door will be opened to you."[64] Much, very much has been given to me ever since those words first touched me deeply when I was thirteen years old. Therefore, I can trust that more will be opened to me until the end.

In the last few days, I have been thinking about the power of God in my prayer. What a great source of power is the sun, how much more powerful is its Creator! I have not only thought about it, but also felt it. It is a very serious thing to approach God and think that this limitless power is love at its core. In this sense, it is easy to understand that we also, as friends of God, become gods through mercy.

Saturday March 29, 1986
In Finland the people are preparing for the Paschal night service. It is probably the Archbishop's last Paschal Liturgy as an Archbishop in service. Many memories come to my mind. The Archbishop's house during Pascha: bright, peaceful joy; yellow daffodils on the table; and in the middle of it all, that radiant, holiness-and-humility-reflecting figure, my Archbishop. Everything in this world is temporary. Mother Abbess is gone, soon the Archbishop will leave also, and soon I will follow. There, in the other life, I wish I could sit among the Easter lilies at the feet of Father Archbishop in the light of Christ.

Tuesday May 6, 1986
In the nuclear power plant accident in Russia, two thousand people died immediately and about forty thousand got an overdose of radioactivity. And now the radioactive contamination has reached here in Greece. But nevertheless, my God, I believe that Your energy—the energy of love—is tremendously stronger than even atomic energy. And in the midst of all

---

64. Matt. 7:7 (New Revised Standard Version).

the horror, destruction, and pain, His is still the last word in the history of humankind. The prophecies of the Book of Revelation are beginning to come true, how the waters will become undrinkable, the earth will burn, and the sea will become poisonous.

Feast of the Lifegiving Spring, Friday May 9, 1986
The secret of Father John of Kronstadt begins gradually to become clear to me. With our own strength we cannot do anything. The secret of Father John was the daily celebration of the Holy Eucharist.

Thursday May 22, 1986
For my part, I am in a kind of wait-and-see state of mind. Up until now the basic idea of my activities has been to serve the Finnish Orthodox people with various writings. But now I have noticed that there is little hope of accomplishing anything substantial in this way. I do not know if God wants to use me in some other way, to give me a new point of view.

Sunday May 25, 1986
I began to sit on the balcony in the evenings under the starry sky. We humans fill our heads full of various small things, but with essential questions we stand as question marks all our lives. What do the starry skies contain, where does the material world end? What happens next? What is the fundamental question of it all? I look at the stars and feel both astonishment and bitterness: Am I doomed to keep on wondering all my life? . . . I and billions of other people, from generation to generation, are passing away from this life without getting an answer to the question of what part our globe in the universe has, and more specifically what our part, the part of the human beings endowed with consciousness, in the universe is; what this whole universe is. We are truly the only living beings in the finite infinity of the universe; it is no wonder that in the eyes of the Creator, a human soul is more worthy than the whole rest of the world.

It is obvious that outside this visible universe (or parallel to it) there must be another reality. It is what is called the world of God. Only from there can we get answers to these questions. Science gathers knowledge of details and adds to the wonder, but it cannot give the final answer. Oh, how I wish that before it is my time to leave this planet, I can get some kind of hint of that world of God, some kind of indication of what or what type is the answer to the problem of the universe. It is cruel to have to live one's whole life in the midst of a great mystery with no hope of getting it solved.

Friday June 6, 1986
Tomorrow the choir of the Holy Trinity Church in Helsinki is coming to Meteora, and they want to meet with me. I did not encourage them too much in these efforts—the leader of the trip called yesterday from Chalkidiki. But if the Metropolitan gives his blessing, I will go and meet with them in Meteora.

Later. All the necessary blessings have been obtained, and tomorrow I will lead forty Finns in Meteora and probably here as well. "Lord, do not let those who are waiting for You be disappointed in me." These words give me courage: "For my power is made perfect in weakness."[65] If God wills that those people will benefit spiritually from their visit here, He will organize it in one way or another.

Monday June 9, 1986
A letter from Father Archbishop finally arrived. He had written it in the hospital on May 5 and 7. According to Sister Maria's[66] description, he had suffered another serious heart episode on the 5th, which seems to explain why the letter was left unfinished and not completed until the 7th. His letter, on the one hand, had plans for the future, and, on the other, has a "Yes, if we still continue to be alive" feeling. Silent warmth sighs from the letter.

Day of the Holy Spirit, Monday June 23, 1986
I struggle with the problem of death. It seems to me that I see human life in all its nakedness and tragedy. Indeed, "we are sitting in the land of the shadow of death."[67] Realistically, there is little hope that messages from the other world will be received very often. Mother Abbess is gone, as is the schema nun Seraphima—both probably loved even the wretched me at least sometimes—but the silence is deep. It is reasonable that we people will be forgiven a lot just for the fact that we were made to live under this pressure of death—first to follow the death struggle of our loved ones, and then to go through this furnace ourselves. In Christ, things take on a slightly different color, but the pain of separation and the

---

65. 2 Cor. 12:9 (New Revised Standard Version).
66. Maria Iltola, later the abbess of Lintula Monastery.
67. Isaiah 9:2 (New Revised Standard Version).

event of death remain the same. I do believe, however, that the time will come when I will be experientially allowed to know the reality of resurrection—the one in which I now believe theoretically. Now I understand that the year-round greeting of Saint Seraphim, "Christ is risen!" not only on Pascha, was not only beautiful philosophy, but the conclusion of deep experiences.

Monday July 14, 1986
I looked at our monastery in the moonlight and thanked God for guiding me all the way from the North to these wonderful mountains, to the midst of the warm-hearted people. Maybe he will let me spend my whole life here. Now I am leaving for a long journey. I wonder what it will bring. You feel safe only when you believe that God is guiding your steps. You should be truly attached to only one thing: the will of God. If you do not place your life under God's protection, it will seem like a mixed bundle full of unconnected events. With the eyes of faith, things look different.

Thursday July 17, 1986, in Kuopio[68]
Contrary to the program, Father Archbishop himself met us at the airport. It was a warm, sunny day, and green Finland was in all its glory. Now I can sleep peacefully. I have reached the goal, to be close to the Archbishop.

Saturday July 19, 1986, in Kuopio
In a conversation with the Archbishop, he said that it will be hard to see his life's work destroyed—he meant the liturgical reforms; i.e., the return to the old practice, when the "secret" prayers will again be read in secret—if the successor is a person who does not value it. He said this after noting that the so-called presidential race, the competition to see who the next Archbishop will be, has already begun.

Monday July 21, 1986, in Kuopio
The Archbishop's reception followed. There Metropolitan Alexios was awarded the Commander's Badge of the Order of the Holy Lamb. I was given a book and a medal "because a monastic cannot really be awarded a badge of honor," as Father Archbishop said. The Archbishop asked me about my father's retirement and then said in his loud and magnificent

---

68. Metropolitan Alexios visited Finland July 17–27, 1986. Kristoduli accompanied him as an interpreter.

way, "I will remain in office until I die—to the joy of some, to the annoyance of others."

Saturday July 26, 1986, in Helsinki
Before coming to Finland I was of the opinion that the Archbishop should not be pressured to continue in his work, but seeing the situation now, I am of the view that he should continue to save the church. I mentioned this to him. "But there is a Chief Shepherd, who takes care of everything," uttered Father Archbishop quietly.

We stayed at Mitro's house for a long time. Finally, I said, "I think it is better to leave, it is almost eleven o'clock. And your program has been interrupted." "Well, that is nothing," said Father Archbishop; "it does not happen very often." And so he stayed standing at the entrance of Mitro's apartment. Who knows, maybe we will meet again in October. This matter must be left to God. Metropolitan Alexios says he believes that in Archbishop Paul, we have met one of the saints of our time.

Wednesday July 30, 1986, in Bytouma
What does it feel like to be close to a holy person? Now that I have experienced it personally, I can describe it. When you are close to a holy person, you feel that a light is lit in your heart, evil thoughts and emotions no longer bother you, all the good that is inside you becomes present. You feel deep gratitude to God and compassion for and willingness to help your neighbor. All in all, when you are near a holy person, you feel that you are an image of God.

Thursday July 31, 1986
One has returned to the daily struggle of monastic life, where often one can hardly stand up from fatigue, limbs ache, and even nerves are taut from the strain, and one feels like sinking into a void, as if one is the most worthless of all human beings, and can only cry out: "Lord, have mercy!" At the end of the day, it is precisely this hard struggle, both physical and spiritual, that is the workshop from which the soul will one day fly like the phoenix. It is there, being "toasted" by many temptations and pains, where our Savior addresses the soul.

Archbishop Paul and Sister Kristoduli at breakfast in Bytouma, May 1985.

Friday August 22, 1986
I received a very beautiful letter from Father Archbishop. He did not give me a specific answer, but somehow this letter consoled me a lot, although it also reflects that the situation of the church is getting more and more critical. "May our Savior and the Mother of God protect their church," the Archbishop writes. "The situation is now so critical that it is not possible to withdraw peacefully from everything, although the time has come to let go of everything." And then he adds in a touching way, "May God grant you a long life so that you will have time to grow and strengthen." On September 17, Sister Maria from Lintula is coming. We will certainly have very interesting conversations.

Of course, I replied to Father Archbishop's letter immediately—with a thick felt-tip pen while he could still see.

Wednesday August 27, 1986
I am just thinking that I can actually be very peaceful. I have promised to go and take care of the Archbishop, which would undoubtedly involve a lot of other work for the Orthodox Church in Finland. But if God sees that I am too immature for such a task, I must be content to continue my less demanding life here in the monastery. One should not push oneself anywhere, but rather should be more content, the less responsibility one has on one's shoulders.

Monday September 1, 1986
Again, a truly merciless wave of longing swept over me. At the evening meal, the sisters talked about the Archbishop. I remained silent on purpose, because I was afraid that if I mentioned him, I would begin to cry. I saved those tears for the cell. Mother Abbess has left, and the spiritual atmosphere of the monastery is getting more and more alien to me.

Feast of the Elevation of the Holy Cross, Sunday September 14, 1986
"Lord, with the thief make us worthy of your kingdom," we sing at the Feast of the Cross. Yes, Lord, together with the thief. You look deeply into our hearts. The value you place on our so-called good deeds is reflected in the fact that you appeared in paradise with a thief as your companion. And what a wonderful moment for him: After all the terrible sufferings of the cross, he could enter Paradise on the same evening with the Son of God. How different God's thoughts are from ours! What power true repentance has, which is inseparable from the humble endurance of punishments and trials.

Thursday September 18, 1986
I sit in my cell with the letters from the Archbishop and from Mitro on my lap, and I watch in deep, overwhelming silence the great acts of God. The Seminary will not be closed, and theological education will not be transferred to the University of Joensuu. Oh my God, thank you! Why is there no stronger word? Thank you, THANK YOU!

Friday October 10, 1986
In fact, I like very much this isolated life that I now lead. The Metropolitan accused me of "taking sisters for a confession," and in that connection

also forbade me to have anyone in my cell or to go to the cells of others. And so, my obedience task as a nurse came to an end. I did it gladly, but, on the other hand, I have nothing against not having such a responsibility and duty. Of course, I did not go to the cells of others in any capacity.

Wednesday October 15, 1986
The absence of the sisters (two sisters left the monastery) and above all the triumph of injustice that has occurred in connection with these things has filled my soul with a silent, impenetrable melancholy. Even heaven seems to be tightly closed. I would like to get a hold of the thread of life again and feel that God after all has a plan for me and that nothing happens by chance. I still live in hope that the sisters would come back after all.

Tuesday October 21, 1986
Yesterday came the newspaper clippings of the Clergy-Laity Assembly meeting. Ah, Father Archbishop, what You have to endure! Despite all the fuss and slander against the Archbishop, the fact remains that the Joensuu plan has at least been delayed, and we can be satisfied with that.

Monday November 3, 1986
We all stumble worthlessly toward Him, and in this endeavor, we should help each other. If I happen to be on a little firmer ground, I should try to reach out my hand to my brother or sister who has splashed into a mud puddle and is in danger of getting stuck there, so that he or she can do the same favor for me when my turn comes.

Friday November 14, 1986
Abbess suggested yesterday that we call Father Archbishop tonight to ask for a blessing for the Nativity Fast. It was easy to get through to Kuopio, and the coverage was very good. I asked how the Archbishop was. "Pretty good," he said. He had written to the Metropolitan that he would very much like to come here again. I mentioned it to him, but he said that it was "rather unlikely." The situation there had calmed down a bit, he said. My father had excelled by writing a small article to the *Kotimaa* magazine on the newspaper articles written against the Archbishop, which the Archbishop had forwarded to *Aamun Koitto*. Father Archbishop asked us to remember him in our prayers. Most likely, he was moved by this call.

Saturday November 15, 1986
Here I am again thinking and pondering. I have never particularly liked phone calls. They confront the person unprepared. And a phone call from here to Finland is like a sprint with a stopwatch ticking fast at your ear. With letters, it is different: Both the sender and the recipient can take their time to think about what they want to say.

Monday November 17, 1986
Lately I have been reading the letters of the apostles with a special joy. Many passages have touched me deeply. In the First Letter of the Apostle Peter, he encourages us to leave all worries to God and then still adds those sweet words that have been translated into Finnish as "hän pitää teistä huolen."[69] But actually, the meaning is "hän välittää teistä."[70] There is the answer to our eternal complaining: "Nobody cares about me." There is One who cares.

Wednesday November 26, 1986
Today was the big day when Philokalia II arrived. I am holding it in my hands, thinking of the years of work that went into this 300-page book. Work, the joy of work, challenges, prayers . . . And now it is ready. The Philokalia is at the halfway point. Something to be thankful for. Although, even after a quick browse through Philokalia II, you can see that there is a little bit of this and that that is not from me, but rather against instructions. For example, reason, will, and emotion have been smuggled in despite my resistance, which makes the text quite deficient compared to using the intellectual, desiring, and incensive powers of the soul instead. This has been noted in the footnotes, although it does not help the situation much. There are some other stupidities in the footnotes, but most likely it is so spiritually rich that in the end, these lapses will not bother the ordinary reader too much.

Feast Day of Saint Nicholas, Saturday December 6, 1986
Next week I will for the first time get to serve as the chief cook for my obedience. Because of the sisters who left, kitchen duties will be more frequent.

---

69. "He takes care of you."
70. "He cares about you."

Tuesday December 16, 1986
Kitchen duty went surprisingly well, although it took quite a bit of strength. So far this week, I have been "convalescing." I have not yet returned to my normal daily rhythm.

Yesterday was a historic day for our monastery because the cows were sold. Now we will focus more and more on the work indoors.

Friday December 19, 1986
Father Archbishop carries out his duties in an atmosphere of ridicule and contempt. Others who think like him have kept their mouths shut. The church is becoming a kind of cultural community. I do not want to know anyone but Christ, and even Him crucified!

Christmas Eve, Wednesday December 24, 1986
Father Archbishop sent his new book *Uskon pidot*[71] (*The Feast of Faith*), which is about the Divine Liturgy. I saw the manuscript in the summer, and there is a little of this and that also from our conversations. There is no doubt that the book is very necessary. I hope that Father Archbishop has also sent it to my father.

Tuesday December 30, 1986
Today, a bright idea came to my mind, quite forcefully, to translate Father John's[72] letters into Greek, and to have them published by our monastery. The abbess agreed, and I got right into it: The introduction and the first letter have been translated. My mind was excited to the extent that I began to wonder why. Father John must have something to do with it, although, on the other hand, I hear him say, "Do not get too excited!"

Thursday January 29, 1987
I received an extraordinary letter from the Archbishop. The central content was the plans for the church at the "skete" (his former apartment in Suokatu, where the "best place in the world" was the chapel, where he took me for confession). The large hall will be made into a church. In his letter of January 23, he writes: "This morning I received the certainty that the church needs to be dedicated to the memory of the Annunciation." It would be very interesting to know how he received this certainty . . .

---

71. Arkkipiispa Paavali, *Uskon Pidot* (WSOY, 1986); Archbishop Paul, *The Feast of Faith*, (St Vladimir's Seminary Press, 1997).

72. Saint John of Valamo.

Tuesday February 3, 1987
These quiet winter days are marvelous. I work away on the translations in my cell, get up periodically to prostrate before the icons, eat an apple or a mandarin that the miller Vlachoioannis generously brings us. Deep thoughts of the Holy Fathers, prayer. Gratitude fills my mind as I think about both the past and the future. What could separate us from the love of Christ?

Saturday February 14, 1987
It is pouring rain, and fog covers the surroundings. Even though I feel like I am at the bottom of a wave, it does not bother me too much, because I have learned from experience that the sun will shine again. Sometimes I even walk in the fog with hymns of praise rising from my heart, and it is as if even the fog itself is praising the glory of God, but this time it is not like that. I murmur to myself that I am bored all the time just living in faith, not in seeing. For years we have been searching and reaching for the other reality, the only real reality, but what have I found? These kinds of thoughts aim to weaken enthusiasm. On my own, I certainly would not have bothered to even wake up this morning, let alone to pray, but as a monastic, I obediently wandered to the church at 5 am, and there undoubtedly a few sighs of prayer emerged from my heart.

Sunday February 15, 1987
For the first time in my almost fourteen years of monastic life, I feel homesick for Finland. This can be interpreted as (a) a temptation from the Devil to disturb my life; or (b) a sign of God's guidance that I should move to Finland. Fortunately, I do not have to make decisions myself; others will do that.

Wednesday March 11, 1987
Suddenly it started to snow very heavily. I have never seen so much snow here. I trudged through the snow up to my waist to feed the chickens. A state of emergency was declared for the entire province of Trikala.

Friday March 13, 1987
Today a helicopter came to bring food for the sheep and goats. We watched from the balcony as it landed near the shepherd family's house. There was something very moving in it, to the point of tears. How we humans—this time those of us drowned in the snow—need each other.

Where else can we expect help but from other people? This is how God's help also reaches us most of the time.

There was a flood last night, when the ice in the frozen and damaged pipes melted. Some sisters worked until midnight in the attic, where the pipes run, to stop the flow of water. Part of the house is now without water.

Tuesday March 31, 1987
This eventful March is coming to an end. And April will begin with a bang: Tomorrow twelve of us will travel together with other nuns from the diocese to a demonstration[73] in Athens. It will undoubtedly be a day to remember for the rest of one's life—if one does not stay on that journey forever; anything is possible here in Greece.

Thursday April 9, 1987
I received a letter from the Archbishop today. It is somehow moving when he writes that this may be his last letter with his "own eyes." These days he has only one eye, which means he is almost blind. It is actually quite strange that we have to live in the two extremes of Europe. In other words, that a person has a truly related soul, with whom there is a deep understanding even without words, and that person lives on the other side of Europe. This is how God's providence has arranged it. May the Giver of Light give him the light of his eyes!

Holy Pascha, Sunday April 19, 1987
A radiant sunny day enhanced the joy of Pascha. It did occur to me, however, that the atmosphere of the Great Lent fits better for this life. We will be able to completely partake of Pascha only in the next world. Here we wander in repentance.

In the evening, I called the Archbishop. I tried the number many times, and we got the connection only after a prayer. "Χριστός ἀνέστη,"[74] Father Archbishop," I said in Greek. "Ἀληθῶς ἀνέστη," he replied. We both sounded very joyful. "Thank you for your letter. It was fun to read and gave a good picture of the situation there," said Father Archbishop. I had given my best in describing the demonstration in Athens; I thought that it would undoubtedly interest him. Of the eye operation he said that

---

73. The demonstration was against the new Church law dealing with the Church's land ownership.

74. "Christ is risen . . . Truly he is risen." This is the greeting during Easter season.

the professor affirmed that all had gone according to plan. Now he is gradually beginning to see something.

Friday May 22, 1987
We have just returned from a very colorful trip to Thessalonica. The deepest heavenly blue was the meeting with Father Paisios. On Tuesday evening we headed by car towards the monastery of Souroti. After a long wait, the sisters smuggled us past the people to meet Father Paisios in a dim room, where he was sitting in the corner on the bench. He stood up to greet us. This time I looked into his eyes, and he looked at us with a special, deep, searching look. From his words one piece of advice especially stuck in my mind: "Do not think evil thoughts." His own simple bright being sealed his words.

Saturday June 6, 1987
I thought with sadness that now "the years will begin to run, of which we say: I do not like them." But we should not give in to such earthly feelings of depression. When you look at things from a spiritual point of view, joy and hope will always remain, even in death. I also have to try to orient myself completely spiritually, to wipe away the cataract that this world has made to grow in my eyes, which prevents me from seeing the love of God. One must move to another, real, spiritual world. Only then can I endure when the bomb is dropped of Father Archbishop's departure from this life. After that, it would be my responsibility to carry on the legacy I have received from him, but I wonder if I have the strength for that . . .

Feast of the Holy Great Martyr George.

Wednesday July 1, 1987
The contact with Father Archbishop has a strange, beneficial effect. Although we did not say anything in particular on the phone, the confusion and chaotic atmosphere that had been inside me lately were gone. Silence landed in my thoughts, and prayer began to work.

Friday July 31, 1987
Today is a significant day in the history of the Orthodox Church in Finland: the last day of the service of Father Archbishop. This blessed time has lasted altogether twenty-seven years. Yesterday Mitro sent newspaper interviews with him. In them he speaks so beautifully, and in a heart-moving way, such that I shed tears. They vividly brought to mind the atmosphere that surrounds the Archbishop.

    I have kitchen duty. In addition to the monks, there are six to ten extra people to feed, workers and guests. Tomorrow I will sail with my last strength to the port of Saturday—on Sunday there will be another cook.

Saturday September 12, 1987
I finished the revision of Niketas Stethatos (texts of Philokalia III) stylized by Marjut.[75] We can be thankful for finishing that work without a blood vessel bursting in the brain. It is such a difficult text.

Tuesday September 15, 1987
I wrote to Father Archbishop that I, for my part, would be ready to come to his skete.[76] I also wrote to him about my thoughts on the matter, and the rest I will leave to his spiritual discernment. He knows me better than I know myself.

Wednesday September 16, 1987
I will not send that letter after all. It would be an exception to the principle of not taking one's life into one's own hands. I have made it known to Father Archbishop many times that I would be ready to come and help him. That is enough. If we start with the hypothesis that God exists, we must also take it into account in practice. Initiatives must come from Him. His will must be manifested in one way or another.

Tuesday September 29, 1987
Unfortunately, I am very far from seeing the image of God in everyone and thus loving him purely. Perhaps this kind of indifference is influenced—from a human point of view—by the fact that I do not live with the people of my own country. The thinking, the problems, the difficulties, as well as the joys of one's own people, can be understood with a completely different depth than those of foreign people.

Tuesday October 6, 1987
I have no one to turn to here in Greece. A very strange feeling of rootlessness; I am like a wanderer in the fog.

Saturday November 14, 1987
The Nativity fast begins. I have decided to rethink my philosophy of life a bit. Attempts to become a hermit did not really yield results, and now I am slowly changing in a more social direction. It is too early to reach for

---

75. Marjut Matveinen, later Sister Siluani, Monastery of Saint John the Baptist, Athens.

76. The Archbishop planned to establish a small sisterhood in connection with his Suokatu apartment.

the moon, and for the time being, it is better to struggle with things like denying my own will.

Saturday November 28, 1987
It is good to struggle in a monastery because one can go through different, even painful, states of the soul. There is no responsibility to help others. When doing active work in the church, a priest or teacher is in a difficult, even tragic situation if he feels God's grace leaving him.

Thursday December 3, 1987
These days I can especially identify with expressions such as "miserable" and "wretched" in liturgical texts. Many times a day, I throw myself into the will of God. Sometimes, however, I wonder if God has any "will" for me; in other words, perhaps the rest of my life will be spent in a daily routine without any special mission or progress in prayer—on the contrary, even greater regression and anxiety of unbelief.

Friday December 4, 1987
Today is my name day. For the occasion, the sisters made doughnut-like pastries fried in oil. The weather has become truly "barbaric"—perhaps the credit goes to Saint Barbara, whose feast day is also today. My internal landscapes suddenly began to clear. How much fun it would be if someone would call from Finland. It is in vain to even dream about it; hardly anyone would remember that it is my name day, because it is not on the calendar.

Independence Day, Sunday December 6, 1987
The rugged and powerful country of the North, Finland, is celebrating seventy years of independence. Lately, this country has become strangely beloved to me. I would not hesitate at all if I were given the chance to work for these seldom-spoken, serious people in the midst of great forests and lakes.

Tuesday December 8, 1987
I like to read articles about astronomy—whenever I happen to see one. When we pray, it is safe to remember to whom we turn: The One who created billions of stars, those mystical solar systems hurtling at a terrifying speed—where? So there is no point in presenting things that are not worthy of the great Creator, when He is listening even to us in the midst of those billions of stars.

Saturday December 12, 1987
How necessary it would be to have an elder to go to and to return with renewed enthusiasm. That is what we did when Abbess was alive and had her strength. I am sending out SOS signals in the spiritual universe in the hope that some saint, either still here on earth or a member of the rejoicing church, will hear them and come to my rescue.

Friday December 18, 1987
Something is finally happening. The phone rang, and there was a miracle indeed: Mitro was on the phone, then Father Archbishop, then Aunt Rauha, and finally Father Matti. The blessing of Rauha's house was in progress, and the whole group had gathered there. I was the only one missing.

My SOS signals were heard last Saturday. Even as I was sending them, I felt unexpectedly strongly that the Mother of God came to console me. There are such starry moments in the ascetic struggle. Then all suffering is forgotten. And now things began to happen even more concretely.

Thursday December 31, 1987
Once again, we have reached the last day of the year. I cannot really give an assessment of this past year. This is the first time here in the monastery that I have seriously begun to think about returning to Finland. Fortunately, it does not depend on me. The future—and perhaps already the near future—will show whether there is a divine plan behind it or not. I cannot wish for myself or anyone else that we would do anything but spend the coming year pleasing to God.

New Year's Day, Friday January 1, 1988
The peace and rest of the Nativity Feast was really needed because the week started with full speed: on Monday Eleftheria called from Thessalonica, and on Tuesday I paid a quick visit there. We went over some difficult passages in the translation of "Valamon vanhuksen kirjeet." I also had the opportunity to see the cover picture of the Greek edition, which is very impressive indeed. In the picture Father John is surrounded by church towers. If not next week, then the week after, the book should go to the printer and be published. I have added some additional facts and some quotes from Tito Colliander[77] in the foreword.

---

77. Finnish theologian.

Tuesday January 26, 1988
I notice that I have begun to use Finnish more and more in my private prayers. The words of the mother tongue touch the strings of the soul more deeply. Only the New Testament I always read in its original language—it loses in translation.

Thursday January 28, 1988
It seems that my mission is to be a kind of step that can help others to come closer to God through translations and perhaps letters, but who herself will always remain low. I have soon been fifteen years in the monastery, and what progress have I actually made? Prayer is as scattered as before except for a few moments—I am outright tired of the eternal churning of thoughts. Let us see what the reception will be like in eternity.

Saturday January 30, 1988
Even though this is already my fifteenth winter here, these spring days in January are still one great miracle to me. It is a great luxury for a Finn to sit down on green grass in the warmth of the sun in January. It is also rare here, although there are such "kingfisher" days in the middle of every winter.

Thursday February 4, 1988
Yesterday I received a very deeply moving letter from Father Archbishop. It began in a strange way: "Honored in Christ . . . " I felt like I was shrinking into nothingness. The Archbishop certainly has no reason to honor me. On the other hand, everyone is "Honored in Christ," even the least of us. The Archbishop spoke sparingly of his sorrows about the state of the church: the liturgical changes—his life's work—were immediately thrown out the window as technical details, the autonomy of the church is being systematically crushed. May God give him strength!

Sunday February 7, 1988
I spent today "walking with the Lord." Silent joy touched my heart in Holy Communion, and today I simply enjoyed the presence of my Savior without asking anything or worrying about anything.

    Tomorrow we will go to Thessalonica to get the Greek edition of the *Valamon vanhuksen kirjeet*. I believe we have Father John's blessing for our trip.

Saturday February 13, 1988
The book is now happily here, and a copy has been given to various people. Metropolitan Alexios said that it was "wonderful." There is life and warmth in the advice of Father John. I believe that if only the book becomes known here in Greece, it will become widely popular.

Lazarus Saturday, April 2, 1988
We have happily finished Lent—Holy Week is another matter. Festive enthusiasm begins to fill the mind. With the car full of nuns, we descended near the olive grove, where we will quarry porous stone for the exterior insulation of the church tower. In the car, the sisters sang at the top of their lungs: "By raising Lazarus from the dead before Your passion, You did confirm the universal resurrection . . . " and "Today the grace of the Holy Spirit has gathered us together . . . " They are so sweet, for sure the Mother of God herself was moved watching this monastery.

THE LAST MEETING AND THE DEATH OF THE ARCHBISHOP

Wednesday April 20, 1988, in Kuopio[78]
We were at the Archbishop's for the liturgy. Twice during the liturgy he had to go and rest. "I remembered the ancient times" when he was still leading the church, and tears began to flow. There were about ten people present. I hear more and more terrible stories about the present situation. Obviously, people want to lighten their hearts, but sometimes it overflows for me . . . no matter, it has to be suffered and endured.

Thursday April 21, 1988, in Kuopio
In my conversations with the Archbishop, I fully realized what I already knew: that God does not expect me to do anything here in Finland. I can continue my work in peace in my own cell, in my own world in Bytouma. Glory to You, Lord! I recognize the silent life as my own element. One can concentrate inwardly.

Friday April 29, 1988, in Kuopio
This was my last day in Kuopio, and today we perhaps had our last conversation, Father Archbishop and I. Now I have to preserve this balance

---

78. Kristoduli made a personal trip to Finland in April of 1988.

that was born in my relationship with the Archbishop during this visit. Otherwise, as Father Archbishop said in our conversations, the world will be judged according to the Gospel, and there is a reason to maintain balance in the Christian life; that is, to be oriented towards love of God and love of the human person.

**Last meeting between Sister Kristoduli and Archbishop Paul, April 1988.
The Chapel of the Annunciation, Kuopio.**

Thursday May 5, 1988
My mind is filled with an unfathomable peace. The trip to Finland indirectly gave me a solution to many things, and various worries no longer bother me. I feel myself to be free in a way. The scaffolding is gradually falling away, and I hope that the face of Christ will appear. I was looking for You, Lord, also in people.

Thursday May 12, 1988
Yesterday we paid a visit to the Monastery of Koson close to Karditsa. It was an altogether awful trip, at least from the point of view of the driver. The car broke, and the engine stopped frequently. At one point the car had to be pushed and whatever else. Miraculously we did finally arrive back at the monastery (Bytouma) at midnight with our coughing car, after we first had left the Metropolitan in Trikala, who enthusiastically sang throughout the trip.

Wednesday May 18, 1988
Perhaps the most important outcome of the trip to Finland has proved to be the further strengthening of the bonds of intercessory prayer. How many pray for me, a sinner! Lord, lead me to salvation for their prayers. How beautiful everything is: Leaning on the prayers of others, we wander towards the kingdom of heaven.

Saturday May 21, 1988
I received a letter from the Archbishop. He wrote about ecclesiastical matters, such as the closing of the Seminary now that clergy education has been moved to Joensuu. There were beautiful pictures of my trip to Finland in the letter. I will not give the Archbishop such a detailed account of my inner thoughts. I do not feel the need for it anymore . . . Besides, I realized that the Archbishop is weak and tired. There is no need to tire him. I will leave the relationship between him and me to God without thinking too much about it. He alone knows how deep it was or not, and whether there will be a continuation in the next life.

Friday June 3, 1988
Tomorrow the church choir of Kuopio will arrive. They will sing at Vespers in Trikala and spend the night here. On Sunday Father Matti will celebrate the liturgy here, and the choir will sing. Tomorrow I will also go to Trikala with the abbess and some other sisters. The choir singers need an interpreter. Thus, I will have to "perform" a lot next weekend, which does not appeal to me. The most important thing is that the choir members enjoy the trip and are spiritually refreshed. At least their reception is well prepared for both here and in Trikala.

Sunday June 5, 1988
The visit of the Kuopio choir was a great feast; both sides were satisfied. Glory to God for everything! Such visits make me even more aware of my responsibility before God—my responsibility to not waste my time in vain, but to spend it on really essential things, my responsibility to intercede for everyone...

Birth of John the Baptist, Friday June 24, 1988
It is just before 4 am. The all-night vigil of over six hours has just ended. As a child, I was always enchanted by the descriptions in children's stories of fairies walking along the moon bridge or some other ray of light. Now, however, I feel that this fairy tale theme has become true in my life. This way of living is such that sometimes I do feel like a fairy walking on a bridge of light.

Wednesday August 31, 1988
It is as if the inner connection between Father Archbishop and me has been cut. I wonder if it is a temporary interruption or a permanent condition? Was my last visit to Finland a kind of detachment encounter? As happened with Mother Abbess: Before her departure, I had separated from her inwardly. But in the next life I hope to have a connection with both of them.

Tuesday November 22, 1988
I have resigned myself to the fact that deep spiritual states are completely beyond my capacity, and I do not have the strength to strive for them. And even when I am not doing anything good, neither are raging passions bothering me. So, I live in a kind of lukewarm state. It is a kind of aimless drifting.

Saturday November 26, 1988
I am likely living in a phase of which Archimandrite Sophrony writes that God seems to be far behind the nebulae, and it seems as if prayers evaporate into a void; they are not heard or even considered. There is no sense of God caring for and feeding the soul, bowing down and examining one's needs. However, Father Sophrony writes, that these feelings are not true, that later, one can see how even during this time the loving care of God has followed one's steps.

Friday December 2, 1988
Mitro called tonight at 7:15 pm and said that the Archbishop died about fifteen minutes ago. Father Archbishop, from now on I place myself in your hands. You can see me and guide me from where you are now. Father Archbishop, now more than ever you are my shepherd.

Monday December 5, 1988, in New Valamo
Father Archbishop's coffin is closed; at night I go there and read the Gospel. Tomorrow the coffin will be opened, and I can see him. I am not really crying because Father Archbishop has gone to another world, but rather, because I have stayed here.

Finland's Independence Day, Tuesday December 6, 1988
At night I read the Gospel next to Father Archbishop's coffin from 2:30 to 3:30 am, and in the coming night I will read from 3 to 4 am. It is so cold in the old church that even the snow brought in on the shoes does not melt. The coffin is closed. At 1:30 pm there was a panihida,[79] and the coffin was opened. I looked at the cold hand of Father Archbishop that had also blessed me countless times.

After the funeral I will go to Kuopio, and Heidi[80] even nobly suggested that I could stay overnight at the Archbishop's apartment. My purpose is to go there and get the letters that Father Archbishop has kept. I have heard that such letters exist. This correspondence is not for the eyes of strangers.

Monday December 12, 1988, in Helsinki
This was my last night in Finland. Today I wrote a column in the name of my father to *Kotimaa* magazine. The title is, "Isä esipaimen on poissa,"[81] and it turned out really well. I am grateful that I was able to do this task. Tomorrow I will leave to go back to the monastery. I wonder if I will ever come back to Finland . . .

Monday December 19, 1988, in Bytouma
I listened to one of the two audiocassettes that Father Archbishop sent. They have now become unexpectedly valuable. At the end he talks very beautifully about death—he says he never calls it death—and expresses

---

79. Memorial service.
80. Heidi Vaalisto, the Archbishop's caretaker during his last years.
81. "Father Chief Shepherd is gone."

the wish that we would still meet, if not in this life, then in the next one. Not death, Father Archbishop! I truly felt a deep consolation today.

LONGING AND PONDERING IN THE EVERYDAY LIFE OF THE MONASTERY

Tuesday January 17, 1989
The days have been wonderful and sunny for most of the month of January. I go out every chance I get. Especially in the evenings, after the church bells ring, I jump up from my writing assignments and go out for half an hour. I climb up the meadow and run and jump around. The sun has already set, but still illuminates the mountain peaks in the distance. The brook is roaring full of water; from somewhere far away you can hear sheep bells.

Wednesday February 22, 1989
In the monastery, it is easy to see how much the changes in your mood originate from within. Here it is not so easy to blame or credit others. Others are not the cause of the bad mood, but they are often the target of venting.

Saturday March 4, 1989
Kitchen duty is happily over. The job of the head cook is a real torture, and only the thought that it lasts just one week gives strength. The work begins shortly after 6 am, during the day there is a break for a few hours, and then it is hectic until about 9 pm. I can usually go to church only in the morning.

Wednesday March 8, 1989
When you are internally left alone in this world, you can really see your weaknesses. All human support is missing. Oh, how much strength and warmth there is in the awareness that there is at least one person in the world who is following your phases with compassion and interest! I feel it now when there is no one.[82] I do not know how my life will continue. On my own initiative, I am not going to seek help from others unless someone is sent. Fortunately, I have this "kindergarten" here around me, which in a way keeps life organized, even though there is no opportunity

---

82. Because Archbishop Paul and Abbess Euphemia had died.

for deeper discussions. For such an immature person like me, it would be good to meet a mature person occasionally.

Saturday March 11, 1989
Be that as it may, the departure of Father Archbishop has deepened my life. I no longer have the feeling of drifting aimlessly. The goal is firmly anchored in the new life, in that new way of being, where they all are already, the first of whom was Christ Himself.

Saturday March 18, 1989
Today I had a thought that guided me towards concentration: The heart should be seen as a room with a door in the ceiling. There is no door for thoughts coming from the sides. If visitors enter that room, they all come from above.

Thursday March 23, 1989
I would like to learn two things: (1) to stay with the Jesus Prayer when I am doing physical work; and (2) to stay with the Jesus Prayer even when I have things to think about, so that the "other thinking" could not separate me from Him. That I could always keep the inner silence . . .

Holy Wednesday, April 26, 1989
The pace of work is getting faster and faster. I did not even have time to write notes. As such a constantly busy person, you feel a certain satisfaction, you feel that you are important, and you can put aside with "good conscience" what is most important: spiritual reflection and the struggle of prayer.

There are still fifty pages remaining of Gregory of Sinai. Three parcels have already been sent to Finland.

Holy Friday, April 28, 1989
The last few days I have been thinking that I no longer have anyone here on earth to share spiritual joys with. When there is sorrow, you can find people to console you—because everyone has more or less experienced sorrow. But few can understand spiritual joy.

The Great and Holy Pascha, Sunday April 30, 1989
I was watching people at the night vigil, children with ribbons in their hair, candles in their hands, joy and light! It is pointless to fight against

the joy of Pascha! There is no system that can erase Pascha from the life of Orthodox peoples. That has been observed even in the Soviet Union. "There is no one in the tomb!" cries Saint John Chrysostom enthusiastically—but a little prematurely. But now we are already living it: no one in the tombs, not even Father Archbishop. Glory to You, Christ, our hope, glory to You.

Gardening.

Tuesday May 9, 1989
I am working in the garden—it is in fact hard work, but very pleasant. These are the simple joys of human life: work in the midst of nature, after which food tastes wonderful and healthy fatigue gives a deep sleep. The mind is clear, free from complex circles. Why can't all people live happily and simply?

It seems that the experience of Pascha brought a firm and deep consolation to the longing for the Archbishop—and not only that, but the wounds in the soul begin to heal. The human person is fundamentally built strong! The somewhat cold saying that time heals is true. Not that a deceased loved one is forgotten, but the thorns of grief stop stinging. One must remain logical in one's faith: "Christ rose from the dead!"

Monday May 29, 1989
How much evil can a man do when he forsakes his conscience! Rough and cynical people are ready to stain even the most sacred and beautiful things with their filthy thoughts. Therefore, it is better to stay out of their reach.

Saturday June 17, 1989
I feel the need to lead an increasingly secluded life. I even plan to reduce my correspondence. Such a person, who immediately goes off the rails when her regular pace of life is disturbed, is not ready to help others—and we monastics are usually considered spiritual authorities. I am beginning to realize more and more clearly that God most certainly does not expect anything special from me.

The Feast Day of the Apostles Peter and Paul, Thursday June 29, 1989
Work—especially physical work—is gradually becoming like opium for me. It is nice to tinker in the garden. This tinkering also has its own spiritual coloration. I help the plants to grow, but the giver of growth is God. In my prayer life, a state that can be described with the words: "My soul waits for God in silence,"[83] is becoming more and more dear.

Friday July 14, 1989
Today I began to translate into Greek the latest book of Abbot Panteleimon, *Valamon Paterikon*, the Synaxarion of the fathers of Valamo. The last one in it is Father Archbishop. My heart is moved to be able to serve in such a task: to make the monks of Valamo known in the Greek-speaking world. If I cannot follow their example, I can at least share their experience with others. However, the work before me is great, and I have to do it in between gardening and translating the Philokalia. Saint Sergey and Saint Herman, please pray for us and for me, so that I can complete this beloved work.

Sunday July 16, 1989
In the world, people usually spend their Sundays and holidays with their loved ones in the family. I have begun to apply this approach also. And since my loved ones are in the other life, I try to sit at the feet of Christ on Sundays with my beloved deceased. In addition to Father Archbishop

---

83. Ps. 62:1 (New Revised Standard Version).

PART II: IN BYTOUMA MONASTERY 253

and Abbess, there are a few saints who are close to me, although I have no way of knowing if they will accept me into their family circle. Yes, I cannot be sure about that. My own spirit, however, enjoys being in their company.

The Feast of the Transfiguration of Christ, Sunday August 6, 1989
These days I am reading Christ's farewell speech from the Gospel. I especially stopped at the words, "By this everyone will know that you are my disciples, if you have love for one another."[84] So there, that is the sign and there is no other. Maybe I can gradually learn what is meant by this love. Not a restless panicking for others, but rather a deep, heartfelt, hopeful compassion.

We had many pilgrims today. I was especially touched by the old folk women, these thin, sunburned, and work-hardened people, in whom humility and dignity are united.

Saturday August 12, 1989
The garden has produced an exceptionally good crop this year. No wonder, I guarded it like the apple of my eye. It takes work, watering, and harvesting. Tiredness is setting in as the fast comes to an end, and I just hope that the whole pilgrimage feast will end happily. Then I would have to focus seriously on translating. With all this hustle and bustle, it is hard to live inwardly, and when the inner life weakens, the whole life flattens out. Yesterday I sat in the twilight in front of the cellar door behind the house—it was the only quiet place—and listened to the night breathing of creation.

Thursday August 17, 1989
The pilgrimage feast (The Dormition of the Virgin Mary) is happily over, but I have not yet had time to return to my writing: the cleanup is taking its time. There is plenty of cleaning to do, even along the riverbanks. A few moving moments remain in my memory. Two little girls came earnestly to ask for a blessing. A couple in their nineties had set up camp at the gate of the old building. I made coffee for them, and we had a relaxed chat sitting on the stairs. My obedience task was to serve the guests: In the evening I served our famous tomato soup, and in the morning shared loukoumi sweets.

---

84. John 13:35 (New Revised Standard Version).

Tuesday September 5, 1989
Perhaps I have already made a statement that translating the Philokalia into Finnish can be compared to unraveling a hopelessly tangled ball of thread when you live in constant fear of losing the end of the thread altogether. I do not mean that the teaching of the Fathers is confusing, but rather the way and the language in which they present it, and to express all this in the rich language, the language that has been born from the different ways of thinking of the staid inhabitants of the North. This work reinforces my conviction that I cannot do anything properly! (Although hardly anyone else could, either.) For a change, it is fun to grow beans, which will give a bountiful harvest without any additional quirks, as long as you fertilize and water them well.

Feast of the Nativity of the Theotokos, Friday September 8, 1989
As I get older, I feel, or maybe it gets easier to notice, that it is harder and harder to separate the spiritual and physical sides of a human being—they are just so intertwined. It is easier to imagine eternal life after the universal resurrection, when the body is back in the picture. These are God's mysteries, and there is much Biblical evidence for the church's teaching that personal existence continues between death and bodily resurrection. There is no "night of non-existence." Even the wise robber did not go to paradise in his body.

Saturday September 9, 1989
Nowadays I feel like I am internally living in a pale, soft mist. I do not feel bad at all; it is not dark, but it is not light either. It is a great blessing to be amid holy people in one's lifetime,[85] but it is also a cause for great worries. When they leave here, the world feels so empty. There is a memory of light and joy, but you cannot find it anymore.

Sunday September 10, 1989
Seldom does a week go by without a catastrophic plane crash in some corner of the world. They are always catastrophic because there are hardly any ways to save oneself. It is a terrible death—the mere thought of what it feels like for the people in that plane as it plummets to earth is terrifying. I have a habit of praying specifically that there will be no plane crashes. It is hard to pray with a real focus on the matter, and it is also the

---

85. Kristoduli is referring to Archbishop Paul and Abbess Euphemia.

kind of prayer whose results we can never know in this world. But when God asks for our cooperation, it is worth praying, if it would prevent even one crash.

Monday September 11, 1989
Today I read in the encyclopedia that the sun goes around the center of the Milky Way at a speed of 250 km/s. And in addition to our Milky Way, there are millions of galaxies. How wonderful the dance of these spheres must be—everything is circulating, everything goes around. But on the other hand—for the one who experiences the wonders of the spiritual world, it makes no more impression than a particle of dust floating towards us. The spiritual world is something else—outside of space and time. It is probably not a good attitude to try to reach far away when praying for the deceased and when asking for their intercession. It is a question of the state of spirituality; if one's inner state is close to theirs, they are here as well as beyond the stars.

Tuesday September 26, 1989
Yesterday the mail brought the happy news that Mother Marina will be here on Friday. She is expected in a spirit of general enthusiasm.

On Sunday, I wrote three articles for *Aamun Koitto*. In her letter, Heidi[86] asked me to become a columnist for the magazine.

Somehow it seems that there is always something to do, in which time flies as on wings, and there is little left to stop and pray. May the Lord help me to pray more. That is, after all, what is needed most.

Tuesday October 3, 1989
Mother Marina left for Athens yesterday and flies back to Finland tomorrow. I hope the visit here was refreshing for her. Of course we talked a lot about Archbishop Paul.

Saturday October 7, 1989
I fell on the cellar steps—I thought they were finished, but there was still one step left. I sprained my left foot badly; my eyes were black with pain. To make sure, I was taken to the regional hospital of Trikala for an X-ray. Fortunately, there were no fractures, but the foot is very sore, and I cannot walk on it at all. The doctor said that a rest of about ten days is

---

86. Heidi Vaalisto, editor-in-chief of *Aamun Koitto* from 1989 to 1992.

needed. I can only move by hopping on one foot or crawling on all fours. So, I have a ten-day retreat ahead of me. I hope I can use it right.

Monday October 9, 1989
For some time now, when praying in my cell, I have had the habit of saying with special reverence, "Lord, in the phases that You know best, save me! In Your hands I place myself entirely." I say the same now. The only worry we have, monks and nuns, is whether we will feel the grace or whether it will abandon us.

Sunday October 15, 1989
I went to church this morning and received Holy Communion. The foot swelled up even more, but you have to take care of more than just the foot.

Thursday October 19, 1989
Here we are, living the beautiful, bright fall days in silence and peace, especially me, who because of my foot am still in my cell, except for services and meals. In other parts of the world, the earth is shaking—not only in California, but also in China—planes are falling, political disputes are raging. It is as if we are on a paradise island: Only the distant rumble of these events reaches us on the radio.

Saturday October 28, 1989
For patients, there are some side effects associated with being sick in the monastery that I have observed over the years, and that I am now confronting. If you try to talk about your illness or accident in a brisk and cheerful way, you will soon hear whispers and will be made to understand with little stings that your situation is not too serious, and you are exaggerating your condition because you want to skip work. This is probably the reason why the groans of most sisters when they are ill rise all the way to the ceiling . . . The consequence of this, in turn, is that they are scolded for lack of patience.

Friday November 24, 1989
Yesterday I began to seriously examine the new Finnish translation of the New Testament. I became seriously concerned. A kind of scholarly enthusiasm was born—if not an ambition! I began to write comments on the Gospel of Matthew, which I, one way or another, will bring to the

attention of the translation committee. As far as I am concerned, I have something important to say. I do not think there is anyone else in Finland who has such a feel for the Greek language as I have gained through years of experience. If it were not a question of such an essential text, I would outright enjoy, for once, commenting on the text of other people—not always my own. Now the main concern is that the Finnish people will not get a lukewarm New Testament to read. The situation is most shocking regarding the letters of the Apostle Paul.

Wednesday November 29, 1989
Today I finished the commentary on the Gospel of Matthew. I will send it to the Lutheran Bishop Toiviainen in Mikkeli—let him send it where he wants. Let's see if there is any feedback. In any case, I feel that I have done my duty.

Monday December 4, 1989
I have seriously considered that the life of a Christian, and especially of a nun, should be a continuous labor on two themes: love of God and love of neighbor. Curling up around one's own inner wounds and emotional bumps cannot be included in either category, so it is a vain waste of energy. Neither God nor people expect this from us. We should not have personal concerns.

Tuesday December 5, 1989
This is the great day, when—according to the information of Mother Marina—the first monks will settle in Old Valamo. May the Mother of God and Saint Savva give them strength. They are brave souls. Winter storms are howling on Lake Ladoga, everything is lacking, the buildings are worn out, the inhabitants of the island are hostile. It seems to me as if the joyful warmth of spring is resting on the whole land. A new era is dawning there as well.

Tuesday December 19, 1989
Recently I have vividly felt how this monastery is a "harbor of protection" for me. On this hillside lives the little sisterhood as if in the protection of the wings of the Lord Himself. Thank you, God, for everything!

Thursday December 21, 1989
Bishop Toiviainen wrote and stressed that my comments would be reviewed, and he urged me to send new ones. There will be no question about how to spend my Christmas holidays. I will need to start researching the Letter to the Romans.

Christmas Day, Monday December 25, 1989
Seventy thousand to eighty thousand dead in Romania in ten days. Now the situation is beginning to calm down. This is something that is hard to think about. I am coming to a point where I would like to change the thoughts, but where to find sweet, tender, "Christmassy" thoughts . . . This Christmas I have spent with the people of Romania. It has wounded me so deeply that I wonder if I could go on if another world conflagration were to be ignited. Now I would like to retreat somewhere. Deep, deep into the spiritual world, where a solution can be found that cannot be expressed in words. Deep into the depths, where one can see that things do not happen by chance, but that everything, after all, has a meaning.

Saturday December 30, 1989
These days, I am very interested in the events that affect all of humanity. I would predict that the Chinese will become relevant in a new way in the next decade. And ecological problems will continue to increase. Looking at the affairs of the world from this mountain, I see the world as a boiling pot. Restlessness and selfishness dominate today's societies and individuals.

Tuesday January 16, 1990
I have been writing a lot of letters lately, and the diary has received less attention. Outwardly, and sometimes also inwardly, the days have been peaceful, relaxed, as much as translating the Philokalia into Finnish can be called relaxing—it is such difficult work, but one also gets used to the difficulty. Especially today I had the feeling that Father Archbishop was following my work.

Thursday February 8, 1990
Today, with renewed interest, I began to browse through the translation work. I finished the most extensive text of Philokalia IV, the detailed treatise of Kallistos and Ignatios Xanthopoulos on hesychasm.

Tuesday February 20, 1990
What an unpredictable creature a human being is! From the low states of tiredness and depression, she can very quickly go to other emotional states. This has happened to me. I feel myself full of joy and enthusiasm and bursting with strength. Where did this change come from? Perhaps the physical work amid summer nature has helped; these past few days I have been hoeing a strawberry field. Undeniably the weather has a great influence, and that is why God cannot judge the people of the north and the south with the same yardstick. When the sun is shining and nature so beautiful, who can be without joy!

Saturday March 17, 1990
Yesterday there were masses of pilgrims—six busloads—at the Akathistos service. It is good that I did not get burned by my task of organizing and blowing out the candles. Everyone saw it as their duty to light a few candles, some even many more. How will they all fit! In the overcrowded candlestands they begin to melt, stick together, burn with a large flame.

Holy Friday, April 13, 1990
And so, once again, we celebrate the memory of humanity's most shameful act. When one gets to know human nature a little better, it does not seem at all as a "strange" achievement that we crucified our Liberator from death. Have mercy on us, Lord, forgive us!

Saturday April 21, 1990
Pascha has been celebrated, and on Wednesday, an event hailed as historic took place: the meeting of all the monasteries in Greece. There were about four hundred monks and nuns from forty-five men's and twenty-seven women's monasteries. Much could be written about the meeting, and I will for sure feel it in my inner landscapes for a long time. In a way, it lifted you to a different atmosphere.

Wednesday May 30, 1990
On Sunday we attended the unveiling of the statue of Papa-Euthymios Vlachavas in the Meteora area. Papa-Euthymios was one of the first to rise up against the Turks in Thessaly. There were also folk dances at the celebration. I deeply understood how even dancing is one of the ways in which human beings can express themselves. The movement in the music's tempo almost lifts the heavy body above the earth. I agree with the

English mother, Maria of Normanby, that in paradise we will dance—as in the present world it has not been included in our experiences.

Pentecost, Sunday June 3, 1990
The Holy Spirit will lead us to the "whole truth."[87] For myself, I am beginning to see the world as more complex and such negative truths, such as that righteousness hardly ever wins in this world, and that often unworthy people who have resorted to questionable means often prosper outwardly. On the other hand, these issues—namely whether injustice has been done, or whether one is successful or not—begin to feel more and more unessential. Only eternity is essential.

"As many of you as have been baptized into Christ have put on Christ . . . "[88] The flowering meadows, the grass fields of Räsälänlahti swaying in the wind, a seventeen-year-old girl in whose inner being these words sounded like a symphony of joy and offering. These views come back to me every Pentecost.

Friday June 15, 1990
I am gradually beginning to understand, among other things, because of the publications I have received here, the way of thinking that is being spread through all channels and that is manifested most strongly in the New Age movement. And I no longer wonder at Christ's words that the chosen ones will be led astray. The central idea and starting point are the human being and that the purpose of life is all kinds of pleasure and enjoyment. Everything is subjective—nothing objective exists. Similarly, the goal of life is not ascesis and elevation to an objective reality above the human being, but rather the satisfaction of needs and wants. Although the practice has shown that people become even more unhappy being separated from God, this does not seem to disturb those who represent this way of thinking.

Saturday June 16, 1990
I continue the previous thought. Yes, such thoughts are sweet poison, and after reading a magazine on the subject this week, I feel myself to be mentally ill. I am trying to do what I can from here, and that is why I need to get a handle on such things, so that I can understand their effects and

---

87. John 16:13 (New Revised Standard Version).
88. Gal. 3:27 (New Revised Standard Version).

find a remedy. A mere intuitive certainty that people are completely off the rails is not enough.

Feast Day of Apostles Peter and Paul, Friday June 29, 1990
Archimandrite Sophrony writes in some contexts that God does not pity—at least, not the way we do. Humanly speaking, of course, it feels very cruel that a young, tender, and enthusiastic girl was hit so hard. Even a small tear may appear in the corner of the eye. But God did not see a young, tender girl in me, but a proud, selfish, and hard-hearted human being who had to be given challenges and hardships so that it hurt. Or now, after abandoning all the worldly joys and enclosing ourselves in a monastery, we may sometimes appeal to God's pity, and He will not allow it. "Nonsense," says God. "For you the world was one long fit of anxiety, and you have not enjoyed its joys, so you have really not given up anything—on the contrary, you changed an uncomfortable state into a more pleasant one. As for seeking grace, you could do much more, which you do not, you lazy one."

Sunday July 1, 1990
God's mills grind slowly. Now, after more than twenty-five years, I am finally beginning to understand ontologically why the Archbishop had a habit of saying that all we have to do in prayer is repent. Theoretically, I of course understood it before, but now I feel and see my own darkness and filth compared to God's light and brightness. Thank you God for letting me finally see that. Now I do not see the filthiness and sinfulness as a consequence of some deeds and thoughts but rather as a kind of permanently stained state.

Wednesday July 25, 1990
Summer is a time of work and heat, but it is also a time of great joy and fullness of life. Special this summer is a big harvest party. Both the wild and the cultivated fruit trees are overflowing with fruit, and even the strawberries have started a new cropping cycle. Soon you will feel like a fruit jar! The summer evenings, when the sun begins to set and it gets cooler, are also wonderful: a cool respite after the heat of the day. Also, all the rheumatic aches and pains of winter heal, and the whole body opens up in the warmth. Thank God for all His abundant gifts!

Thursday July 26, 1990
You have to be completely humble and sincere in front of young people. This could be one of the remaining tasks in my life: to support the youth that God sends my way, as I was supported in my time.

Sunday August 5, 1990
These days I often think about two things:

1) I am trying to find out—what it is that is permanent in a human person and transferred to the new life? These days I feel that the body with its ordinary daily needs (food, rest, sickness, or health) is quite a tyrant that rules over our states of mind. Only once—when I was ill in early spring—did I clearly experience that there is something else that cannot be reached by the body's pains and needs. This is what I would like to "fish out" from within myself.

2) What is the role of this world in eternity? Is it just a transient phenomenon, or will it perhaps be renewed with the human being and become incorrupt? Today I was thinking about timelessness. I thought that in the eternal state, existence is not sequenced by time, but rather by the changes of power in the streams of love originating from its primal source. In a sense, such thoughts simplify the human being. But more important than these thoughts is standing before God in the spirit of repentance. This is the first commandment of the Gospel: Transform your state of mind.

Saturday August 18, 1990
It would undoubtedly be most peaceful to not follow the news. But on the other hand, I see that it would be somehow cowardly to live in one's small circle, ignorant of the plight of the rest of humankind. We monastics need to throw ourselves between destruction and humankind as the first victims and say to God, like Moses: "If you are going to destroy them, destroy me first."[89] In such situations praying is very difficult, like bleeding. You are put in the position of those you are praying for, and you become a victim yourself.

---

89. Ex. 32:32 (New Revised Standard Version).

Thursday August 30, 1990
If I am no longer needed here, Lord, take me to You. Lately, though, I have begun to feel God working occasionally through me. I notice it, for example, when writing letters. Some kind of unexpected inspiration comes. I wonder what the effect is on the recipients . . . Sometimes I hear that it was helpful—not me, but the grace of God through me.

Sunday September 9, 1990
Be that as it may, this body is quite a millstone for us, limiting the spirit's aspirations at every step—and as Father Sophrony says, "trying to make it a party to its own mortality." The body prevents us from reaching absolute perfection in anything. But perhaps that is its function: to give us the opportunity to seek and to transform. If there were no body and the spirit could instantly realize everything it wanted, we could also instantly end up in evil, from which there would be no return.

What is all of the knowledge acquired by people: mere fragments beside all that we do not know. We do not know even the most fundamental issue: how was this universe, where we live, born; where are its limits; what is behind them—here we are already moving from science to metaphysics. Not to speak of knowing where it is going and what its end is—according to all logic, matter cannot continue its life as matter forever, and everything that moves goes somewhere, unless it moves in a circle—and what comes after. Somehow, we can cope with the fact that we do not know what has not yet happened; but we do not even know what has already happened! Those who do not believe in God are truly "mindless," as the writer of Psalms aptly puts it.

Monday September 10, 1990
I received a letter from Mother Marina. She has been elected as the acting abbess in Lintula. That is how the compatriots advance in the hierarchy, while I have not even been tonsured in the small schema! I say this mainly with humor. I would not exchange the possibility of a free inner life, free of all external responsibilities, for any kind of formal position. I am simply not suited to tasks that require a lot of interaction with others. I believe that the choice of Mother Marina will be good for Lintula.

Saturday September 29, 1990
What a day! This is one of those days in my life when the heavens opened for me. Our Patriarch, Demetrios,[90] who was visiting the diocese, is somehow a deeply moving, frail figure. I received his blessing twice over the day. In my understanding, it is a great blessing for Orthodoxy that we have a person like him, a humble, kind, natural figure as a Patriarch, a human being without a trace of a church prince. That is what the modern world needs; it has had enough of rhetoric and pompous gestures. The very being of the Patriarch is a strong sermon.

Thursday October 11, 1990
Irinja Nikkanen writes from her trip to America, from New York, and suggests that I come to Finland in connection with Philokalia III. I think I need to go, perhaps already at the end of this month. I do understand myself that it would be very useful if I could take another look at the whole of Part III. It will be more successful to write even the definition of terms after that. Indeed, the work has been going on for so many years that despite the notes, I cannot control everything. Let the matter be left to God.

Wednesday October 24, 1990, in Frankfurt Airport on the way to Finland[91]
Going to Finland feels like going to a well-kept, pleasant, artificially lit cave—but one whose inhabitants are unaware that outside the cave there is sunlit nature, a bottomless blue sky. This is completely irrespective of the so-called religious devotion of the cave dwellers—namely, devotion and experience are two different things. If you mumble something to the effect that there is something else besides the cave, you sound like a deranged fool to them.

Monday November 12, 1990, in Frankfurt Airport on the way back to Greece
I notice that I am becoming more and more interested in people. For example, I find it fun to have a conversation with my fellow passengers. In some sense, people seem more and more moving to me.

---

90. Patriarch of Constantinople from 1972 to 1991.
91. The purpose of the trip was to finalize the last part of Philokalia III.

Saturday December 15, 1990
The mere mechanical quoting of the Jesus Prayer has not filled my soul, it alone is not enough to conquer the army of thoughts that slush around in the heads of us twentieth-century "intellectuals." You must find something to delve into that surpasses all other research topics in its level of interest . . .

Saturday December 29, 1990
The exhausted cook has managed to finish her work. On the one hand, it is wonderful to serve the sisters, but at the end of the week, one's physical strength is truly exhausted.

Wednesday January 2, 1991
Today is the feast day of St. Seraphim of Sarov, and I spent my whole day in his company, so to speak. Very necessary and beneficial company! Perhaps I have begun to get too involved in worldly events and the destinies of humankind. There is a reason to remember that I am, first and foremost, responsible for my own soul. The world has always been and always will be in turmoil. I asked Saint Seraphim above all to strengthen my faith, so that it would not be affected by changes in my environment or, more generally, by anything. With this, I do not mean that one should end up in some subjective fanaticism, but that one should really find Christianity as the objective truth. Amen.

Wednesday February 27, 1991
I have rediscovered the good old morning and evening prayers, where all that is essential is expressed so well. I doubt if I will ever progress in the Jesus Prayer in its classical form. It is very hard for us modern, educated people of today, to strip ourselves from thoughts . . . In a way, I find myself concentrating better when there is a certain content in the prayer. But there are also variations. Sometimes you get tired of a lot of words, and then a short sigh of prayer feels better. And sometimes the name of Jesus tastes so good.

Holy Monday April 1, 1991
One of the most magnificent things you can experience in this life, to my understanding, is to work and strive, with a like-minded person inspired by the same ideals, towards some elevated value. And what would be more elevated than the spread of the Kingdom of God—with this, I

do not mean so much preaching, but experiencing it, and through that bringing it to the life of humankind.

Holy Tuesday April 2, 1991
The fog is still creeping over the earth, the rain is pouring, and it is cold.

In the church and elsewhere I try to look at the heavenly state. It is illumination, indescribable beauty, lovely music, pure bright love, translucently light, opening and expanding perfect knowledge . . . In a word, ever-deepening gazing at the brightness of God.

Holy Saturday, April 6, 1991
The Persian Gulf War consumed so much strength that it is hard to think of anything war-related after it. However, it may be that the most horrible phase began after the war, when the Iraqis were left to fight each other. Saddam has even used chemical weapons against the rebellious Kurdish citizens. Yesterday it was said that about thirty thousand Kurds are surrounded by Saddam's troops and are dying of hunger, cold, and bombing by helicopters. And the world does not care . . . The main point is that we ourselves have escaped the threat of war. The Kurds and the Palestinians are the most unfortunate peoples in the world. Nobody wants to give these people land to live on, and they are not wanted citizens in the countries where they live. What should they do, move to the moon?

Saturday April 20, 1991
Yoga and other Eastern meditation techniques have never interested me personally. Somehow, ever since I was a child, I have clearly felt that there can be no "technique" which can lead you to union with God. The basis of genuine union with God can only be a struggle to fulfill God's commandments. I feel that people are looking for some kind of easy way to happiness through these Eastern techniques. Even this corresponds to the modern person's principle of making the least effort, this time in the spiritual realm.

Saturday April 27, 1991
I continue the review of Philokalia IV. The church papers in Finland mention that Philokalia III will be published in April, but it has not reached here yet. If someone reads my diaries, he or she will probably wonder why I cover the Philokalia fairly little in them. In short, translating the Philokalia makes me feel like a worm on a hook, like a crab in tongs. The

work is overwhelmingly difficult. This does not mean that I am not grateful to be able to serve in this task. There is only a small amount of new translation to be done. Systematic work on the Philokalia will probably come to an end within a year—after that there would only be the checking of Matti Jeskanen's stylizations, whenever they come. My time in a "bench-vice" will soon be over. After that I should begin to read the texts I have translated and apply them in my life. In this phase I am thinking of them mainly from the point of view of expression, and there is little strength left to admire their deep, soaring meaning.

Tuesday May 7, 1991
The stapled edition of Philokalia III arrived in the mail yesterday—the bound one is not ready yet. I was moved to see the result of many years of work. As for the text, I have the impression that the level is improving part by part. The whole team is gaining experience. Now only part IV remains.

Saturday June 1, 1991
In June, summer really came. The weather got warm, the air is fragrant, everything is growing, God's blessing hovers over nature. We are eating strawberries in solemn silence. Beginning strawberry production was one of the best ideas I have ever had.

I keep myself busy in the garden all day, hoeing and watching, planting and sowing. You do not have to wait for sleep in the cell: you cannot help closing your eyes in the evening as well as during the siesta. I have begun to organize the library, but only a little time of the day is left for it. I rejoice deeply for all of this, in spite of the fatigue. We are God's co-workers.

Tuesday June 18, 1991
Today I have completed forty-six years of this earthly wandering. I thank God for everything! I really feel that life becomes more beautiful with the years; in other words, the curtain that separates us from the deepest, eternal reality becomes thinner, and we start to see more and more.

Later. This evening, we served the Small Compline outside on the balcony. Stars began to appear in the still-illuminated sky. But the translucence that is characteristic of the summer nights in the North, when the mist floats on the lake's surface, is missing here. The white lilies, the "virgin lilies" as they are called here, that are blooming right now are probably the most beautiful things that exist.

Sister Kristoduli at the Chapel of the Mother of God and Saint Seraphim, January 1992.

When I work in the garden, I sometimes sit down in the shade to rest. There is something special about sitting on the grass, on the ground, in contact with the earth. The earth—our great dining table, the earth from which we have gotten our beginning. A human being sitting on the earth lifting her eyes towards the sky is a human being in her most authentic state.

I feel love for this globe that God has given us to live on. It is a pity that it will be doomed in ten billion years, when the sun begins to cool down. But I do not believe that tragedy is the last word on the fate of creation. The last word is love.

Sunday June 23, 1991
White virgin lilies bloom in the courtyard. I wish one day I could be with Father Archbishop in the virgin lily meadows of paradise! I wonder what it is like over there, Father Archbishop? Let me anticipate!

Monday July 1, 1991
A very dear place to me on our monastery grounds is a small chapel dedicated to the icon of the Mother of God, [titled] "Quick to Hear," at a well where our river begins. In winter and spring, water gushes from many directions. The chapel is surrounded by large sycamore trees. The care of it has somehow fallen to me. Once a week I go and clean it up. The presence of the Mother of God is very strong there.

Wednesday July 10, 1991
Today, as I entered the chapel to pray, it occurred to me that we could place a small icon of St. Seraphim of Sarov in the chapel of the "Quick to Hear" icon of the Mother of God. From idea to action, I presented the idea to the abbess and received the necessary blessing. Holding the icon close to my breast, I walked along the stream to the chapel and sang in Greek, Finnish, and Russian: "Holy Father Seraphim, pray to God for us." The icon was given to me by Mother Marina during my visit to Finland. I have a feeling that St. Seraphim will visit our little chapel often.

Sunday July 14, 1991
With God's help, you have to try to control your tongue. I usually do not get upset no matter what the sisters say to me—and they do say quite a lot. But that is probably because I react quite strongly in my "clever" way, so that I usually get the last word. I of course do not yell or argue, but use other, more subtle stabs of the dagger. But this is not in line with the spirit of Christ. If there is nothing kind to say, it would be better to be silent.

Thursday August 1, 1991
The Dormition Fast of the Mother of God began. One of the greatest gifts a person can receive is peace—a deep inner peace, which is rarely a permanent state, but which touches the soul from time to time. Our chapel is a lovely place, "a little wilderness" of St. Seraphim here in Greece.

Thursday August 8, 1991
I was baking bread this morning, starting at 4 am. After finishing the work and having made it to the end of the Matins service, I slowly came up to my cell. A silence overtook my mind, and in the silence a thought shone: "God is also pure reason—Ingenuity beyond everything." Often the name of God, whose name we should not mention too often, is associated with various emotions, as love and goodness, which is of course

quite right. But for us, intellect-worshipping people of today, it is also good to remember that He, in the universe—and outside of it—is the one whose IQ is infinite. When you wake up every morning, you can think trustingly, "He, under whose leadership I have given my life, is infinitely good and infinitely genius. There is no reason to worry about anything, just be grateful."

Saturday August 17, 1991
For my part, I still stay away from people and, if possible, from all strangers. Undoubtedly, this attitude is influenced by the fact that I myself am a "stranger," a foreigner, and do not want to be a showpiece. But, in general, being a kind of "spiritual guide" to lay people does not attract me at all. I leave them, as well as myself, to the care of God's goodness and do not want to interfere in the lives of others. In relation to others, I usually wait for some kind of inner encouragement. Sometimes, a strong thought comes to me to write to someone in such and such a way. I am ready to give that kind of help, if the Lord wants to use me for such tasks. It is quite different from trying to talk to visitors in a godly way and somehow being artificially "beneficial" to them.

Sunday August 18, 1991
Of all the words used to describe God, I am most attracted to truth. God is "Truth"—we do not worship a creation of our imagination, but stand in holy awe before Him who is "Truth." Pure truth, bright truth, truth that is the core of everything. I am convinced that when you divide an atom into smaller and smaller particles, what is ultimately indivisible is truth, truth that burns so brightly that the human brain will be dazzled. And truth is also in the macrocosm. Truth is God and God is Truth. Other characterizations of God derive their value from this basis. Truth is Love . . .

Wednesday September 4, 1991
It has been a while since I tasted inner silence. I do not mean that there are storms going on, but life has somehow become external, which dries you up inside. The whole world is in turmoil, and it affects even us. The civil war in Yugoslavia is raging more and more, although peace agreements are periodically made at the diplomatic level. They seem to have no practical significance.

After the summer chores, I am making a "comeback" to the Philokalia. The result: a headache and enormous yawns. I thought today that when I finish the Philokalia I will not really look for new writing assignments. I will let various parties know that I will be available to delve into liturgical texts, but not on other assignments. It would be a pity for the church if I do not get any assignments, since no one there has as much experience with this work and with the Greek language as I do—but it would be a relief for me. There will always be work in a monastery for those willing to do it.

Tuesday September 10, 1991
We have won! Even the last step has been taken: today Metropolitan Seraphim was appointed Metropolitan of Stagoi and Meteora. This is a great miracle; after seventeen years we have our bishop back![92]

Sunday September 29, 1991
I am trying to focus on my inner life. Lately I have spent too much time "outside."
    Later. Just now, in the evening, I was walking in the yard under the bright starry sky, looking at the stars. Beautiful, magnificent is the creation. But it just occurred to me that it is not for nothing that people say a human being is more valuable than the whole world. The stars, the whole material creation will disappear one day, but we will not; we are eternal by the grace of God. And eternal is always more valuable than mortal.

Sunday October 13, 1991
Light and life are fundamentally one and the same: light is life, and real life is light. What comes to me is that I remember people mainly by the degree of their lightness. I do not remember clothes or other special characteristics, but lightness stays in my mind, just like darkness. And the people who have attracted me or continue to attract me have all been particularly strong reflectors of light. And that in turn was a consequence of their generally high quality of life.

Feast Day of St. Demetrios, Saturday October 26, 1991
I have tentatively begun to learn the duties of a secretary and am going through the papers of the monastery.

---

92. The dispute that had torn the diocese apart for years came to an end when it was divided in two. Meteora area and Bytouma were placed under the pastoral authority of the ousted Metropolitan Seraphim. Alexios remained the chief shepherd of the Trikala part of the diocese.

Oxi Day, Second Independence Day of Greece, Monday October 28, 1991
I have continued to go through the papers. This task of a secretary is not spiritually uplifting, but someone has to do it. There are all kinds of strange things revealed in these papers.

Thursday October 31, 1991
It has been pouring for days. It is even nicer to be in one's own cell. Joy swells the heart. It is early in the morning after a divine service. Haritini is in the kitchen frying doughnuts to cheer up the day. The world outside is boiling, but life in the monastery continues in its idyllic, warm way. And in the idyll, there is also great heroism.

Tuesday November 5, 1991
All the heavenly sweetness has landed on our monastery! Thank You, God, for everything. Today Metropolitan Seraphim received the whole sisterhood one by one. Everybody's face was radiant, calm. A new era has begun in the life of our monastery. And also in my life. I have great responsibility in the monastery, and I know the Metropolitan expects a lot from me. Help me, dear Mother of God, the protector of our monastery.

Saturday November 30, 1991
I have begun to see the image of God in people and at the same time the unique persona of each person. And what a beautiful sight that is!

Wednesday January 22, 1992
Much has happened. Mother Marina arrived on Friday as promised, and we had a lot to talk about. Yesterday she left for Athens. We visited both Metropolitan Seraphim and Metropolitan Alexios, for whom Mother Marina had a letter from Archbishop John.

Wednesday January 29, 1992
Monastic life is truly something wonderful. Today, in the early evening, after lighting an oil lamp in the chapel of Saint Seraphim, I walked down the mountain road. The mountains were glowing with snow, the sky was bright. And there was also a brightness inside me. I literally jumped down the mountain. In the midst of joy and gratitude, it occurred to me how many forty-six-year-old women in the world feel the need to jump down a road with a light soul and body. Worries and disappointments do not

clip our wings in the monastery. No matter what happens, we are always in touch with the Giver of Life.

Feast Day of the Three Holy Hierarchs, Thursday January 30, 1992
What made me a little sad in my last conversation with Metropolitan Seraphim was that he began to talk about how I see things differently than others because of my upbringing and because I am more cultured than people here.

I hope that I do not categorize people according to their nationality. I try to see the persona in everyone, whether they are Greek, Finnish, or other. Because everyone, regardless of their nationality, is basically a human being who in many ways has similar needs and goals and problems, and at the same time everyone is their own persona. Apart from that, nationality is a secondary factor.

Sunday February 2, 1992
Translating, or rather, "twisting" the Philokalia into Finnish is getting more and more laborious. Fortunately, we are at the final draft stage. Instead, I wrote a ten-page article for *Aamun Koitto* in just a few hours. No doubt it is easier to function as a "freelance writer" than as a translator.

Spiritually it has been mostly good. Christ has felt close. A piece of advice from Father Archbishop that happened to catch my eye has helped me a lot: "In prayer, speak to God as to a person in the same room." God is here and now, there is no need to try to reach heights.

Sunday April 12, 1992
In the afternoon the phone rang, and it was a person from the radio station of the Greek Church who explained that they were making a program about the Easter celebrations in different Orthodox churches and asked me to participate in the discussion as a representative of Finland. So, I should be in Athens next Wednesday when the recording takes place. The matter will, of course, be decided by Metropolitan Seraphim.

Tuesday April 14, 1992
And here I am in noisy and dirty Athens with Sister Thekla. Our apartment is in a terrible state because no one has been here for a year. The first thing we did was to clean it.

The twenty-nine-year-old interviewer, by the name of Smaragdi, will come here for a visit tomorrow evening before the beginning of the interview. There are Orthodox people from fifteen different countries in the program. There will be interesting acquaintances!

Thursday April 16, 1992, in Athens
Now everything is all happily over. I spoke in a live program of Holy Thursday and of Pascha in Finland, and I stammered this and that about the history of the Orthodox Church in Finland. I do not know how it all went and sounded, but they suggested that I come back sometime.

Palm Sunday, April 19, 1992
I remember the evening when "God looked down from heaven" on me, then a young schoolgirl, and led my steps to St. Nicholas Church to warm up from the cold. How did I ever know that I would be warm for the rest of my life? I was coming home from the Kuopio City Library, but for some reason wanted to do a bit longer walk and passed by the church park. How could I have anticipated that Christ Himself would guide my steps and answer my hunger for truth? From that evening on, the adventure of my life began.

Tuesday May 26, 1992
Yesterday our father confessor, Father Isidore, came spreading joy and peace around him. Together we visited both the small church of the Holy Trinity and "my" well church, the Chapel of the Mother of God and St. Seraphim of Sarov.

During my confession, Father Isidore said that he hoped that I would always be joyful and spread joy around me. With the prayers of my confessor, let the Lord allow for this to happen.

Friday May 29, 1992
In the last few days, I have been thinking that death is really just an episode in life that continues. Even Christ does not give it great significance: "Do not fear those who kill the body, and after that can do nothing more."[93]

Pentecost, Sunday June 14, 1992
We can see all people as one. We are all different manifestations of the same material—and in this "different manifestation" is the personality. The word "individual" has a bad echo in the words of the Holy Fathers,

---

93. Luke 12:4 (New Revised Standard Version).

because it refers to being separated and detached from others. It describes a false and wrong way of being—a human being is not a separate phenomenon but rather a personality connected to the whole humanity by a common human nature. It is precisely this distorted tendency to see ourselves as individuals that is the mother of envy and thus of all the misfortunes of humanity. If we saw ourselves as part of the whole of humankind, we would rejoice for everybody's achievements and success, because they would be ours as well. And on the other hand, we would sympathize with the pains and misfortunes as shared wounds from which all humanity suffers. This thought is behind Christ's commandment: "You shall love your neighbor as yourself."[94] This is Christian communism.

And yes, I thought about the fact that even in the time before the Second Coming of Christ, when we are separated from our body, our body is not dead material, but its parts become trees, leaves, grass, flowers. Even I, when the time comes, want to give my body to the cycle of nature and not be buried in a marble box or under cement.

Thursday June 18, 1992
I spent my forty-seventh birthday shopping in Trikala among these smiling and friendly Greeks. In a study of twenty-four countries, Greece ranked last in suicide statistics and in other mental health issues. No wonder—life here is interesting and fun. People do not get bored.

Tuesday June 23, 1992
Yesterday was the abbess's birthday, and sisters from the Saint Stephen and Roussano monasteries came to visit. We also went to the chapel.[95] As we, a large group of sisters, wandered along the riverbank under the branches of the plane trees toward the monastery, singing "O Gladsome Light," it was like a moment of a lifelong pilgrimage toward the Kingdom of Heaven.

Friday June 26, 1992
The moments spent in the morning in the chapel of Saint Seraphim are a source of strength for me. There I also remember all the "protectors of my life" and ask for their help. They are the Mother of God, my guardian angel, Saint Seraphim, and Holy Shepherds Paul and Dionysios.

---

94. Matt. 22:39 (New Revised Standard Version).
95. Chapel of the Mother of God and Saint Seraphim.

Monday July 27, 1992
Now that the work of the Philokalia is coming to an end—although there is still some work to be done—I feel that my monastic life has come to a turning point. What comes next? Mother Marina wrote in her last letter that when the new wing[96] in Lintula is completed, she would like to invite me to spend some time there. I replied that she can ask Archbishop John to write about it to Metropolitan Seraphim. I have to pray hard that the Lord will lead the way and show me what He wants from me after the Philokalia.

Friday August 14, 1992
I have been listening to the news during the day. The situation in Yugoslavia is becoming more and more tense. The sword is once again piercing the heart of the Mother of God: on the one side, the Serbs are calling on the Mother of God for help, and on the other side the Croats are calling on the Holy Virgin—both for the destruction of the other.

Wednesday August 19, 1992
Today I went to Trikala for a short visit. When Salome and I went to get the car from the parking lot, a young boy—maybe about seventeen years old—appeared and said politely in a foreign accent: "Some bread, please." I found some cookies and a bag of pumpkin seeds in my bag, where I usually keep a little something, and gave them to him. "Thank you very much," he said. "Albania?" I asked, and he replied with a bitter smile: "Yes, Albania . . ."

Monday August 31, 1992
Whenever we are confronted with difficult administrative matters, such as the drafting of separation papers for our former forest ranger, the abbess always turns to me. Certain bitter thoughts begin to circle in my mind: "You ask me for help, but you do not want to tonsure me to the small schema. I would love to give up being a secretary. Let's see where you can find an assistant then!" If I cannot be trusted enough to be tonsured as a nun after nineteen years of monastic life, then I cannot be trusted to take care of the affairs of the monastery either. But then I realized that this is a temptation. So far, I have followed the fundamental principle of obedience; that is, I have not taken the reins of my own life into my own hands. That must have some meaning.

---

96. Expansion of the convent building for the sisters, completed in the summer of 1993.

Friday September 18, 1992
I am working on the last rough translation of the Philokalia. Then there will be proofreading and checking of the texts, and the project will be finished.

Wednesday October 7, 1992
Yesterday I was in Meteora guiding the iconographers of the Diocese of Oulu, of whom only two were Orthodox. A paradoxical phenomenon: an iconographer who is not Orthodox! They were really nice people to guide, and once they warmed up, we had a really good time.

Thursday October 15, 1992
Today I typed on a typewriter the final version of the last lines of the Philokalia, where the Greek compiler of the Philokalia, Saint Nicodemos, asks the reader for prayers for his wretched soul. The translator of the Philokalia into Finnish also joins in this plea.

Saturday October 17, 1992
Today I went completely crazy. Abbess asked me to write the lease agreement for a piece of pastureland during our midday rest break while the lessee was waiting. Tired from yesterday's trip to the mountains to collect chestnuts and from the morning's work cleaning the chicken coop and one of our houses, I said that I did not have the strength to write the agreement now, but I asked the abbess to ask the shepherd for all the necessary information so that I could write it in peace, as we usually do. I said that I would only make typing mistakes. This caused quite a commotion. I heard a cry regarding my "satanic stubbornness" and other such things. The abbess also mentioned something about removing me from secretarial duties. But I beat her to it: in the afternoon I gave her the key to the office and said that I would resign from the secretary's post. I had wanted to do this already for a long time, and now an opportunity presented itself to do so.

Tuesday October 20, 1992
As I had expected, the Metropolitan did not want me to resign from the secretary's post under any circumstance. And I had already sighed with relief!

Tonsure to a nun, December 14, 1992.

Friday December 4, 1992

Today began a series of celebrations that will not end until Theophany. We Orthodox love to celebrate! Today is the feast day of Metropolitan Seraphim (and also mine), but at the moment, after participating in serving the festive meal, I am so utterly tired that I cannot write any more.

Monday December 14, 1992

Tonight, God willing, will be my tonsure to a small schema. It will happen during the all-night vigil. I do not, as such, have the feeling of a final decision, because that was already made for the monastery a long time ago.

I am interested to see how God will guide me going forward.

Tuesday December 15, 1992

There were several priests at the ordination, maybe as many as seven, some of whom stayed for the all-night vigil. After the vigil we had a meal together. Father Metropolitan even asked me to say something. I said about monastic life that in it we put our life dependent on invisibility—it is like a leap into emptiness, which does not turn out to be empty. We can really see that God is no longer as theoretical knowledge, but as an experience, and that life in Christ produces the fullness of life. In a monastery, values are in the right order, and the soul feels at home, and this is also felt by the pilgrims.

Saturday December 19, 1992
Today, in the ancient Church of the Mother of God in Kalambaka, there was a joint meeting of the monastics. Father Metropolitan had asked Professor Ioannis Foundoulis, a specialist in liturgics, to be the speaker. Nuns from all the monasteries and most of the people of Meteora were present.

Christmas Eve, Thursday December 24, 1992
"Today a Savior is born to you." I paused at the word—Savior. It was with this name that Christ was first made known to humankind. A Savior is born to us. There is no more need for despair: in all difficulties, both external and internal, we have a Savior. Death and even aging do not lead to a dead end: the Savior saves us, showing that even these are only relative phenomena and that the truth itself is elsewhere.

Today Father Metropolitan was present at a long service, and he himself celebrated the Liturgy of Saint Basil. I stood in the church, and waves of transcendental joy washed over me. The presence of our Chief Shepherd and praying together with him warmed my heart in a very special way.

Thursday December 31, 1992
I am here trying to give a kind of report on the past year. It has been relatively calm for the sisterhood. We had many spiritually uplifting events. I have counted that Metropolitan Seraphim visited the monastery twenty-three times; in addition, I met him personally in Kalambaka about ten times. There have been eight all-night vigils, remarkably more than in previous years.

For myself, I can say that Father Isidore, our Father Confessor, has given wings to my ascetic efforts. In addition, I have received the long-awaited tonsure to the small schema.

THE PHILOKALIA IS NEARING COMPLETION—
WHAT THEN?

Monday January 4, 1993
The snow disaster with power outages continues. On today's program was cleaning a meter-thick layer of heavy snow from the side roof of the

church. We also took all the food items from the freezer in the kitchen out into the snow. The third cold night begins. And even I spent many years here when it was always like this in winter, because the cells had no heating. In those circumstances I even translated the Philokalia in my cell. It was a miracle that I did not catch a deadly disease. Fortunately, we Finnish children were accustomed to a hard life.

Thursday January 7, 1993
The power came back yesterday, and even the road has been plowed a bit, although it will be a long time before you can get here by car. Kir-Vasilis came yesterday, and we slid down the slippery road to his car to pick up the sacks of fruit he brought. It seems that Kir-Vasilis loves the monastery even more than we do.

The condition of Sister A. of Saint Stephen Monastery has worsened. When a person has always experienced, or has supposedly experienced, in line with human logic, that God takes care of her, it is a kind of shock that this friendly God suddenly makes her suffer. But if you have experience that "His ways are not our ways,"[97] and that He can often lead us, according to our logic, in very cruel ways, "through fire and water," but in some inexplicable way for our own good, then you are in a way differently prepared to undergo even a physical death.

Wednesday January 13, 1993
The basic vibration in my own mind is deep peace. God, whom we have been asked to call our Father, is holy, mighty, and immortal. These qualities of God even adhere to us when we are close to Him.

Sunday January 17, 1993
The basic problems, the basic needs, the basic questions to which human beings seek answers are the same in all cultures and in all times, as long as *homo sapiens* has inhabited the surface of the Earth: "From where, to where, and why?" These are the essential questions. Eternity . . . Everything else that has little to do with it is secondary.

Thursday January 28, 1993
Finnish television (TV1) would like to come here and make a program about monastic life. The matter has to be discussed with the Metropolitan.

---

97. Isaiah 55:8 (New Revised Standard Version).

Sunday February 7, 1993
In my youth I sometimes hoped for special experiences, something "supernatural." Now, all that does not have much of an impact on me anymore. The main thing is to live the miracle of the present life according to the will of God, to develop in these circumstances, to mature, to move on to the new form of life, which has its own miracles. The present life has been given to us for this development, and therefore the present conditions are fit for it. The warmth of grace in the heart, the feeling that life is under God's guidance—these are sufficient and already undeserved gifts.

Tuesday March 23, 1993
Lately, my life has resembled that of a doctor on call . . . Today I brought all the medicines from Trikala and distributed them to the sisters, advising each one on how to take them.

Saturday March 27, 1993
Today a small miracle happened in our monastery: The abbess was agonizing this morning, even to me, about how to pay the salaries of the construction workers. Sister Agne's brothers are still here, repairing the damage caused here and there by the snow. Shortly before noon, a young man by the name of Panagiotis came and gave the abbess five hundred thousand drachmas.[98] He lives in Germany and had a burning sensation that the monastery needed money. And so he traveled here quickly—he comes from a nearby village.

Holy Thursday, April 15, 1993
Oh, how much even I personally owe to the mystery of the Holy Eucharist! How innumerable times have the Body and Blood of the Lord pulled me up from the darkness of despair (even before coming to the monastery), opened the way out of a dead end, filled me with new strength, joy, and confidence. Glory be to You, Lord Jesus!

Tuesday May 4, 1993
Yesterday I mailed off the second-to-last review of the stylized copy of the Philokalia. There is still one more to go. It has been a kind of foundational work of mine for the past nineteen years. I wonder what I will do in the

---

98. About $2,174 in US dollars at the time.

future—what God wants me to do. Maybe it is time to put the Philokalia into practice.

The camera crew of Finnish TV1 has been in contact with the Metropolitan through the embassy. They are coming here at the beginning of next month and want to use me as their interpreter. Good that the matter has some kind of formal background.

Sunday May 9, 1993
Everyone wanders along their own path. To some, God gives many great gifts of grace (usually accompanied by heavy crosses), and when the occasion demands, they can also help others. For others, He gives less, but He also protects them from severe hardships and bad diseases that almost always follow supernatural gifts of grace. Everyone fights in his or her own league—the main thing is that they fight.

Thursday May 20, 1993
I have finished the last final review of the Philokalia. It is over now! Nothing holds me in this life anymore: Father Archbishop has left from here, and the Philokalia is finished—it would have been a pity to leave it unfinished. In any case, even if you live to be one hundred, it is good to live so that nothing holds you back here. To celebrate the completion of the Philokalia, I will eat an apple. In itself, this is nothing exceptional: I usually eat a fruit in the afternoon.

Saturday May 29, 1993
My aunt Rauha arrived already on Friday of the week before last. She brought some of my daily journals from my youth with her. It is self-evident that God answered the burning search of a young girl. Whoever knocks, the door will be opened. Everyone can see it in his or her turn. I also want to assure the youth of the future generations: knock, and the door will be opened to you; search to the edge of despair—and you will find. I am living proof of that.

Last Monday we went to the mountain tops to gather herbs. The beauty was like in a fairytale; you did not want to leave.

Thursday June 3, 1993
The television men are coming tomorrow. Father Mitro, whom they had chosen as their interpreter, will also come. Personally, I feel relieved that he is coming: he can fight for the filming permits here, and my part will fortunately be reduced.

I am mostly doing gardening work and am very content. If you study the lives of ascetics, it is easy to see when God wants to use someone for a special mission. His guidance and revelation are very clear in that person's life. What I am trying to say is that since there are no such manifestations in my life, I do not need to stress myself by thinking that maybe God wants me to do something more than what I am doing.

I received an invitation from Finland to give a keynote address on the Philokalia at the twentieth anniversary celebration of the Friends of Valamo on November 6. The Friends of Valamo will pay for the travel.

Saturday of Souls, June 5, 1992
I came here to the chapel to clean it and at the same time to pray a little and to think. Lately my life has been a little bit like aimless wandering. Now that the Philokalia is practically finished, I am pondering whether I will have another real mission in life, and especially in the Orthodox Church in Finland. I would like to know God's will. If it is that the rest of my life will be spent in practical tasks and inner vistas, I would be happy with that. But I would like to be sure.

Friday June 11, 1993
The days have been eventful. I never imagined that filming could be such hard work—both for the filmmakers as well as for those being filmed. Hannu and Tom wanted to do a good job, and that meant I had to walk back and forth along the river ten times! God did intervene in many ways and blessed the attempt. First, the sisters were willing to cooperate and played their part naturally and with a smile. We were able to film most of the activities in the monastery, the knitting room, the rabbits, the bees, the garden, the chickens, the services.

The next day was dedicated to filming the Philokalia work and my interview. The abbess remained gloomy (at first her attitude was positive, but then she changed her mind). Hannu and Tom cold-bloodedly continued their work whenever an opportunity presented itself. The sisters were quite upset by the abbess's behavior, and despite it, they continued their friendly cooperation with the film crew.

Yesterday's program included an interview with the Metropolitan in Kalambaka. He was wonderful, as always. He had visited here on the Holy Spirit Day, and his reception in the courtyard of the monastery was filmed, and pictures were taken of him and the sisters and youth who accompanied him. His interview went very well. He expressed himself and spoke without a trace of tension. Apparently he was able to influence the abbess's behavior, which changed yesterday afternoon. Father Mitro and I did our best, and it so happened that Hannu and Tom were able to film the Small Compline service where the prayers of the sisters were accompanied by a nightingale's singing. It was a real icing on the cake. It is certain that no other Greek women's monastery has ever been filmed so thoroughly—nor will it ever be. I believe that the film will be a great blessing and will have a future, not only in Finland, but also abroad.

Wednesday September 15, 1993
Now it really feels like I am going to be one of those millions of pilgrims who have wandered to holy places throughout the times. Now, however, the "wandering" will take place in an airplane, in air-conditioned buses, in first-class hotels . . . But in any case, I am going to the Holy Land! I look a little wistfully at our monastery, which for me has been Jerusalem, Tabor, and perhaps in the future even Golgotha. A lot will have happened before I see it again.

Tuesday September 21, 1993
Our memorable visit to St. Catherine's Monastery in Sinai was crowned with the Holy Eucharist this morning. The monastery with its rocky mountains has made a deep impression on me. It is no wonder that the holy fathers focused on inner prayer here—life here is somehow bare. One feels the need to purify, to simplify. Somehow you feel that you are sinking into God, the Creator of everything, mighty, immortal; and everything that vanishes is forgotten.

Tuesday September 28, 1993
We returned to our home monastery full of joy. Only yesterday afternoon I sat on the high reception terrace of the St. Mary Magdalene Monastery and looked at the old Jerusalem in front of me. I was able to be alone there for an hour and a half, thanking Christ, my Savior, for this unforgettable experience. How deeply the events of the New Testament now live; the Church of the Holy Sepulcher is the source of our faith. From these places the streams of immortality began to spread.

Friday October 9, 1993
A visit to Jerusalem is not a travel experience, but rather a spiritual experience. As such, it does not leave behind a longing for a particular

geographical space, but rather it lives on. One could say: once in Jerusalem—always in Jerusalem. I "stayed" on Golgotha, the place where suffering culminated, where love was infinite, and where love inspired suffering, conquered death, and brought eternity into our lives.

Thursday October 14, 1993
Today Philokalia part IV, the last one, arrived. It is now finished. I took the book to the church and silently thanked Christ and His Holy Mother for the joyful completion of the work. I will still make a search index.

Saturday October 29, 1993
It seems that the pilgrimage to Sinai and the Holy Land was a kind of milestone in my inner life. I do not trust in any emotional stages—I know how changeable a human being is—but I truly trust in the mercy of our great God and Savior Jesus Christ.

Sunday November 28, 1993
In fact, the entire inner ascesis needs to be focused on clearing space in the mind for Christ. When that happens, we are already on the winning side. Our Lord and Savior begins to act and work in us.

Monday January 31, 1994
I wish that the Lord would help me to get rid of the condemning and critical attitude, at least now in the last phase of my life. Has anything resulted from all the criticism and condemnation?

Saturday February 5, 1994
The proclamation of Christianity began at just the right time, when people still had time to listen. Nowadays, people are so immersed in complicated, supposedly important matters that no one bothers to really listen to even the most interesting things, or else hears them with only one ear.

Monday February 14, 1994
Today I was finally able to meet Father Paisios.[99] He was resting on his bed, tired (cancer had spread to his liver and to his only lung), but serene and peaceful with a clear look in his eyes. He mentioned something about

---

99. In February, Kristoduli was in Thessalonica taking care of the sisters who were in the hospital there. Fr. Paisios was in another hospital in Thessalonica at the same time.

our monastery, and I said that we have "some problems." "Problems..." said he; "life is for passing entrance examinations." I asked him to say something to me, a sinner—in his presence I really felt like a big sinner. He said, "Patience, obedience, and saying the Jesus prayer." At the end of the conversation, he grabbed small crosses out of a bag, seven in all, and looked at me somehow joyfully. I already sent two of them to Finland, one to Mother Marina and the other to Mother Johanna.

Wednesday February 16, 1994
Father Paisios was discharged from the hospital today, but he was still there when we arrived. Christina, a social worker, took us directly to Father Paisios, especially Justina, who had never met him before, but the rest of us naturally joined in. There was a large crowd of people standing at the door. Father Paisios was resting on his bed, fully dressed, waiting for the departure. I realized immediately that he clearly recognized me from the previous visit. It was strange that throughout our visit, Father Paisios looked mainly at me, even though there were many other people in the room. And how he looked! It is hard to explain: a light was lit in his eyes, a kind of joyful light, and a ray of that light hit my eyes as well—as if he had a laser beam in his eyes. How can I put it—it was as if there was a deep understanding between us, a kind of connection of joy and light. Deep humility fills my mind when I think about it: an unearned gift for me, a sinner.

Before I left, when I went to get a blessing, I said to Father Paisios that I had translated some of his words into Finnish and that I was thinking of translating his book about an ascetic on Mt. Athos. "Wait, wait a bit, it still needs something more," he replied, looking at me peacefully the entire time. I have not seen such peace and purity since the days of Father Archbishop. Anyway, Father Paisios is also my intercessor, both in this life and in the life to come.

Friday April 1, 1994
The monastery was populated by seven busloads of people who came to the Akathistos service. Sparks flew from our heels serving this crowd. Coffee and, after the service, bread and olives were given to everyone. The Pilgrims, on their part, brought money and goods. The Metropolitan again delivered a very beautiful sermon using a sentence from the Akathistos hymn as his point of departure. And now we, being very tired, lay ourselves to rest.

Thursday April 7, 1994
Fortunately—oh, fortunately—my time in the kitchen is coming to an end. Today I heard this comment: "Your rice is such that I am almost sick just seeing it." And throughout the week, similar comments rain down on me, either about the food or the state of the kitchen. Glory to you, God! So far, I have endured without losing my composure, and in some ways I have even been thankful. The fatigue weighs heavily. Especially early in the week, I followed my confessor's advice to recite the Jesus Prayer out loud in the kitchen. It has calmed the situation there somewhat.

The Lord's Pascha, Sunday May 1, 1994
Christ is risen! At night I said the Paschal greeting to Father Archbishop, Abbess Euphemia, and schema nun Seraphima. It felt completely natural. They all live in Christ, and certainly much more than I.

In the morning, I have just been walking in the meadows, blooming, green mountain meadows. My friend, the sun, is shining brightly, and we are waiting for Father Metropolitan for lunch. It seems that he is already arriving!

Friday May 6, 1994
On Wednesday I was in quite low spirits. But then I began to think that faith is just that, when the earthly eyes see only vice and injustice everywhere, you still believe, against the visible reality, that Christ has been given all the power in heaven and on earth. You believe and rejoice! I immediately put this thought into practice.

Monday May 30, 1994
No doubt a person in love supersedes him- or herself in many respects, lives in a kind of world of beauty and goodness. He or she has received something on loan from the Spring of Love. So if in many ways limited human love—limited, among other things, by being dependent on one person, with all its negative sides such as jealousy and fear—can elevate and vitalize a human person, what can we say about the sea of love that is in God? The one diving into it will be renewed. "Behold, I make all things new."[100]

---

100. Revelation 21:5 (New Revised Standard Version).

Saturday June 25, 1994
One day I would like to write a book, warm and beautiful, the kind that would fill people with joy. We have done a third printing of the *Valamon vanhuksen kirjeitä*,[101] and it is selling like hotcakes. Orthodox people sense the authenticity. The letters spring from the warm heart of Father John, comforting and encouraging to go forward.

Saturday July 16, 1994
I baked bread this week—good bread. Baking is somehow a sacred process, and I especially like the time when the bread is rising, well covered under blankets. It is a kind of mystery that also has something to do with our lives. Out of sight, in the warmth, in the silence, the transformation of the bread takes place—from sticky dough it changes into fluffy bread, which then gets its final shape in the oven.

Sunday August 28, 1994
I am the hostess of guests this week. Today we had a lot of people. Even a pharmacist, a man, came all the way from Athens, guided by *Valamon vanhuksen kirjeitä*. Many have gained a lot from this book and feel that Father John is their spiritual elder. One lady said this afternoon that she had never seen nuns so happy anywhere else. What can stop us from being happy—we are living as if in paradise. In the evening, I sat on the corner balcony with my legs resting up on the railing and felt cloudless joy inside. Thank you, my Lord and my Savior, thank you for everything!

Tuesday October 4, 1994
I remember from last night, how we sat and stood on the terrace of the outer gate with our Father Confessor. We gave a chair to Father Isidore, who has problems with his feet. I sat on the steps next to him. We waited for the Metropolitan, who was still talking with the abbess. We chatted about odds and ends—we were many sisters. From time to time, Father Isidore would recite the Jesus Prayer aloud. Warmth and peace overcame my mind. It was already dark, and it felt as if Christ Himself had visited us through the prayers of Father Confessor. And surely, He was among us.

Monday October 17, 1994
Today we made candles all day long in the crisp autumn weather and will continue tomorrow if it does not rain. There were all kinds of arguments

---

101. *Letters of a Valaam Elder.*

and exchanges of words. I began to feel really good, and I even put it into words for the sisters: "How wonderful it is that everyone can say straightforwardly what she thinks without fear of being brought before a church tribunal to explain every word! If a person of serious character were to visit our monastery, he or she would take us before the patriarch from time to time . . . No doubt there are monasteries where the sisters must watch every word they say." Fortunately, ours is not one of them.

Wednesday November 9, 1994
It occurred to me today that in the next life there will be complete democracy. There are no fathers or mothers, no earthly or ecclesiastical hierarchy—there are only free souls who are in loving relationship with each other based only on who they are. Your value depends on what you are. Perhaps this is what Christ meant when he said that we should not call anyone on earth our father. Father and child settings, both physical and spiritual, are not maintained in the next life. There we are all, expressed in worldly terms, of the same age—or rather, ageless—and outwardly equal, and so to speak, in the same basic status. Value depends on inner things.

Saturday November 12, 1994
This past week I was a guest hostess. Even two Finns came on two different days. Word is getting around, and more Finns are likely to come. This is probably one of my ministries.

Saturday December 31, 1994
The last news of the year: fierce fighting in Grozny, the capital of Chechnya. I had never even heard of such a place. And now the fighting is going on; i.e., the Russians are going to crush the uprising of the Chechen people. All this shocked me to tears. Lord, next year protect us from ourselves! I deeply feel the unity of humanity: we are different cookies from the same dough. And that is why wars and battles are essentially self-destruction. But it is one thing to realize it and another to feel it under your skin.

Tuesday January 17, 1995
My sister Marja called this evening. A choir exchange visit between Trikala and Helsinki has been planned for a long time. Now it looks like it will finally happen. The Trikala choir will go to Finland at the end of

August, and the Suomalainen Yhteiskoulu[102] choir will come to Trikala at the beginning of October.

Friday February 10, 1995
Often, when I close my eyes for prayer, I see our small world hurtling at high speed around the sun, which itself is also hurtling somewhere with all the things that orbit it. It is unavoidable that one day our globe and the sun itself will be destroyed. Even science says this, not just the Bible. But in some ways, we do not take this fact into consideration at all; our worldview is practically stagnant. We still live as if we were on an eternal pancake that the kind sun faithfully rises every day to light. Listen: everything will be destroyed! I do not mean that a person should stop creating, building, studying, but the gravitational center of life should be somewhere else; or rather, creating, building, and studying should serve the only important thing. And that is, how can we learn to know what there is to know to come into union with the Creator of the universe? From this point of view, wars and all other struggles on our planet seem totally senseless. What is power on this earth? Why fight for power, why establish borders, bans, regulations? We are all here, hunched over for a short time on this small planet of ours, waiting for the next development. Is it not the height of senselessness to use this little time to fight others who are members of the same humanity?

Saturday February 25, 1995
I have received an invitation to give a series of lectures on the Philokalia at the University of Helsinki for the spring semester 1996. Hmmph...

Friday March 17, 1995
Little snippets from this week: a little Roma girl in the stairwell of the Trikala hospital—how her eyes lit up when I dug out a small chocolate bar that happened to be in my bag. Five American tourists today. We had a deep, beautiful conversation. Letter, letters. And then great news: Father Mitro called and said that he will be our Pascha priest from Lazarus Saturday until the end of Holy Week. Aunt Rauha will come on April 7th. We will be a Finnish triplet celebrating Holy Pascha here.

---

102. Helsinki Finnish Coeducational School.

Tuesday March 28, 1995
Lately I have been thinking about the problem of evil, and I even wrote about it to *Aamun Koitto*. Evil will always get its revenge—outwardly it may carry out its plan to the last little detail without God intervening in any way. But the end is not the end. Then the metaphysical phase begins, God's justice begins to act. Conscience is the most terrible tormentor in the world. I am convinced that evil will always get its punishment, even if not in the way we would expect, and on the other hand the victims will always get consolation. That is why our Lord says: "Do not resist an evildoer."[103] There is no need, because the evildoer is more pitiful than his or her victim, even if the victim would die. Therefore, a Christian should not be easily shocked by evil; there is no fear of evil winning.

Holy Thursday, April 20, 1995
Today I received a letter from the Finnish Association of Orthodox Teachers. They have invited me to speak at their summer meeting in New Valamo on August 7–8. The demands are growing. Perhaps the rest of my life is meant for giving. I have little time left for anything but helping others in one way or another. I hardly have time to write the diary—there are always letters to write. Thank you, Lord, that I can serve.

Saturday May 6, 1995
There was peace and tranquility. Thank you God. I feel refreshed. I slept, I prayed. It has been exceptionally cool, but that is good too—it has helped to calm down.

Tuesday May 16, 1995
I called Metropolitan Seraphim about going to the meeting of the Orthodox Teachers Association. He sounded hesitant and negative. It felt bad. Since my youth, under the influence of Father Archbishop, I have been used to the custom that when one is asked to do something for the church, one does not say no. The Metropolitan said that he would answer later. Conflicts appear in my life when I come to observe that my work for Finland is being hindered.

---

103. Matt. 5:39 (New Revised Standard Version).

Saturday May 20, 1995
The abbess told me yesterday that she had discussed with the Metropolitan about my going to Finland, and that he had given his blessing for it. Well, fortunately . . . although I needed to spend a few days in bitter thoughts. I have already started organizing the trip and thinking about what I will talk about.

Midsummer, Saturday June 24, 1995
My fiftieth birthday last Sunday went by like any other Sunday. Birthdays are not celebrated in Greece. Since it was a Sunday, I did receive the best gift of all, Holy Communion.

Sunday July 16, 1995
God is "doing His work in my life," as Father Paisios used to say about himself. But I am very poor at communicating anything to others, except for the little that can be communicated just by being. It is somehow very difficult to say anything to people who are accustomed to living in the dim or dark cave, hesitantly approaching even the thought that there is another kind of bright life.

The speech is finished, I just have to proofread the last pages. Somehow, I have not really internalized yet the thought of actually going to Finland, even though the day of departure is already approaching.

Saturday August 19, 1995, after the trip to Finland
I have missed my spiritual brothers and sisters in the land of birches and lakes. This afternoon, when there was time, I studied my inner state. The fact that in Finland I felt like I was with likeminded brothers and sisters, trying together, being available for God together, was an inspiring experience for me.

Beheading of John the Baptist, Tuesday August 29, 1995
I am regaining my joyful mood, which is not disturbed by thoughts like homesickness for Finland. I just noticed that I think a lot about Lintula and about Finnish things in general—but, without longing. I wonder if my place would be there after all? You must strive to be so close to God that where you happen to be geographically does not matter very much.

Then you can be like God's balloon that He can freely push from one place to another.

Tuesday October 3, 1995
The choir of the Helsinki Finnish Coeducational School visited our monastery today. They had come for a return visit to Trikala when the Trikala choir had visited Finland in August. The high schoolers seemed to like it here in the monastery—in some very special way. In silence they listened to my talks, discussed, asked wonderful questions. It was obvious that the monastery talked to them—that they left here deep in thought... Yes, authenticity speaks to youth. And even I was left in deep thought: God bless them! In the church they sang a Latin hymn "Turhuuksien turhuus,"[104] and later in the guesthouse especially for me, "Kesäpäivä Kangasalla."[105]

Monday October 9, 1995
When we say in the Lord's Prayer: "Thy will be done," we are accustomed to think of our will as the contrast. But this is not necessarily so; the counterforces are all the evil that fights against the work of God.

Sunday October 15, 1995
Tomorrow we are going on a pilgrimage to Patmos, led by the Metropolitan. That means about a ten-hour voyage. The wind is strong in the Aegean, it said in the weather forecast. This is the first time since the Estonia shipwreck that I have had to deal with the sea. Before, it never even occurred to me that cruise ships could sink. Now, however, I find myself constantly planning what I would say to the sisters, if... how would I put the life jackets on them, etc. I hope taking care of their seasickness will be enough!

---

104. "Everything is meaningless," Eccles. 1:2 (New Revised Standard Version).
105. "Summer day in Kangasala," a Finnish folk song.

Sisters of Bytouma Monastery: Theodora, Thekla, Parthenia, Kristoduli, Theodoule, and Agne on Patmos, October 1995.

Sunday October 29, 1995

I believe that dance should be revived as a form of prayer. Dance is first and foremost a form of expression, and if we study its roots, I am quite sure that religious dance, dance before God, is the most original form of it.

Monday January 15, 1996

For my lecture texts I have collected definitions of love by the Holy Fathers. It is good for the Finns to realize that in the thinking of the Holy Fathers, love and dispassion are closely linked. What treasures I have to offer to my countrymen—if only I could offer them!

Forgiveness Sunday, February 25, 1996

I have already been back in the monastery for almost a week. The trip to Finland was a blessing, everything went well. The lectures were well attended, I met many people and heard their stories, beginning during the flight. The visit to Lintula and Valamo in the second week gave me new strength. I spoke on the radio and gave an interview for Helsingin Sanomat.

Thursday March 7, 1996
I woke up early this morning around 3:30 am and got up to pray. At first the Jesus Prayer did not flow very well—there was a dry spell. Then I remembered the instruction of the Holy Fathers to put away all thoughts. I took them away and removed them from my chest like emptying a mailbox. What happened next is hard to describe. Our Lord Jesus Christ came and filled the empty space. Our Lord Jesus Christ lives and is powerfully present—therefore, nothing is impossible. On the contrary: simple, wonderful . . .

Saturday June 22, 1996
Yesterday I was watering the garden, and as I did so, I recited a few familiar prayers, but in a new way, no longer somewhere far away, but in the ear of Christ. I could rest in Christ. In the evening, He drew me even deeper into the core of my being—to a place where only God and the human soul are. I had never gone so deep before.

Friday August 9, 1996
Sometimes I think that as soon as I leave the surface of the earth, the first thing I will do is to find out how the universe came to be and where it is going. Some theologians might be afraid of the prospect of life on other planets—afraid that it would somehow destroy Christianity. I have no such fears—on the contrary, I think it would be very interesting to compare how the living beings on other planets experience God—to the extent that they would have creatures capable of communicating.

Monday September 2, 1996
How quickly the summer has flown by! It is already September—although it is still summer here and one of the best months of the year. Next week, on the island of Aegina, under the protection of Saint Nektarios, the representatives of all the women's monasteries in Greece will meet. Abbess Eusevia will go there and, surprisingly enough, will take me with her. I am very interested in this event.

Sunday September 15, 1996
I was in Aegina. Everything went wonderfully, including the travel, and even with the abbess there were no difficulties. There were two hundred and fifty nuns there, and the whole event was a very uplifting experience.

Most of the speakers were nuns, and one can only feel nothing but justified pride in their presentations.

Entrance of the Theotokos to the Temple, Thursday November 21, 1996
These days I will finish the index for the Philokalia, and then I should still prepare the lectures from last early spring in a literary form, so that they could be published together with the index. After that, I should think what to do next—where to direct myself. Should I write about Father Paisios, should I again translate something else into Finnish, should I perhaps write something "from my own head" (as WSOY has asked me to do)?[106] Or should I finally focus on this, my own sisterhood, which all these years has remained secondary to these Finnish matters? The questions are many.

On the balcony of Bytouma Monastery. Photo Nicolas Karellos.

Friday November 22, 1996
This morning in church I felt that I would be ready to go to Finland—Lintula, if only someone would think of inviting me. As you get older,

---

106. Here, she refers to the Finnish publisher Werner Söderström Osakeyhtiö.

things tend to become simpler, and I have, for example, realized that "a Finn I am, and a Finn I will remain." So you could almost say that I am living a crisis! I like crises because I know from experience that something always comes out of them—you come out wiser. Besides, a monastery is a good opportunity to go through different crises without anyone else noticing. Everyone can go through their crises thoroughly.

Saturday November 23, 1996
Today in the liturgy, I thought about—as if I, for the first time, really understood—the little words " . . . which is for you" in the Eucharistic Prayer. The Lord quietly reminds us that his passion was for us. He quietly reminds us, without bursting into abundant confessions of love, how much He loves us. Those little words " . . . which is for you" are the highest possible confession of love.

Saturday December 7, 1996
For the last few days I have been a quiet girl, and tears have flowed, especially in church. A stranger, alone . . . And when the thought, not suitable for a nun, arises in my mind that I also have the right to be treated humanely (mocking and sniping, especially by certain sisters, is daily bread, instead of Finnish rye bread), it also darkens my mind. It is not possible to put any ideas into practice—and in this way I am flattened; I no longer believe that I can do anything. Well, all of this has been true through the past eleven years and partially even before. But—and this is a big "but"— we nuns simply cannot afford to worry about things that in one way or another focus on ourselves. We have given ourselves completely to Christ our God. And we must stay in Him and believe in Him—even when He does not (or does not seem to) care for us.

Saturday December 21, 1996
We did a lot of cleaning last week. Everything is getting ready for Christmas. My Aunt Rauha called, and my parents called tonight.

I would really like to spend the Christmas holidays without any "should" and "must" feelings. The twelve-day Christmas period is a special holiday time for us. Last year, however, I was very busy preparing lectures.

Tuesday December 31, 1996
This past year has been a turning point in my inner life. My interior has truly begun to live by the love of Christ. In the last few days, my love for God has glowed from the thought that He alone knows me completely, knows every cell and every side of my soul. He does not need explanations. Before Him, one can be silent in deep love. No one knows us like God, who created us and this whole planet for us to inhabit. I entrust myself to His care also in this coming year.

Friday February 7, 1997
The person who enters the monastery has at some point experienced the powerful touch of God's grace—that draws him or her to the monastery, to the atmosphere of prayer and ascesis. Only after that come the theological and other such reflections.

Saturday February 22, 1997
In Trikala I wrote an article requested by WSOY for a book titled *Hiljaisuus* (*Silence*). Such creative writing is very exhausting.

Forgiveness Sunday, March 9, 1997
Recently there has been a complete change in my worldview. Until now I had somehow seen the world developing positively and even people returning to spirituality. But now my eyes have been opened, and I can see and feel the terrible state we are actually in and where humanity is drifting more and more. Drifting, however, is not the right expression: rather, where it is being led. The priests are still preaching as if we were still living in the quaint bourgeois society of the last century, where everyone is now enthusiastically preparing for the physical and spiritual ascetic practices. The cold truth is completely different, even here in Greece.

Apostle Thomas Sunday, May 4, 1997
"Stay in the city until you have been clothed with power from on high."[107] The city, Jerusalem, refers to the "house of peace"—we need to wait in inner peace. Perhaps one day the power from on high will flow upon me too. We should not always think I do not know how, I cannot, I am not capable. The power of God makes everything possible.

---

107. Luke 24:49 (New Revised Standard Version).

Tuesday July 15, 1997
I continue to get to know pain, especially at night. When I wake up in the morning after a bad night's sleep with an aching arm, I feel a deep connection to those who at that moment are curled up in their pain in the streets of Calcutta, under the bridges of Brazil, in the mud huts in Africa. The brotherhood of pain . . . how can I ask for healing, when others continue their lives in pain . . . Pain is like a prison, and trying to get rid of it is like banging on the bars and wasting already-diminishing strength. Instead, one must try to make one's existence in the cell as comfortable as possible, be aware of it and live with it, try to organize the cell as a place where the Lord Jesus Christ can come for a visit. His presence transforms the cell of pain into the palace of the Sun King. On Friday I am going to see a doctor in Metsovo. If the visit to a doctor can really heal my shoulder joint where the pain is, I do not want to forget my suffering brothers and sisters, those who are in pain.

Saturday August 9, 1997
The rich and varied colors of life have begun to enchant me more and more. People, animals, the buzzing of insects, the roar of a stream, plants, trees, warmth . . . Today in church I was thinking about how many kinds of life or memories of life I carry in my material being. It is actually made up of the decomposed remains of plants, animals, and (why not?) people who have lived before, and through daily nourishment you keep increasing within yourself the life that has lived before. The cycle of nature . . . How many deep mysteries this life contains!

Wednesday September 24, 1997
Today I reached the end of the Philokalia; i.e., I finished the last segment of the index titled "Prayer." Above all, I feel relief! The work of twenty-three years has come to an end. I thank God for giving me the strength to serve in this task and for allowing me to bring it to closure. Other tasks are in the planning but of course not as heavy as this one!

Saturday November 29, 1997
Astronomical studies have made it clearer and clearer for me how unique and wonderful, a true rarity, a human being is in the universe. I am no longer surprised that God became man to save this lost crown of His creation. Was it not for us? No one else could study and admire His works, to try to reach Him himself.

Friday January 2, 1998
My parents called tonight. They were very moved by a letter I had sent to them—in November, I remember. In it, I thanked them for the gift of life and for all the care they gave me during my childhood and early adolescence. Sometimes it is good to say things out loud, when those concerned are still alive. Usually, these things come to mind only after the death of one's parents and other benefactors.

Friday February 13, 1998
After the service I turned on the fax machine and found a message from Irinja. Unexpectedly we have become rich: The work team of the Philokalia, Irinja, Maria, Matti, and I, received a grant of 120,000 marks, about 6,400,000 drachmas, from the Finnish Cultural Foundation. I called Irinja to congratulate her. Probably a few million drachmas will come here ... It is fun to realize that my native country appreciates my work.

Wednesday March 11, 1998
Father Mitro called me and said that the Finnish TV invited me to participate in an hour-long panel discussion on "Letting Go" on March 27. The television station would pay for my trip. At first the idea sounded very strange, but since I have other things to do in Finland (to collect the grant money and see my sick father), with the blessing of the abbess and the Metropolitan, I finally decided to go.

Thursday March 19, 1998
I have spoken twice with the TV reporter on the phone—they wanted to make sure that I can still speak Finnish! Well, the skill has not been forgotten. Early in the week I felt my blood pressure rising when thinking about the matter, but now I have—thank God—somehow calmed down.

Sunday April 26, 1998
My repeated mistake in the spiritual life is still that I overexert myself. The right attitude is to remain calm on earth, where we have been placed, and to wait for God to land.

Tuesday April 28, 1998
Today I read a speech given by Patriarch Bartholomew on ecology and was very happy. He is also interested in modern science, quantum physics, and the perspectives it opens up. In fact, over 1,500 years ago, holy

people made the same observation that science is making today: that matter is energy.

Monday June 1, 1998
Early this morning the phone rang in the abbess's cell, where the calls are redirected for the night, and it was my sister Elina. I called them. Little Freja answered the phone. I asked her why mom had called—maybe grandpa was sick? Freja answered in a weak voice: "Did you know that grandpa died?" So Dad has left this world. Just on Friday I talked to him and Mother for a long time on the phone. I have to start preparing for a trip to Finland.

Saturday June 27, 1998
The trip to Finland went well—nothing unexpected happened. Father's funeral was a beautiful and solemn event. The whole extended family was present. The funeral was held in Helsinki, but the actual grave is in Vehmersalmi.

Monday July 6, 1998
Friday night I got my first lesson in using a computer.
When I went downstairs from the office room, there was a shock waiting for me: eighty-seven-year-old Sister Elizabeth had fallen and broken her leg, which I noticed immediately. I went to call an ambulance; Sister Salome and I accompanied her. Sister Elizabeth's leg was plastered from top to bottom, and today again we returned to the monastery in the ambulance.

Sunday August 9, 1998
Life is so beautiful these days that it would be worth writing more about it. It is the fast of the Dormition of the Mother of God, warm and actually hot; the full moon is rising in the sky in the evening. There is work outside, work inside, liturgies, prayer services, visitors. Inner peace and communion with the Lord.

Saturday October 10, 1998
Yesterday I prayed the Our Father in my cell. I realized for the first time that the three "wishes" at the beginning express a surrender, not a request. We make room, we remove obstacles, we give God the freedom to act, we hope that He will do so with all his power. I especially stopped at

the "Thy will be done" wish. Sometimes it is interpreted as us letting go of our will (which, in silence, we may still think is wiser) and submitting with a sigh to the will of God. I understand that it is something much more: Let the Will of God penetrate with all its power, in its full dazzling light, in its purifying brightness, in its indescribable might, into the life of this planet, and especially into the life of its conscious beings, "as it is in heaven."

Thursday October 22, 1998
Today I started writing a children's book. Hellevi Salminen sent me her own book, *Pekko ja Jänis Joplin*,[108] which I liked a lot. It reminded me of my own theme—the main characters are children: Finnish-Greek Lennu and a shepherd boy, Kosta. Of course, I do not expect to get a Nobel Prize for it, but maybe something will come out of the book. There is at least one good thing, that at every stage I can rely on the opinion of a professional, Hellevi. I have to start doing something, and this fascinates me more than translating the church fathers!

Thursday November 19, 1998
After the "basic course" of at least fifteen years in monasticism ended in my spiritual life, I went through different periods. First, there was a time when I was very interested in the affairs of the world—and things did indeed happen during that time: the collapse of communism began. Then there was a period of one year when the love of Christ became real to me in a new way. Finally, I got a little tired of just emotions and asked for some knowledge. And then the knowledge started to flow. Now I feel that I have received all the necessary basic knowledge of the universe, and my thirst for knowledge has been quenched. Of course, any new enlightening knowledge is welcome, but I am not devouring scientific literature as I used to. Let's see what comes next in the program.

Saturday January 23, 1999
A fax came from Father Mitro explaining that the Valamo Association had decided to organize a celebration and a conference in the spring after Easter to honor the completion of the Philokalia series. My presence would, of course, be almost obligatory. I replied that they should write directly to Metropolitan Seraphim.

108. *Pekko and Joplin the Rabbit.*

Sunday January 24, 1999
Yesterday evening, Father Christodoulos, who is writing a book on Father Paisios, appeared suddenly at Vespers. It became apparent why I had seen Father Paisios in my dream! It seems that Father Paisios would like me to translate the book into Finnish. We agreed on the matter with Father Christodoulos, and he gave me the English translation, which is more condensed than the Greek one. I will do the translation into Finnish based on it. I began to feel shivers—Father Paisios himself is clearly involved in the initiative.

Friday February 26, 1999
By the way, it is quite something that monks can very well found a women's monastery, live in it, or go and die in it, but the opposite would be a terrible scandal. Who could imagine a nun founding a monastery of men and serving as its spiritual mother, living there, or going and dying in a monastery of men? It would not work at all, even if all the monks there were doctors. An amusing thought—we are still far from equality in this respect.

Tuesday March 16, 1999
Somehow this gift of life must be used for the glory of God! I want to live without conditions, in a radical way! I will no longer bow down to the weaknesses of people and keep quiet just to keep my own peace. I want to live authentically and fully. No more of that stuffy life! I will not let what is best in me starve for lack of use, for fear that it will cause me trouble.

Monday April 5, 1999
Why should you always be on bright hills? If the Lord wants to keep you in a dark valley, He does not ask you to present yourself to others as a radiant witness of the Gospel . . . It is enough to suffer patiently! Well, these are such luxurious sufferings compared to the sufferings of people who are about to freeze to death, or who are starving, or who have no place to rest their head. Great numbers of such people can be found just across the border! Europe in the last year of the twentieth century.

Saturday April 24, 1999
I have decided to get away from the "shadows" in my prayer life. Why do we try to make our intellect and thoughts non-existent in our prayers? It is a different matter to zero one's will. No Holy Father asks us to zero our

intellect. If our ability to think is something that distinguishes us from animals, then it is meant to be used. This became very clear to me today.

Nativity of the Mother of God, Wednesday September 8, 1999
I spent five days on the beach at the foot of Mount Olympus, swimming about three hours a day! It was magnificent.

Wednesday October 6, 1999
Unpleasant things came up in the monastery, for which G had to leave—for a reason—and we are still living in its aftermath. Strangely enough, this helped me to recover from my own sorrows. So it goes, one being's death—another being's life. I have managed to finish preparing the speech I will give in Finland on October 23. The idea is to travel to the north on Thursday after two weeks.

Friday December 31, 1999
One thing is certain about this new century: long before its halfway point, my bones will be resting in its soil, and my spirit—yes, my spirit—will have begun a new adventure.

Tuesday March 21, 2000
The Metropolitan came for a surprise visit and immediately took the ballots out of his pocket and said that we would now have the election of the board. In the voting, Sister Eupraxia received seven votes, and both Sister Theoktiste and I received five votes each. Everyone had the right to vote for two people. Eupraxia and Theoktiste were elected (because she was ahead of me in the order). Legally, there probably should have been another vote between Theoktiste and me, but the Metropolitan did not want to take that risk. I must admit that I am a bit annoyed now. Anyway, I have to do all the administrative work!

Monday April 10, 2000
Father Athanasios came on the day of the Annunciation to hear confessions. He has also come here on other days. The atmosphere has changed and calmed down. Today we received the Holy Unction, which we all participated in. The healing effect can still be felt in the soul.

Sunday October 29, 2000
Today I finished the children's book I started a long time ago and sent the last chapter to Hellevi for review. We'll see if it is possible to even find a publisher for it!

In a strange way, the characters in the book are starting to live their own lives, as Hellevi says also. I will actually miss Leenu and Kosta and their world, which includes Leenu's sensitive father, Kosta's grandpa, the gang of three (which really exists); i.e., my three nieces, and others.

Monday December 11, 2000
Father Paisios's biography has been published in Finland.[109] I feel relieved, because now help for the spiritual life of Finns is in greater hands. I, as the translator of the book, am a small co-worker of Father Paisios. Finally, I feel that I can be a part of the collaboration, even if the other partner is a holy man of God in the next life. It is really very interesting to see what Father Paisios can do in Finland.

Bishop Seraphim of Stagoi and Meteora (d. 2017).

109. Priestmonk Christodoulos Angeloglu, *Pyhän Vuoren Vanhus Paisios* (Rista ry., 2000).

New Year's Eve, Sunday December 31, 2000
I do not think about anything for the coming year except to constantly cry out for the Lord Jesus Christ. My life has really been simplified: He remains my only anchor and my only hope. Now we can see what prayer means in practice—does it work.

RETURN TO FINLAND

Tuesday January 2, 2001
Tonight, something incredible happened. On Sunday I was upset when in the sermon read in each parish (the rural priests cannot preach, so the diocese sends them a finished sermon), something was said about international Zionism and the Jewish world power. Tonight, the Metropolitan (Seraphim) came to visit, and I mentioned it to him. He had not seen this particular sermon and asked me to show it to him. I found the sermon and underlined the passage that had upset me. The Metropolitan thought it was just right and gasped at me: Are you Jewish? No, I replied. In short, he went on to say that American Jews rule the whole world and that the text was completely correct. Finally, he said that if I do not agree, he would give me a month to think about it, and after that he would expel me from here!!! An exciting thing. What a surprising turn of events! Naturally, I will not change my mind. I told him that there is no reason to drag the greatest shame of the twentieth century, anti-Semitism with its terrible consequences, into the twenty-first century. No worldly power will make me support anything related to anti-Semitism nor the oppression of any other ethnic or religious minority. Today I was again in telephone contact with Mother Marina. She wondered if people here are still living in the Stone Age.

If I have to leave, I will make the matter public, including the newspapers and the prime minister himself, who, poor thing, happens to have Jewish blood from his grandfather's side. This is probably strong evidence that he is part of a raging global power-seeking Hebrew conspiracy! Margot and Anne Frank and many others, this is the least I can do in your memory.

Friday January 5, 2001
The night before last, Father Confessor came to discuss "lively" in front of the whole sisterhood, the Jewish question and other issues. I said what

I thought and explained the discussion I had had with the Metropolitan. From the thoughts of Father Athanasios, I was astonished to realize how deeply rooted anti-Semitism is here. He was also absolutely sure that the Zionists were running the destiny of the world; he even said that they deliberately created mad cow disease to destroy us! Something totally imaginary. Father Athanasios thought that I should go to the Metropolitan and ask for forgiveness. I said that I could ask for forgiveness for my behavior, but not for my opinion (although in my opinion I had not behaved improperly at all).

Yesterday morning we left for Kalambaka, Abbess Eusevia, Eupraxia, and I. When we then entered the Metropolitan's office, I kissed his hand and asked him to forgive me for perhaps speaking too sharply. I said that there was freedom of speech in the country, and therefore anyone could preach against Zionists, against Communists, and against capitalists, and I could not prevent it, even if I did not like it. But when I first encountered the matter, it seemed strange to me . . . (as the reader will understand, there was a little hidden irony in this statement). The Metropolitan lectured me for about an hour and a half on how I did not fit into the sisterhood, how I caused trouble, how I despised others, how only about eight hundred thousand Jews were killed (wrong, as I know very well; the real figure is closer to six million), how the Greeks hid and saved many of them, how Zionism is trying to control the whole world and its center is in Brooklyn, how I am idiorhythmic and practice individual fasts, etc.

It is really a difficult challenge not to have anyone in the monastery with whom one can discuss deeper issues. I discuss with the sisters practical matters and ascetic topics, but of course there are issues the sisters do not know about. The Metropolitan said that I should not be like a rooster on a hill and [should not think] that things should always go as Kristoduli says. (These are probably the fruits of the abbess's complex accusations. My own impression is that what I say never happens.) A few times in between everything, the Metropolitan said that I came there, not truly repenting, but rather because Father Confessor had told me to. I do listen to him, but it in no way influences my opinions (in which he is right!). Northern Europeans are supposedly like that; even in all the meetings they never change their minds: "This is how we are, and this is how we will remain." Yes, why should we change when we have been taught critical thinking, something that is sorely lacking elsewhere? And yes, then he went on to say that I despise the sisters and think of them as simple and uncivilized—again this is outrageous!—when they are so good and useful. Again he added that whenever I say something, for example, during bus trips (sometimes I have erred in doing so) or in other contexts, there is something foreign to the Greek Orthodox tradition in my speech. As a result of all this, he is of the view that I should leave Bytouma, and if I do not want to leave, I have to give a written assurance that I will change my way of thinking and be like the others (Hah!). And to be even more sure, so that the matter will remain in history, as he said, he had made a written report where these points were recorded, with the grand conclusion that I should move to Finland! So, I am a victim of anti-Semitism! Today in the liturgy I felt that the souls of many Jews killed in the Holocaust were floating around me.

Summa summarum: After returning to my cell, I thought about this amazing chain of events. Then suddenly a great silence fell upon my confused mind, and I understood: This is the answer I have for so long prayed. God wants me to go back to Finland.

Saturday January 13, 2001
A lot has happened. The tickets for next Wednesday are ready. My cell and my papers have been cleaned, clothes washed and partially packed. Next week, God willing, I will probably already have a sauna in Lintula.

Sunday January 21, 2001, in Finland in Lintula
I am in Lintula, already since Thursday. I am in Finland! In my serene, peaceful fatherland. Thank you, Lord. Glowing snowbanks, frosty trees, birches, spruces . . . Finland.

Christmas Eve, Tuesday December 24, 2002
I have not written much because I feel that since I left Greece my life is no longer mine, but that God is using it for other purposes . . . My task is to make myself available, humbly and obediently.

Wednesday April 12, 2017
I was today, on this lightly cloudy day, in Valamo for confession—before confession I went to the Valamo cemetery to Father Archbishop's grave. It was a cloudy day, but not dark. While standing by the grave, an image of a rectangular snow plate appeared on the grave; it was made by the sun. After a while it disappeared. I looked at the site, and soon it came back to the same spot. Soon it also disappeared as it did the previous time. But suddenly it came again, stayed for a while, and disappeared.

So, there were three of these images appearing one after another on the bright snow, the same shape in the same place. Strangely enough, an explanation occurred to me right away: "It means, that you will still live three years in this world, and then you will get to see Father Archbishop." I do not need to wait for too long to see if it really is so!

Sister Kristoduli, weakened by Alzheimer's disease, died on December 23, 2020, and was bid farewell with the prayers of three sisters. Those present said that they had never seen such a happy expression on the face of a dying person.

Sister Kristoduli on her 70th birthday in Lintula, June 18, 2015.

www.ingramcontent.com/pod-product-compliance
Lightning Source LLC
Chambersburg PA
CBHW051629230426
43669CB00013B/2231